ASK **NORM**

250 answers to questions about your home from television's foremost home improvement expert, Norm Abram

First Edition, ISBN 1-929049-35-8

About This Book For more than two decades, master carpenter Norm Abram has been fielding questions from homeowners all over the country. And since 1997, he's been answering them in the pages of *This Old House* magazine in his hugely popular column "Ask Norm." The questions in this book come from that column. Norm would be the first to share credit for its success with all those involved readers who took the time to write with their questions. He'd also point out that there's more than one way to solve most construction and repair problems. The answers he offers here are simply his way, informed by years of experience on the job site and in his shop.

You can read this book for general knowledge or consult it like a reference book. Or you can just open it at random and browse around. To organize the book we've divided it into twelve chapters, but as befits the complexity of a house, some questions and answers don't fit neatly into a single category. That's why you'll find cross-reference boxes throughout the text—their job is to guide you towards related chapters.

If you'd like to learn even more, we invite you to visit *This Old House* on the Web. While there you can read up on a technique, track down a product, or just revisit lessons learned from one of the projects the show has covered in more than 22 years on the air.

But if you don't find the answer you're looking for, you know what to do: Ask Norm. Direct your mail to *This Old House* magazine, 1185 Avenue of the Americas, New York, N.Y. 10036.

—*The Editors*

Contents

INTRODUCTION

Dear Norm: Having been on *This Old House* for over 20 years, you must have been an accomplished carpenter by your early twenties. How did you get your training? Don't you have some background in engineering as well? And is "master carpenter" a labor-union designation or is it an informal title obtained through years in the trade?

Shawn Weiman, Thornton, Colo.

There's no getting around it: I'm incredibly fortunate to have this career, but it didn't happen overnight. As a teenager, I worked with the same construction firm as my father and continued right through college. Yes, I did study engineering, but it hasn't been nearly as useful as the practical know-how I got from hands-on experience. I believe strongly that you learn by doing; there's no substitute for practicing a craft and learning first-hand what works.

So by the time I started my own contracting business in 1975, I had a wide range of serious projects under my belt. Through several strokes of good luck, and by being in the right place at the right time, I was asked to help out on the early episodes of *This Old House*. The rest, as they say, is history.

Now, about that "master carpenter" title. It's an informal distinction recognizing many years of work at a craftsman level, and I'm honored that others think enough of my skills to bestow it. Truth be told, I'm still thrilled that I get to do all this on TV and in print. But even if I wasn't this lucky, I'd still be making sawdust because that's what I love doing.

Norm Abram

General Remodeling + Repairs

Most people call in a house inspector when buying a place, but I prefer the advice of specialists. After all, who would be better than a plumber to check pipes, or an electrician to assess the wiring?

Evaluating Fixer-Uppers

I'm thinking about investing in a "fixer-upper" that I can work on and sell. How can someone like me, who is not a contractor, know if there is any damage to the structural system of a house? Is there any quick way to spot potential trouble in other areas?

Charles F. Bogues, Dorchester, Mass.

I admire your enthusiasm, but anyone looking for a quick way to size up houses without hiring a pro or taking time to learn about them risks buying a flawed structure.

Most people call in a house inspector when buying a place, but I prefer the advice of specialists to that of generalists. After all, who would be better than a plumber to check pipes, or an electrician to assess the wiring, or a pest-control expert for spotting bug damage? If you have specific concerns about a structural system, I'd recommend that you hire an engineer who is experienced in residential construction. For everything else, go to contractors you've worked with in the past, ask them to accompany you on a tour of the house, and pay them for their time.

If for reasons of time or money you choose to go with a house inspector, look for one who was once a builder or remodeling contractor. He'll have a better view of what can go wrong. I'll give you one key tip, though: Look for any signs of water damage, from the roof to the foundation, because water is the number one enemy of houses. Look for peeling paint, rotting wood trim, stained ceilings, crumbling plaster, mildewed bathroom walls, or a wet basement. You'll be able to spot many of the problems an inspector would point out.

Framing With Less Lumber

My wife and I are planning to build a new house in Tennessee, and I've been reading up on house building. One book refers to a method called stack framing, where you frame the walls with 2×6 lumber instead of 2×4s and space them every 24 inches instead of every 16 inches. According to the book, this leaves more room for insulation and it is a more efficient way to build.

Richard Bussone, Albuquerque, N.M.

Your description is correct, but I don't buy the book's implication that this is the best way to build or achieve energy efficiency, or that it's always more cost-effective.

The idea behind stack framing (which is also called in-line framing) is to have the rafters line up directly over the studs. That way, the loads are transferred in a straight line from the roof to the foundation. In standard 2×4 frame construction, more lumber is needed to shoulder the loads. As a result, a stack-framed exterior wall doesn't require as many studs and the walls need only a single top plate (the horizontal board that caps a stud wall) instead of a doubled top plate.

It's true that stack framing uses less wood and saves energy because of the extra insulation you can pack in, and it generally is allowed by building codes. (Check to make sure it's approved in your area.) But there are downsides, too. The 2×6 studs and plates will shrink more than 2×4s, unless they're the more expensive kiln-dried variety. Without a doubled top plate, there's less wood for securing the top edge of the drywall. You'll

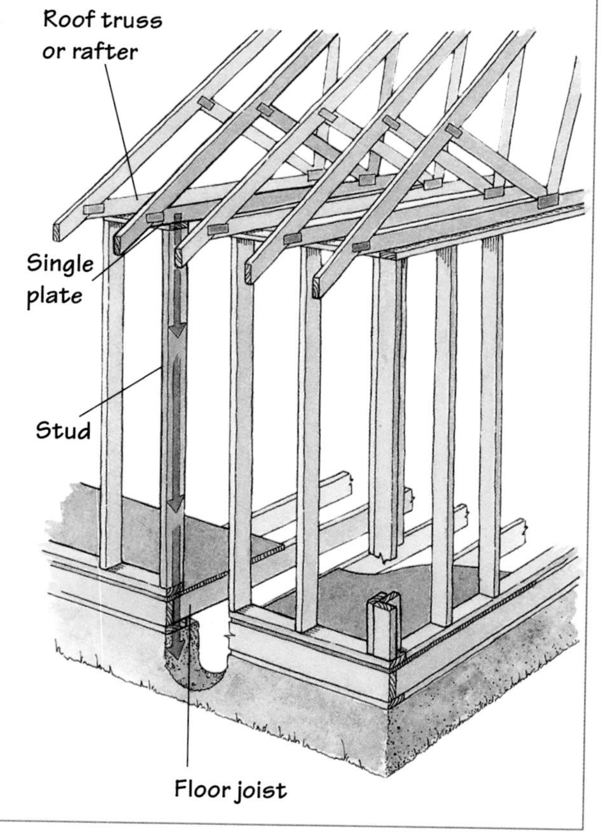

FREQUENT DISCUSSIONS *as the work progresses iron out problems that could derail the project.*

also want to use wall sheathing rated for 24-inch, on-center spacing, and that translates into ⅝-inch plywood or oriented strand board instead of ½-inch, and you'll also need aluminum H-clips to stiffen the joints. Indoors, you might notice that a wall covered with building-code-approved ½-inch drywall doesn't seem quite as solid because it spans 22½-inches between the studs. I'd probably use ⅝-inch drywall instead.

If it's just energy savings you're after, consider using SIPS (structural insulated panels). But for the best combination of energy efficiency and tried-and-true framing methods, I'd go with 2×6 walls and standard 16-inch spacing and then spray in low-density polyiscynene foam insulation. It's expensive, but it does a much better job than fiberglass of sealing wall cavities. If the foam had been available when I built my house, that's what I would have used.

Attic Fly Infestation

My wife, son, and I renovated a house that was originally built in 1898. We installed new windows, re-sided two walls, and insulated, rewired, and replumbed everything. Our problem now is with flies. When the weather gets

THE BEST *way to begin any major remodeling is to access what's there. Here, Norm checks for rotten beams on the Tucson project.*

cool outside, they come inside—in droves. We can't see how or where they're getting in and can't figure out what to do. Please help!

Paul Mertz, Goodwin, S. Dak.

Good news: You can be rid of them with some caulk, some screening, and some patience. According to Fred Baxendale, professor of entomology at the University of Nebraska, you're probably dealing with cluster flies, harmless critters a little larger than a common housefly that usually appear in late fall and on warm days in early spring. Baxendale says that the adult flies, which start life as parasites inside earthworms, like to overwinter in sheltered areas. As a result, they're experts at finding cracks and crevices that lead into a house, especially into attics. (In fact, they're sometimes called attic flies.) Unfortunately, they're not so expert at finding their way out, so they accumulate indoors.

The best way to fight them is to keep them from getting into the house in the first place. Patch torn screens, seal holes around electrical or plumbing penetrations, and caulk even the tiniest joints between trim and siding, especially at the eaves. Do this during the summer and early fall, before the weather turns cool. Baxendale says that cluster flies don't breed indoors, so if they can't get out, they'll eventually starve to death. And because famished flies aren't very quick, that's when you can suck them up with a vacuum cleaner.

Your roof might also be providing a hideout for cluster flies. Slate roofs, for example, are commonly infested with cluster flies. Slates are often laid directly on skip sheathing or boards with no felt-paper underlay. That leaves a great number of small openings, exactly what the flies are looking for. Cedar shingles can also provide hiding places, as I've discovered firsthand.

FOR MORE ON SHINGLING TURN TO CHAPTER 5: ON AND AROUND THE ROOF

Tool Starter Kit

What are the first tools someone who is interesting in doing home projects should get? Do you have some kind of shopping list for the novice?

Ben Kronish, New York, N.Y.

If you're talking about do-it-yourself repairs rather than woodworking projects, I'd suggest starting with a 7¼-inch circular saw and a good electric drill with a ⅜-inch chuck; if you're going to do any serious amount of work, the drill should have a power cord rather than be a cordless model. Then add a good random-orbit sander for refinishing work. After that, get a jigsaw. To get the most out of the tools, be sure to buy top-quality bits, blades, and sandpaper (the hook-and-loop kind, which is user-friendly, not the adhesive-backed kind, which isn't).

Bombardment by Noise

What can we do to reduce the noise from an adjacent turnpike? Our house was built in 1928, but it has new windows and insulation.

John Dryjowicz, Ludlow, Mass.

If the number of letters I get on the subject is any indication, noise aggravates an awful lot of people. There are various ways to muffle noise generated inside the house, including the use of carpeting or throw rugs. But when it comes to blocking noise from outside, the solutions are more complicated.

The most cost-effective strategy is to block what are called "flanking paths"—gaps that allow sound waves to enter a house unobstructed. You can stop a lot of flanking-path noise simply by weatherstripping doors and windows. (You'll improve comfort and energy-efficiency, too). Then pull out the caulking gun and fill the gaps around hose bibs, wiring penetrations, and any other place you'd seal out air or water. If the house isn't insulated, I'd have insulation sprayed or blown into wall and ceiling cavities. It forms a blanket that soaks up sound. We used expanding Icynene foam on walls and ceilings in the media room at the Watertown project—a house quite close to a busy road—and we really noticed the difference. According to Gary Ehrlich, an acoustical engineer at Wyle Laboratories, if your windows are single glazed, the most effective way to reduce outside noise is to replace them with double-glazed acoustical units, which have built-in storm panels and an STC rating of 40 or higher. But if wholesale window replacement is not appropriate or within your budget, try installing storm windows. Ehrlich says the best ones are well-sealed and have panes of ¼-inch laminated glass. Remember to keep them closed; you'd be surprised how many people forget to do this, even in winter. Masonry walls or earthen berms can block or deflect a fair amount of sound, as long as they are taller than the line of sight between you and the source of the sound. Or how about a small fountain? When you're in the yard, the sound of running water is a soothing way to mask unwanted noise. As for me,

If the number of letters I get on the subject is any indication, noise aggravates an awful lot of people.

A CIRCULAR SAW *with a carbide-tooth blade is essential for most remodeling work.*

well, I'd probably head for my shop—there's nothing quite like the whine of a table saw for blocking out other sounds.

Moving the Family Home

I would like to move my grandparents' 1895 house from Pennsylvania to New York State and then restore it. The house is approximately 3,000 square feet and is in wonderful shape, including all the pocket doors, molding, and parquet floors. Even the plumbing and lighting fixtures remain. Could you give me the pros and cons of taking on such a project?

M. Jackman, Armonk, N.Y.

Let's start with the pros. I probably don't need to tell you that a house as nice as the one you describe would be expensive to build from scratch. And no new house could match the particular blend of family and architectural history that surrounds this one. It's also in good shape, which gives it a better chance of withstanding the rigors of a move. The cons for any move include street lights, steep hills, and telephone wires, not to mention trees, traffic, and tunnels. You get the idea. Because these obstacles seem to multiply with every mile a house has to travel, the longer the move, the more difficult and expensive it will be. You might even have to pay for a police escort to handle traffic problems and spectators. (A house in my town was moved a while back and it caused quite a traffic jam.) Technically speaking, almost any building can be moved, and over the years structural movers have relocated everything from lighthouses to brick school buildings. By comparison, your place shouldn't be much trouble. A local house mover—one that's licensed and suitably insured—can give you an idea of what your options might be, and how much they will cost. For instance, sometimes it's easier to cut a house into two or three sections and then put it back together on its new site than it is to move it in one piece. One thing you won't be able to take with you is the foundation; so don't forget to add the expense of filling it in and building a new one at the new site.

FOR MORE ON FOUNDATIONS TURN TO CHAPTER 2: BASEMENTS, CONCRETE, AND CHIMNEYS

A bermed house isn't much different from a house with a walk-out basement. In both cases, you want crack-free walls below grade and a floor slab provided with proper drainage.

Sizing Up a Bermed House

I'm thinking about buying a bermed house in southeastern Iowa, and wonder what you think of this type of construction. The back of the house is made of poured concrete set into a small hill with only about 3 feet of wall extending above grade. The above-grade portion has siding, but there are no windows in back.

Louise Haney, Glendale, Ariz.

The basic idea of a berm is to use the earth's mass to insulate the house from cold and hot weather and to protect it from wind. The earth also reduces sound transmission into the house. But in terms of construction, a bermed house isn't much different from a house with a walk-out basement. In both cases, you want crack-free walls below grade and a floor slab provided with proper drainage. If the builder did his job right, there should be drains buried in gravel along the footing, and porous backfill sloping away from the house. Inside, you want a sump pump standing guard against water emergencies. Fire safety and ventilation are other issues to consider. Building codes require that all bedrooms have a window large enough to be used as a means of escape in case of fire. Your local building inspectors can determine whether the rooms in this house meet local codes. And because this kind of house may not offer much in the way of natural cross-ventilation, make sure the mechanical systems supply enough fresh air, or about 10 changes per hour.

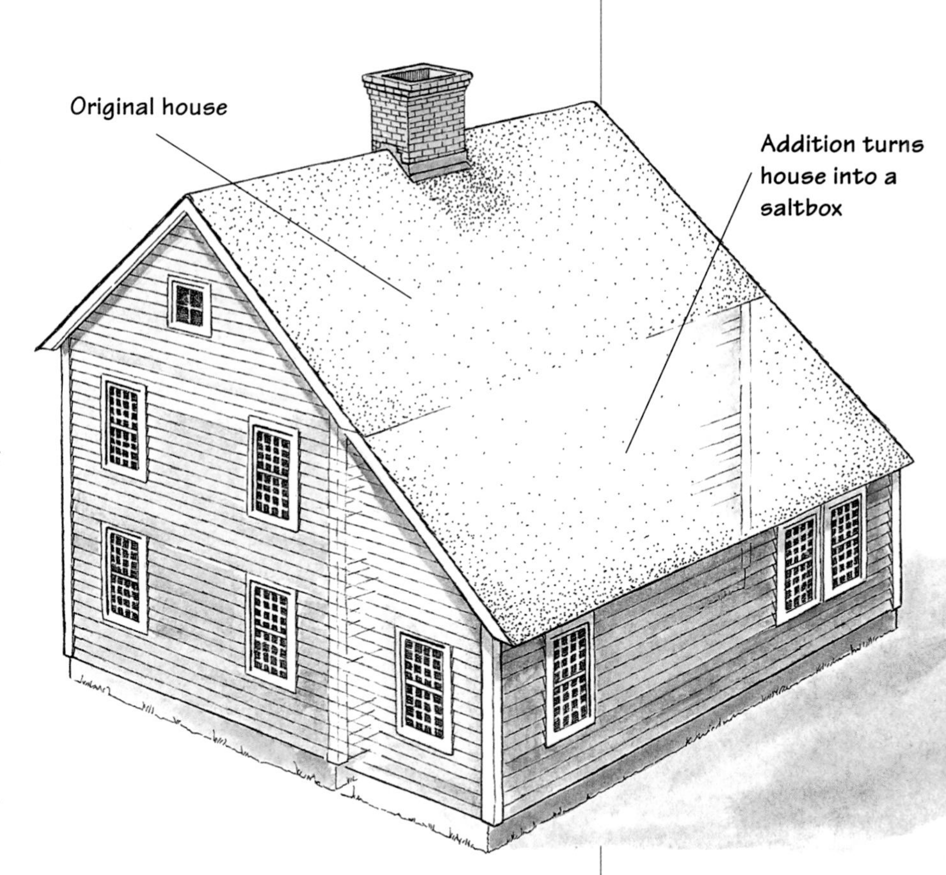

Wrong Color Shingles

My house is only seven years old, but I'm already unhappy with some of the colors I chose. I wish my asphalt shingles were blacker and my mortar redder. Is it possible to stain shingles? If so, what kind of stain will work but not bleed onto my white trim? Is there any way to tint mortar? It's a natural color now, but I'd like it to be rose.

Laura Tungett, Bethalto, Ill.

You can get blacker shingles when you get a new roof, and not before. Mortar can be tinted when it's mixed, but I don't know of any way to tint it afterward. Painting it isn't out of the question but would look awful, be a miserable job to do, and leave you with a maintenance headache.

Adding On to a Saltbox

We've been renovating our 1820s saltbox in order to get more space, but we can't quite figure out how an addition would fit in. We don't want to lose the beautiful lines of the house. What can you suggest?

The Huddlestons, Columbia, N.J.

The saltbox, which was quite popular in colonial New England, actually owes its origin to remodeling. It's just a standard two-story Colonial, with gable ends and a central chimney, and a one-story addition extending out all along the back (see drawing above). The long, sloping roof connecting the back of the house to the addition is the most noticeable feature of this style. By doing a little homework—studying some of the books on saltbox architecture—I'm sure you'll get some ideas that look good from the outside. But if the new floor plan is poorly arranged, even the best-looking addition won't be successful. This is where an architect (or architectural designer) comes in. I'd lean toward hiring one on this project, and you should make sure he or she has experience designing Colonial-style houses.

Historic Once Moved?

My wife and I purchased an old house with a rather interesting history. Built in 1765 in upstate New York, it was slated for demolition after many years of neglect. The family who saved the house—the folks who sold it to us—painstakingly moved it piece by piece to its present location, along with the original foundation stones. Is there any

chance we can put up a historical plaque to commemorate our home's history?
Jim Cronin, Waccabuc, N.Y.

The rules for recognizing houses vary from town to town, so you'll have to check with the historical society in your area. Remember, though, that the historical significance of any dwelling comes in part from its roots in the community, so a house that's been moved from another town might not qualify for recognition unless it represents the work of a significant builder or designer. You can find most local historic preservation groups through the phone book or through one of the six regional offices of the National Trust for Historic Preservation (www.nationaltrust.org). You also might want to take a good look at what the National Register of Historic Places has to say about the subject; their Internet site is quite informative.

Design Help on a Budget

Our house has a large concrete slab in the back that's covered by a shed roof. We thought it would be nice to enclose the area, but we're not sure exactly what we want done. Would a contractor be able to help us decide what the options are, or should we be talking to an architect?
A. Hatfield, Harrisburg, Pa.

When the job is relatively small and your design budget is limited, start with a contractor. Some are more design-savvy than others, but most will be able to suggest several possibilities, as well as tell you how long the job will take and approximately how much it will cost. Ask for photos of similar jobs they've done, or go take a look at them yourself. Your budget will be a deciding factor in any project, of course. If you're still not satisfied, you could discuss the work with an architectural designer who specializes in residential and small commercial projects. Though they usually aren't trained as extensively as architects, their services are less expensive and they're more likely to take an interest in small remodeling projects.

When the job is relatively small and your design budget is limited, start with a contractor.

Uninvited Attic Guests

For the past three months I've been finding little piles of sawdust in my attic. My brother and I think the cause is a mouse, squirrel, or chipmunk gnawing at the rafters. We've tried to trap and even poison the little invaders, but with no luck. Is there some way we can treat the wood to make it unpalatable to rodents?
Ed St. John, Midland Park, N.J.

Treating the wood with some kind of poison? I don't think that's an option; maybe you need to get yourself a pellet gun. The source of the problem is access; if you leave it open, they will come. Look outside and see whether you have tree branches hanging close to your roof. And look for holes around the foundation. Mice can get through very small holes, which means you have to look very carefully. Of course, once you deny access, what about the animals still inside the house? If it were me, I'd call in a professional—a squirrel desperate to escape can do a surprising amount of damage in the attempt.

Best Colors for a Bungalow

I own a 1918 Arts and Crafts bungalow. Where can I get information on the appropriate colors for this kind of home?
Lynda Gerken, Liberty Center, Ohio

You can find information about bungalows through various books and websites. Many people ask about authentic colors for painting bungalows, and for that I defer to bungalow expert Robert Schweitzer, who says to choose colors from an autumn palette. Browns, tans, dark yellow; even dark olive green would be fine. He adds that vintage issues of magazines like American Home, House Beautiful, or House & Garden are good places to find the color choices of that era; look for them in a large public library. "Just steer away from bright Victorian colors," he says.

Burst Pipe Aftermath

Just after I moved into a new house, the hot-water line in the bathroom burst, flood-

A KITCHEN *is the most complex room in any house and remodeling requires detailed drawings.*

ing the master bedroom and closet. What damage can I expect to the OSB (oriented-strand board) subfloor and drywall ceiling? Both were wet for at least seven days. I have already been told the carpet will rot. How soon must repairs be made, and what should be done? The builder is acting as if this is not a problem, and has said nothing about repair under the warranty.

Robert Rovegno, Brevard, N.C.

It's time for some straight talk with your builder. If this happened within the one-year warranty period typically provided by builders of new houses, this is clearly his responsibility. All those water stains you probably see are just a sign of worse things to come: The soaked OSB and drywall are certain to eventually break down, de-laminate, or turn moldy. You need to replace the soaked elements and thoroughly air out the spaces around affected walls and floors, and the sooner the better. Repairs now will minimize problems down the line and probably save the builder from getting soaked by additional costs and trouble. This seems like a simple choice for all concerned.

FOR MORE ON PLUMBING TURN TO CHAPTER 10: ELECTRICAL AND PLUMBING

Attic Truss Clutter

I've heard you say that a truss roof renders the attic unusable because the cross-bracing gets in the way. But for my new garage, I used box-scissor trusses to create an attic space that's roomy enough to use as living space. What do you think of the idea?

Doug Puckering, Lummi, Wash.

I was comparing standard trusses to ordinary stick-frame roof construction. Sure, you can design any kind of truss for any kind of purpose if you're willing to pay for the trade-offs. Your truss, for example, requires an enormous amount of lumber, and leaves you with a small attic best used for storage. Judging by the headroom you described, I'll bet it isn't up to code for living space.

YOUR CONTRACTOR *should be able to answer any and all questions about the project.*

First Things First

I have the opportunity to buy the house I'm now renting, but I'd like an expert's opinion first. Although I'm eager to become a first-time homeowner, the house is more than 50 years old and needs lots of work: insulation, new windows, a new kitchen and bathrooms, and landscaping. I look forward to your advice.

Joanne Goldbeck, Westfield, N.J.

Don't jump to any conclusions. Your house doesn't seem old enough to be completely uninsulated; you may only have to add some insulation in the attic. And if your windows are basically sound but just need some repair, perhaps all you need are new storms. As for the big jobs, I recommend doing them first. Having a workable kitchen and at least one good bathroom done up front will provide a sense of satisfaction that will help you through the rest of your renovation.

Build Up or Move Out?

My family and I purchased our 100-plus-year-old home a few years ago after a "love at first sight" visit. We have made many cosmetic improvements, but now our family is growing. We're considering either adding a garage with a room above it or building another home. I would love to have your input.

Heather Brizendine, Georgetown, Ind.

The photos you sent show a charming house, though one that's a bit on the small side. That makes it especially important to consult an architect before constructing an addition; you don't want the addition to destroy the proportions of the house, which could actually devalue the property. Compare the cost of adding on to that of building new, then consider the inconvenience involved in either choice. This process will help you decide; the hard part is the possibility of leaving a house you've put so much of yourself into.

Roof Framing Sags

Our old house is not as old as its parts. My grandfather built it in 1940 using lumber and slate roof shingles from a demolished railroad roundhouse, and flooring and trim salvaged from various old houses my uncle tore down. Although Grampa helped build the Panama Canal, he apparently didn't understand framing. How else to explain the attic floor joists that go in the wrong direction (parallel to the ridge) over half of the house? Because of this, the house sags considerably. A structural engineer suggested that we not try to straighten everything, but just stabilize the structure by cabling the front of the house to the back. In addition, the roof slates are breaking away—Grampa's Yankee thrift didn't allow for copper nails. Should we tear off the roof and rebuild it with proper framing, venting, and insulation, none of which we have now? If so, can the 100-plus-year-old slate be reused?

Darlene Sines, Bolton, Conn.

Your grandfather was probably trying to get the most out of whatever lumber he had on hand. It's an honorable approach, but he obviously used the material in ways that shortchanged the house's structural integrity. With no ceiling joists connecting the ends of opposite rafters to eath other (see drawing below), the weight of the slate pushes the walls out, your walls bulge, and your roof

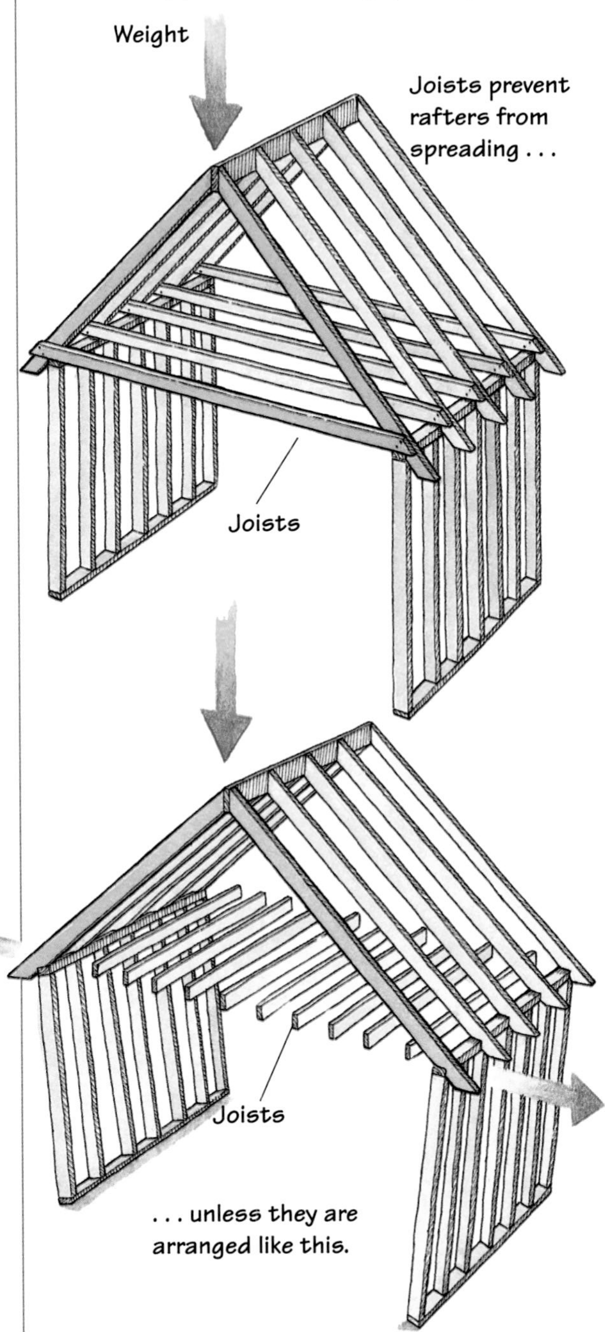

can get a bad case of swayback. In some houses, wood collar ties help to reduce this problem. But in this case I doubt they'd do enough to help. If your budget is tight, I'd defer to the engineer on this one: Straightening bowed walls and a sagging roof is an expensive and complex proposition. If you have the money, though, get your engineer to draft a complete rehabilitation plan and find a contractor who specializes in fixing up old houses. When the time comes to rebuild the roof, it's not a problem to reuse old slates, provided they're not crumbling and flaky. An experienced slater should be able to tell if they're still sound.

Signed Craftsmanship

I found an old scrap of maple attached to a beam in a century-old barn. Dated 1897 and very faded, it seems to have a written message from one of the original builders. Is there a way to make this neat artifact more legible without damaging it?

Ken Janowski, Beach Lake, Penn.

Lots of old buildings contain such relics because 19th-century craftsmen often, and quite literally, signed-off on jobs. A colleague once found both the plasterer's and the framer's signatures in his 1888 house in Pennsylvania, and I've heard of people finding notes in the hollow newel post of staircases. So you have an interesting little project here. The first thing I'd try is photocopying, with the machine adjusted for maximum contrast. If you don't get a legible copy, check with your local police department: someone there might be interested enough to show you how police labs "raise" old or damaged messages and serial numbers.

Chemical Sensitivity

Friends of mine suffer from multiple chemical sensitivity, which has already driven them out of two houses. Now they've got a piece of land on a hilltop high enough to give them air that's free of pesticides and pollution. They want to build a chemically safe house but don't know where to start.

Pat Slowinski, Knightsen, Calif.

Your friends can start by checking with their doctors. After that, they can head for the Internet. The Healthy House Institute has a Web site that covers multiple chemical sensitivity (MCS), as well as topics related to making houses more comfortable for people with asthma or allergies. The site is well organized and easy to use, and includes articles, a bookstore

Straightening bowed walls and a sagging roof is an expensive and complex proposition. Get your engineer to draft a complete rehabilitation plan.

Anything is possible in construction, but that doesn't make it legal or cost-effective.

with an annotated list of related publications, and an extensive list of links to other sources.

Adding a Basement

We're thrilled with our new house and its historic location: Our township was the site of New Jersey's first Indian reservation and forms the largest part of the Pine Barrens/Wetlands Preservation Area. The house has everything we were looking for—except a basement. We don't know why, but it's the only one in our development that has a crawl space. Is it possible to put in a basement?

Ryan and Karen Stradling, Shamong, N.J.

Anything is possible in construction, but that doesn't make it legal or cost-effective. My house has only a partial basement because I decided not to spend a fortune blasting through solid bedrock at one corner of the foundation. Maybe the water table beneath your house is high, or maybe there are restrictions on your lot that relate either to the wetlands or to the former Indian reservation. Perhaps your developer was trying to save a few bucks on a spec house—ask him, if he's still around. If everything checks out okay with the town building and zoning department, get several bids and weigh the expense against the advantages of gaining extra space.

Looking for Craftsmen

My wife and I bought a circa 1795 Colonial in Townshend, Vermont. Although the house has been updated, we would like to remodel. Can you recommend craftsmen of various trades, including carpentry, heating, roofing, windows, and others?

Stephan A. Velazquez, Denver, Colo.

If I gave out all the referrals I'm asked for, I wouldn't have time to eat, let alone work. And it wouldn't be fair. Craftsmen I know and respect would get so many calls they'd have to unplug the phone. Meanwhile, fine craftsmen I've never met would be ignored just because I hadn't recommended them.

Whether you do a renovation blitz or spread the job over many months (so you can pitch in and build some sweat equity), you'll need a good general contractor to handle scheduling. He or she should be able to find the specialized tradesmen you desire and to oversee their work. Ask neighbors and friends who they've used as a GC, then invite several of the most promising candidates over for individual chats.

Money for Fix-Up

We are currently restoring our third old house. It was nearly destroyed by the previous owners, but it's sitting on 2½ country acres and we couldn't pass up the deal. Do you know of any programs that will help us? On our last fix-up we didn't make much of a profit, even though my husband and family members did all of the work.

Cindy Young, Clio, Mich.

I'm afraid the outlook for a grant, or even a low- or no-interest loan, is pretty dim, because there's no historical significance to your house. Though Michigan might be among the states granting "energy-saver" rebates for added insulation, it's unlikely that anyone (besides relatives) will loan money to fix a house you plan to sell for profit. For your next rehab, however, consider a federal 203(k) mortgage, which combines purchase and renovation funds in one package.

Searching for Salvage

My friend is building a house and would like to incorporate some old architectural details into it, so we're planning a trip to New England to look for salvage yards. Can you provide me with some names?

Marti Horm, Cranford, N.J.

These yards aren't hidden: They're often tourist attractions whose names are mentioned in guidebooks and brochures or available through local chambers of commerce. But I have to say, just because it's New England, you shouldn't expect a trove of pristine artifacts. The best stock is snapped up in a flash, and the rest is often poorly stored or damaged by none-too-gentle removal. And if you happen upon a fabulous find, it probably won't be cheap. Yard operators are real horse traders: You see a dinged-up, paint-covered old mantelpiece; they see the focal point of your living room, and charge you what they think you're good for. Dressing down won't fool them; they know who's local and who is, as New Englanders say, "from away." I don't mean to sound like some cranky Yankee protecting his sources—*This Old House* encourages reuse of old material—but I do want you to be realistic. My advice: Pack a picnic, take your time, and enjoy the hunt, whether you find anything or not.

Victorian Overload

My wife and I purchased a 102-year-old Victorian during its centennial year, and now we're settling into a maintenance program. We have already replaced the coal-fired boiler with a high-efficiency natural-gas unit. We'd like to re-roof, but that's just an aesthetic notion—the roof is in good shape. So now we're looking at the electrical service. We have two 60-amp fuse boxes and want to upgrade to 200 amps with breakers. What should I look for as an indication that the wiring in the house needs to be replaced? Also, the woodwork has never been painted, and we really like the deep red patina the finish has taken on, but not its wrinkles. Is there anything we can do to smooth them out and save the finish?

Max D. Sterrett, Greensburg, Ind.

Good job on separating the important work from mere cosmetics—there's no need to bother a roof that isn't bothering you. If your finish is wrinkled, you either have varnish, which will have to be stripped, or shellac, which can sometimes be rubbed smooth with alcohol. Your wiring shouldn't be much of a problem, even if it's the old-fashioned knob-and-tube type. It doesn't need replacing unless it's been so heavily overloaded that the insulation falls apart in your hand—just be sure to cut power before investigating. Electrical contractor Allen Gallant applauds your move to 200-amp service ("Welcome to the 20th century," he says). He suggests putting new wiring in the kitchen and laundry room for the heavy-load appliances, and to any outlet within 6 feet of a tub or basin. These outlets can then get ground-fault protection, which he calls "the best invention of the last 50 years."

Planning a Big Rehab

My cat and I have a new old house, a 120-year-old two-story shingled Victorian with a square tower for a third floor. It's beautiful but sadly neglected. I've begun working with an architect and, unskilled but willing, I plan to participate in all phases of the renovation. Here's my wish list: Rebuild most of the porches. Repoint the mortar, repair the sill, and shore up the beams. Replace the current heating system with a gas-fired, hot-water baseboard system. Tear down the porch/mudroom and replace it with a one-car garage, with workshop and storage areas. Expand the kitchen. Redesign the first-floor bath and laundry. Add a sec-

THE REBUILT *structure of the Santa Barbara house had to withstand seismic forces.*

ond-floor bath and a third-floor half bath. Tear down the second-floor walls and redesign the floor plan to provide two bedrooms and closet space. Remove both chimneys, converting one to a dumbwaiter. Paint exterior trim, level the sidewalks, landscape the grounds, and add herb and vegetable gardens. Breathe an enormous sigh of relief and satisfaction, then move in. What do you think?

Stephanie Ann Carr, Ocean Grove, N.J.

That must be some cat, if you need all that house for the two of you. But it sounds as if you have a rewarding project here. I notice you don't say much about infrastructure. Before proceeding, be sure your roof and plumbing don't hold any surprises, and move sill repairs and shoring up beams to the top of your job list: You want to work on a sound structure. Indoors, it's a good idea to update from the ground up—such as install new heating, plumbing, and wiring—and do the finish work from the top down. This way, you don't have contractors dragging their stuff through your finished rooms. It's good that you're working with an architect, but I'd recommend that you compare his estimate with your contractor's. If the two aren't close, you need to settle that issue early.

I think it's great that you want to become involved in the renovation, but I urge you to be realistic about what you can do. No offense, but during a full-bore renovation, when lots of jobs are going simultaneously, unskilled labor seldom saves money and often wastes some by getting in the way of skilled tradesmen.

It's good that you're working with an architect, but I'd recommend that you compare his estimate with your contractor's.

Flat-Roof Warning

We're building a house in Reno, Nevada, using structural insulated panels (foam sandwiched between oriented-strand board) for the roof. The builders are hesitant about our flat-roofed design because of Reno's snow loads, but many commercial buildings there have flat roofs, and we want to have a roof deck. What do you

think? Also, would you recommend a roof snow-melt system like those used for driveways?

Cathy Beaver, Carnation, Wash.

Sure, many commercial buildings have flat roofs, but many of the products they use and the systems they employ to fend off leaks are foreign to residential construction. I've never been a big fan of flat roofs on houses anyway. Even when built of the best materials, they tend to leak, especially in regions where heavy rain and snow are common. And any leakage in structural-insulated-panel roofs is disastrous. Their wood skins don't tolerate moisture. Whatever the builders say, it's the panel manufacturer's obligation to confirm that the design will handle the loads expected in your area, and it's the local building department who has to approve the plan. Forget about using a snow-melt system to reduce snow load. A building inspector will veto any roof design that can't carry the full load. And adding a deck? I don't like that idea on a flat roof. You run the risk the deck will interfere with drainage, concentrate loads in small areas and abrade the roofing material as it expands and contracts.

More Basement Headroom

The basement in our 1913 house has six and a half feet of headroom, and we'd like more. We've thought about lowering the floor, which appears to be a concrete slab 1½ inches thick. The basement walls are fieldstone. Can this be done?

Chuck Udzinski, Stewartstown, Pa.

Sure, but you're looking at one substantial project. A new floor should be 4 inches thick laid on 8 inches of gravel. That means excavating a foot below the desired headroom. Lowering the floor undermines the foundation, particularly if it's stone, so get engi-

HEAVY LOADS *are best handled with help. At the Tucson project, this replacement for a rotted ceiling beam steadily rose into position.*

neering advice and proceed carefully to avoid digging your way toward structural collapse. You'll have to jackhammer the existing floor, dig beneath a small part of the foundation—praying you don't hit bedrock en route—and pour a concrete footing and wall section. Repeat this process all around the foundation; then pour your floor. If you ask me, a root canal sounds like more fun. You can avoid all this inconvenience and expense by simply raising the house. Disconnect plumbing, heating and electrics, and have an experienced house mover jack it up. Then add to the top of the foundation, lower the house, and reconnect everything. Then do some regrading and landscaping to hide the work.

Arrogant Contractor

We will probably be building a new house soon, and we would like to have the name of a reputable contractor who knows what he is doing on all aspects of building a quality home. We have talked to several contractors so far, but they are either very arrogant or too busy to care. My brother-in-law has had several homes built in this area, and he's had the same response.

Dale Alexandre, Sanford, Maine

Whenever the economy of a region is going strong, it gets tougher to find contractors—maybe the contractors you call arrogant are in fact just busy. The best thing to do is find a contractor you get along with and who has a good reputation, then wait until he's available. You'll probably get a good price and be happy with the job. In the meantime, talk to your brother-in-law. After all, he succeeded in getting his houses built.

The best thing to do is find a contractor you get along with and who has a good reputation, then wait until he's available.

Budget Woes

Can you tell me how to put an addition on my home without going over budget? We're six in our family, and we're currently cramped for space in our three-bedroom ranch. I have borrowed as much as I could, but I still don't have enough for the simple addition that an architect designed for me.

Robbie Penna, Iselin, N.J.

If the financing can't be expanded, either the renovation design has to change or your choice of materials—including finishes, carpeting and the like—has to be reassessed. There's no magic that can get around that reality. It's why the words "cold" and "hard" are seldom far away from "cash." Once you've settled on a plan you can afford, staying on budget entails two things. One is to hire a reliable contractor who will work for a fixed contract price. The other is to avoid making changes once the work has begun. Nothing wrecks budgets faster than sentences beginning: "While we're at it, why don't we . . ."

Sinkhole for Renovation Costs

We've bought a 1970s split-level town house and want to give it a more Victorian feel inside and out. Is it foolish to consider making the house resemble a style from another period? Do you think such changes will increase the property value? I've heard that people who renovate seldom get their money back when they sell. Can you recommend any surefire upgrades that will increase the value of a house when it goes on the block?

Dave Marcopul, Bensalem, Penn.

Short of a total transformation, such as we did on Brian and Jan Igoe's house in Lex-

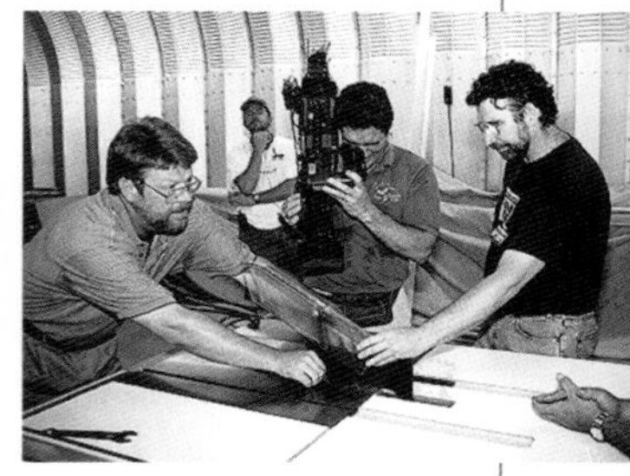

CAPTURING A TECHNIQUE *for the camera often calls for as much effort as the technique itself.*

ington, Massachusetts, a while back, restyling a house from one era to another is like using paint and muslin to make two kids look like a horse for the school play: It requires an indulgent audience. The kind of restyling you're considering probably won't be convincing and could even devalue your house, attracting only bargain hunters. When it comes time to sell, you'll get the most value from simple exterior upgrades that boost a house's curb appeal. Start with the basics. Make sure you clean the house as well as paint and touch up where necessary. And keep the lawn cut and the shrubs trimmed.

Hiding a Concrete Porch

We have a nice 1870 Victorian that still has a good amount of gingerbread and detailing. But previous owners did some modernizing and left us with a concrete porch. I guess they wanted something solid that would not rot, as this porch faces Long Island Sound. The nice cutout posts and brackets remain from the original porch, so we wonder whether wood can be installed over the concrete. We like the sound and authentic antique appearance of wood, and we don't like the feel of concrete under bare feet in summer. What do you advise?

Daniele Lasser, Branford, Conn.

Installing wood over a concrete porch can be done, but it's a bad idea. It will change the height of the top stair and threshold, producing dangerous trip hazards. You would probably end up replacing the steps too. For drainage, you would need 1×2 treated-lumber sleepers. They would run from the house to the end of the porch, making the floor at least 1½ inches higher. And the floor still wouldn't drain or ventilate very well, possibly leading to mold and mildew. My advice: Removing the slab will be a nightmare, so leave well enough alone except to ask around for cosmetic tips on hiding your maintenance-free and rotproof concrete.

Warming Cold Basement Walls

I have two projects. First, I'm refinishing our basement. What's the best way to attach drywall and paneling to a concrete-block wall? Second, because my wife saw photos of driveway pavers in a magazine, I'll be doing a patio this summer. Can I lay the pavers on top of my existing concrete patio?

Lee Bouse, Elkhart, Ind.

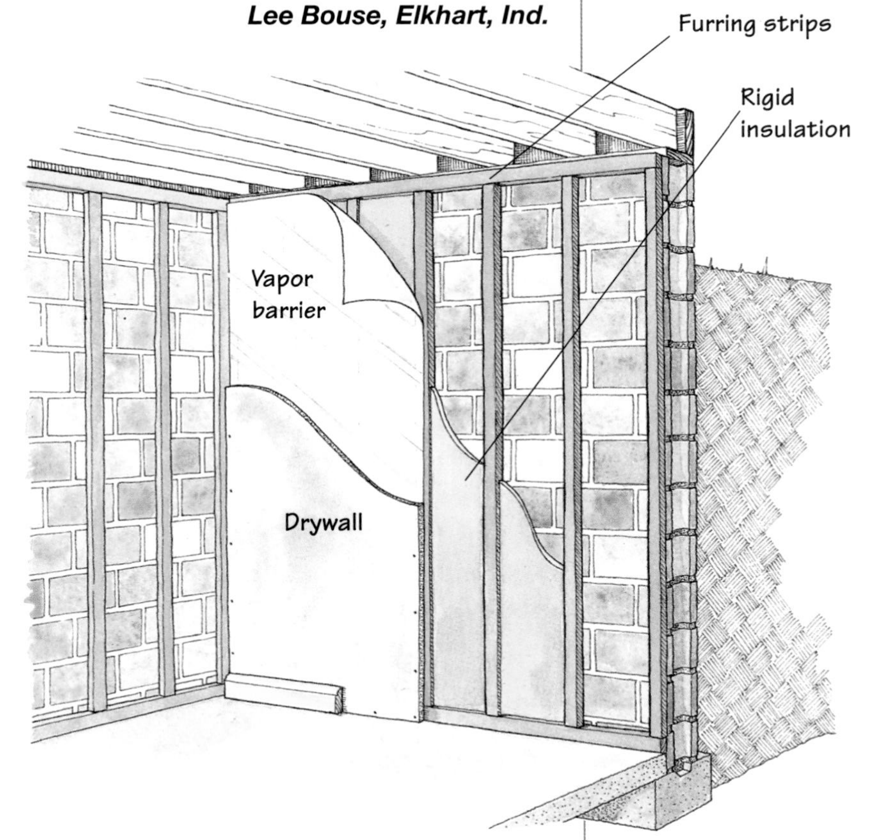

For the drywall, fasten furring strips of 1×2 treated lumber to the walls of your basement, using masonry drill bits and special masonry screws. You might want to put rigid insulation between the strips—even just a little bit will help in Indiana—then add a vapor barrier and drywall on top of that (see drawing above). A better way, if you can spare the space, is to build a stud wall and use batt insulation. Leave a little air space so nothing touches the wall. Ordinary studs will do, but the sill plate should be made of treated lumber in case of seepage.

FOR MORE ON BASEMENTS TURN TO CHAPTER 2: BASEMENTS, CONCRETE, AND CHIMNEYS

As for your patio, freezing might be a concern. But if your present slab has good drainage and you lay interlocking pavers on top of the concrete without mortar, you shouldn't have any problems.

THE CONCEPTUAL *leap from plans to project often calls for some on-site adjustments.*

Floors Transmit Noise

Our house is just three years old but, when we're in the basement, we can hear every little sound made upstairs. There is no insulation between the joists, and the basement ceiling is finished with drywall. Would insulation help?

The Coggans, Washington, D.C.

Trying to contain or muffle noise is never easy. Insulating a ceiling with fiberglass or cellulose will do little to block out footsteps or other noises overhead. Polyicynene, an expanding foam insulation, is a much more effective sound barrier but is expensive and has to be installed by experienced contractors. Acoustic tiles on a ceiling will cut down on echoes within a room, but they're not really suited to cutting down on noise transmission from above. You can reduce the noise level somewhat by putting down lots of scatter rugs upstairs or by carpeting the whole area. Then again, you may just grow accustomed to the noise. The sounds of life are part of the charm of a house. It's unrealistic and, in my view, undesirable to create a tomblike silence.

The sounds of life are part of the charm of a house. In my view, it's undesireable to create a tomb-like silence.

Money for Historic Houses

You've inspired me to refurbish my great grandparents' late-1800s homestead in rural South Dakota. This five-room "little house on the prairie" has been vacant for about 50 years and will require much work. My dream is to make the place livable and put some of the original furniture and fixtures back in. The original claim shack is also located on the property. Do you know of any funding available for restoration projects?

Barbara Raba, Selby, S. Dak.

Your property may have historical importance, so the possibility of receiving financial help from local, state, or federal agencies is worth investigating, starting with the town or county historical society.

Cut Countertop Traps Dirt

I want to run new kitchen cabinets along a wall with a floor-to-ceiling window, and I don't want to break up the counter space. Can you supply details for a solution?

Linda Haldane, Las Vegas, Nev.

Extending the counter space is not as hard as it sounds. The next time you talk to your installer, just tell him you want a cutout to accommodate the window. I have to say I don't really like the idea very much, though, because it will create a trap that accumulates dirt and moisture.

Impractical Basement Addition

We're planning to demolish our home and replace it with a new one. My husband insists that our new home have a basement, but we live in an area where the soil is pure clay and the rainfall is very heavy in the winter. I'm concerned that the constant expansion and contraction of the soil will cause the basement walls to crack and then leak. Is it practical and cost-efficient to have a basement under these circumstances?

Anne Staton, Encino, Calif.

Here's a case where you have to do a balancing act. First, look around to see what your neighbors have done. If they don't have basements—or if they do but wish they didn't—

there must be a reason for it, and you'd be wise to vote with the crowd. On the other hand, building techniques and technologies have changed over the years, and there are new methods for dealing with what once were intractable moisture problems. So you have to investigate to learn what's available. The only caveat I'd add is this: If you find that a solution is available, check carefully to be sure that it isn't a brand-new solution. You want one that's been proved—that is, used successfully a number of times in recent years and in areas like yours. In a case like this, you don't want to be the guinea pig for some new technique that may—or may not—work.

Stone Foundation Sinking

Our 108-year-old home needs leveling. It sits on a slab made of limestone blocks (we think) and has settled considerably over the years. While we're at it, we'd like to add a small basement. Any advice on how we should proceed?

Deborah Womack, Douglass, Kan.

I certainly don't want to be beneath those blocks while you're digging out the basement. What you need is professional engineering help, because only an expert can tell you how to proceed safely and cost-effectively. He can also advise you on the leveling, which may not be necessary. After all, if a house has been settling for 108 years, suddenly jacking it back to plumb and level may blow out the plaster on the walls and cause timbers to fail. Unless there's structural damage, you may be better off leaving well enough alone.

Replacing a Sagging Beam

We live in an Ontario cottage built in 1865: a square, single-story house with deep overhangs. The 8×10-inch main support beam in the basement, which is held up at each end by the stone foundation and in the middle by various brick pillars and cedar posts, has become soft and crumbly in spots. We'd like to replace it, but there are some complications. A wall above and in line with the beam is solid wood—1×4 planks stacked on top of each other—and we worry about supporting all that weight during the replacement. Also, because we recently plastered a ceiling in one of the rooms above the beam, we're afraid that it will be damaged when the beam is removed. How should we proceed?

Debbie Trollope, Brussels, Ont., Can.

I can see why you'd be concerned about the new plaster, but if you don't replace that beam, you'll have much bigger problems than a few ceiling cracks; your only choice is to proceed. First, however, have the beam professionally inspected to determine what caused the wood to become soft and crumbly. If insects or rot fungi are involved, all your joists and mudsills should also be examined. Then, eliminate the problem's cause and repair or replace wood as needed. For insects, call a pest-control service; for moisture, dry out the basement. An engineer should determine a suitable size and material for a replacement beam. Don't assume it will also be an 8×10. These days it might be engineered lumber, or steel. The engineer will also specify the size and placement of the support posts and footings.

Replacing a beam involves several steps. First, temporary steel or wood beams supported by posts are placed on either side of the old beam, then they're cranked up gradually until all the weight is resting on

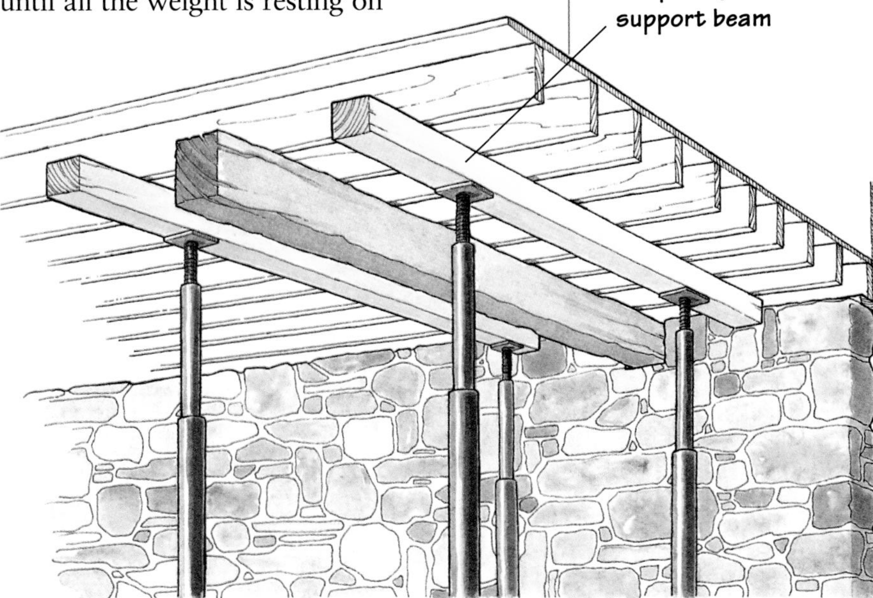

ONE REWARD *of working on old houses is the chance to lay hands on timeless materials.*

the temporary beams. After the old beam is removed, a new one is lifted into place and the support posts placed underneath. When these posts are secure, the floor is slowly lowered onto the new beam. The weight of that solid wood wall won't matter much; I've seen much heavier houses lifted with ease. If the floor hasn't sagged much, and the job is done slowly and with care, your plaster may survive intact. One more thing: This is not a project you should do yourself. Hire a general contractor with the equipment and the experience to tackle this kind of work.

Identifying Load-Bearing Walls

I'd like to open up a couple of tiny rooms in my house, but I'm not sure which walls are load bearing. Is there an easy way to determine this? What kind of specialist should I hire, and how do I protect myself if the advice is wrong?

Barbara Ansley, Edmunds, Wash.

Get what you pay your taxes for. One of the most effective and least expensive ways to find out whether your walls are load bearing is to call up town hall and ask that your local building inspector come by and check it out.

Trusses vs. Rafters

I would like your take on prefabricated trusses. All of the trusses I see these days, including the ones in my own garage, are made of 2×4s fastened with small metal plates. These trusses don't look very substantial to me. Also, they have a butt joint in the middle of the bottom chord. My grandfather was a contractor who always used 2×6 trusses and never put a joint in the middle of one. When building a house, would you use prefabricated trusses? Or would you recommend framing the roof piece by piece?

Richard Ross, Sidney, Neb.

Today's trusses are as good as or better than yesterday's trusses and are more economical, too, assuming you have proper construction and high-quality materials. That's because modern, prefabricated trusses are engineered to do exactly the job that building plans call for and to be well within the strength specifications of your local building code. Back in your grandfather's time, workmen often overbuilt trusses and other structures. To be on the safe side, builders avoided putting joints in the bottom chord, but in fact a joint there is perfectly all right because of the way a truss distributes loads. As for which method you should use when building a house, as always it's a matter of trade-offs. Framing a roof stick by stick is slower and more expensive than using trusses. But a truss roof renders the attic unusable because the cross bracing gets in the way.

Hidden Log Cabin

My husband and I are in the process of moving to an 1836 farmhouse. After we bought the farmhouse, we discovered the original house—a log cabin—had been hidden deep within extensive later construction. Can you give us some advice on how we should go about restoring the log cabin, much of which was covered with hideous paneling? We want to expose the massive logs and show them off.

Sue Turley, Evansville, Ind.

Pray for the best, but prepare for the worst as you open up the walls to see what's underneath. If you're lucky, you'll find the paneling was simply tacked to the walls, leaving nothing but lots of nail holes to patch. On the other hand, you might uncover something like the extensive damage I found when I helped the Forest Service renovate a log cabin in Montana. The cabin was 30 miles from the closest road, but apparently during the Paneling Plague of the 1950s and 1960s, nothing and no one was safe. Somebody had actually hacked notches into all the logs to make room for studs to put up paneling. All those slots—and there were many of them—had to be repaired with filler blocks. The blocks had to be cut and shaped to fit each log, then stained to match.

The cabin was 30 miles from the closest road, but during the Paneling Plague of the 1950s and 1960s, nothing and no one was safe.

Misplaced Laundry Room

I am a fan of yours and have even fantasized sometimes about adopting you. But let me pick at you about something I've seen all too often: Why do you guys at *This Old House* always put the laundry room next to the kitchen? Think about the project house in Milton, for example, which has all the bedrooms and bathrooms upstairs. Where does all the laundry come from? Where do people dress and undress, bathe, change bed linens, use towels and washcloths? Upstairs, of course. Then why is the laundry downstairs? I'll bet your design team is all men—not one woman.

Audrey R. Ricker, Pendleton, Ore.

Just for the record, our design teams aren't always all-male, but that doesn't make the difference. The point is, where does most daily activity occur? If you have a busy first floor—cooking, cleaning, entertaining, children playing—the laundry should be there too, for easy access. Otherwise you have to go up and down the stairs every time you need to start another load or switch clothes from washer to dryer. But if you work at home from an office in a spare bedroom, an upstairs laundry makes sense. There's one downside. A leak in an upstairs laundry will flood the first floor, not just the basement, and ruin the walls too. A drain pan is required under the washer-dryer, and should be connected to the plumbing system. Manual or automatic water shutoffs and burst-proof hoses covered with braided stainless-steel wire should also be used.

Claiming Attic Living Space

We want to get some additional living area out of our attic, which has a finished floor between the knee walls. I know the room needs insulation, but where?

Kurt Maier, Glendale, Ohio

Richard Trethewey and I have the same view of your situation; as he puts it, you should always "insulate—but just as important, ventilate." The goal in your case is to envelop the new living area with a continuous shell of insulation on the ceiling and the knee walls, as well as between the joists that are outboard of the knee wall (see drawing below). Attic spaces need eave-to-ridge ventilation to prevent the buildup of heat and moisture, which can lead to rot, mold, and ice dams. I'd recommend putting foam baffles between the insulation and the underside of the roof to provide a clear pathway for the air to move.

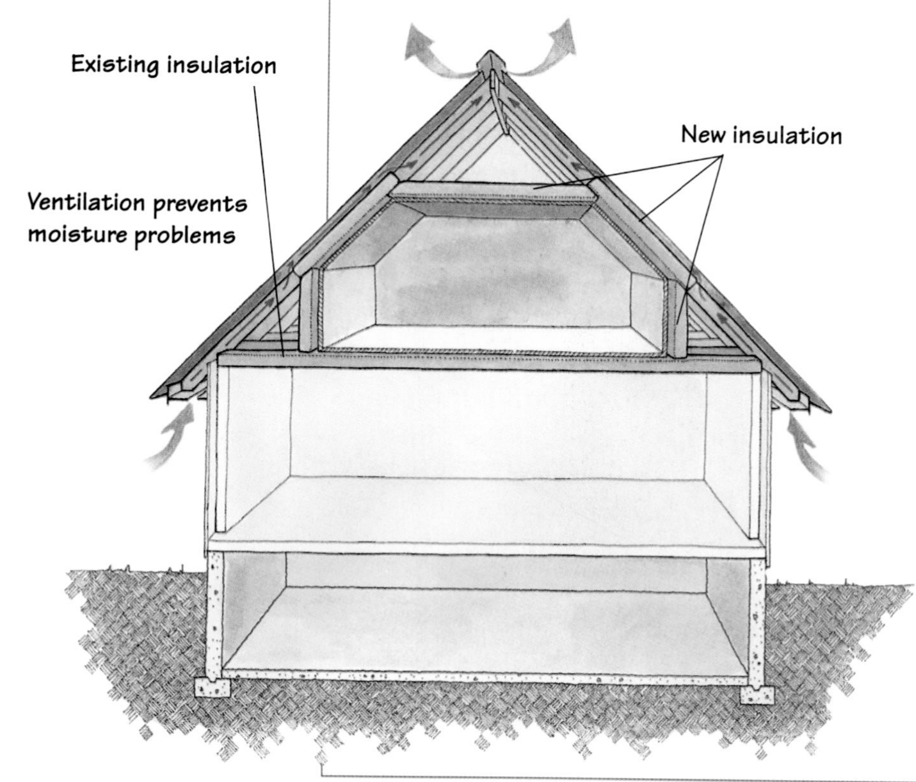

Building a Space-Efficient Shop

I've built a 14-by-17-foot room to use as my woodshop and would like some expert guidance on a layout for my power tools.

Greg Rosol, Rochester Hills, Mich.

I'm reluctant to spout off about anything as personal as a shop, but I will say that when it's small, you'll want to be able to move your tools around. That means putting them on or dropping them into movable bases whenever possible.

Preservation vs. Remodeling

I'm in my junior year at the Savannah College of Art and Design, majoring in historic preservation. One of my pre-graduation goals is to get an internship in the preservation field. Does *This Old House* have any internships?

Katherine A. Bridgett, Savannah, Ga.

Historic preservation is a discipline that moves backward; the aim is to take a house back to what it was at an earlier time. *This Old House* tends to move forward. While we try as much as we can to maintain the historical character of the houses we work on, we also integrate the kind of modern systems and materials that make the difference between the 1890s and the 1990s. I suggest you try the National Trust for Historic Preservation, 1785 Massachusetts Avenue N.W., Washington, D.C. 20036.

Shop Dust Solutions

We will soon be building our dream house, and we've planned a space for my husband's shop in the basement. Do you have any suggestions?

Marie Andrews, Mount Pleasant, Penn.

My preference is for a stand-alone building, but that's not possible for everyone. All openings between the shop and the rest of the house will have to be sealed, and you should consider installing a whole-shop vent or an air-cleaning system. At the very least, try to buy tools that have been designed to hook up to a shop vacuum. But no amount of special equipment will be enough if the workshop isn't cleaned after every use. One final piece of advice: Be sure your husband dusts himself off thoroughly before going upstairs.

Building a Space-Efficient Shop

I've built a 14-by-17-foot room to use as my woodshop and would like some expert guidance on a layout for my power tools.

Greg Rosol, Rochester Hills, Mich.

I'm reluctant to spout off about anything as personal as a shop, but I will say that when it's small, you'll want to be able to move your tools around. That means putting them on or dropping them into movable bases whenever possible.

IT'S NOT WORTH *using stock that isn't straight. The best way to check is to sight down the face and one edge.*

Remodeling Muddled

I wonder whether I was possessed when I recently purchased a 102-year-old Victorian. I always wanted an old house and fell in love with this one the first time I saw it. But I didn't realize how many problems I'd have to deal with. The breaker box was new but not the wiring, so I had to hire an electrician to redo the entire house. To keep sand out of the house and protect my laboriously refinished floors, I had to have my driveway paved. After a few days of rain, I discovered that the "new" roof was simply new shingles over old ones, with rotten sheathing underneath. Pipes from the added-on upstairs bathroom aren't connected—they simply drain out onto the roof. Not one of our 38 windows closes completely, and some won't budge at all. The walls need insulation, the brick piers that support the house are crumbling and sinking, and the heating system is shot. There's rot hidden beneath the paint, and the kitchen floor slants severely. Any advice?

Ann Weaver, Bamberg, S.C.

I don't know whether you were possessed, but you certainly were distracted when you bought the house, and you've made matters worse by not prioritizing the jobs. It's a very common mistake: New owners often try to make a major rehab tolerable by first fixing up inside to avoid the feeling of living in a construction site. But refinishing floors and paving the driveway could have waited—and should have. That's also true of rewiring. What you need to do now is step back and get organized. Job one is to call in a structural engineer. He may tell you that the piers have sunk about as far as they're going to and that all you need to do is repair the masonry, jack the house up and shim it level. He may also suggest adding one or more piers. This will stabilize your house and may alleviate some other problems. For example, windows may fix themselves once the footing levels out. Your other priority should be to start work on your roof—leaks and rot can't be tolerated. I gather you're new to the area, so you're going to have to put in a lot of time finding a contractor. Talk to your neighbors. Find out what work they've had done recently and whether they were satisfied, and don't just take their word for it—inspect the results yourself if you can. Materials suppliers also know who does good work. ■

It's a very common mistake: New owners often try to make a major rehab tolerable by first fixing up inside to avoid the feeling of living in a construction site.

CHAPTER TWO

Basements, Concrete + Chimneys

An insulated basement floor will be good for your comfort and good for your wallet, but first you've got to solve any moisture problems.

Lining an Existing Chimney

I'm interested in learning more about a repair I saw on one of your shows. An inflatable tube was put down the chimney; then mortar was poured in around the inflated tube, forming a new flue liner.

Debbie Hayward, Stephenson, Mich.

This system works, but there are a few things you need to keep in mind. If you have an old chimney built with soft lime mortar, the new mortar for the lining should have the same expansion-contraction characteristics. If the chimney is weak, the weight of a concrete liner could cause a collapse, so have an expert assess the risk. *This Old House* contractor Tom Silva recommends one-piece stainless-steel liners instead, saying it's worth the cost to get a top-quality one. Repair or repointing of the chimney will be a separate job.

Sidewalk Patch Washout

We used a bagged cement mix to patch our sidewalk. Two days later, after an unusually heavy rainstorm, we noticed that the patches were crumbling. Should we blame the rain for the bad patches and try the same mix again, or is there a different product we should try?

The Reisners, Meadville, Penn.

I assume you had small depressions or shallow potholes in the sidewalk, in which case you were trying to do something that's very difficult. Did you remember to wet the area before applying the cement? Was your mix too wet and applied in the sun on a hot day? Thin patches don't generally work well, and ordinary bagged cement mix is too coarse for this job. Visit a mason's supply for a product designed specifically for this condition.

Cracked Brick House

We have a beautiful brick house on 8 acres in rural Missouri, but we also have a crack that starts low on the front wall, then extends to the corner and up one side to the roof. At first it's just a little crack, but it eventually widens to about 1½ inches. Our house moves so much we can't keep drywall tape on the wall at the ceiling. We've been told that's because our house sits atop a large cave filled with water. Should we take down the cracked walls and rebuild them? Can we jack up the house and build a new foundation?

Ruth E. Wise, Bourbon, Mo.

When a geological feature like the one you describe is the cause, there's no quick fix. Putting in a new foundation may not stop your house from moving, because the ground itself is in motion. A civil engineer could advise you about how to make the foundation more rigid and spread its load over a wider area.

Damp Basement Floor

Our 1840s house has a fieldstone basement with a dirt floor that never completely dries out but never puddles, either, even after big rainstorms. We'd like to insulate the floor above the basement, but everyone has a different opinion about how to do it. Some say this is a good idea; others say it will trap moisture and rot the joists. What do you think?

Andrea Mischel, Groton, Mass.

DIRECT CONTACT *between concrete and most species of untreated wood eventually causes rot.*

An insulated basement floor will be good for your comfort and good for your wallet, but first you've got to solve any moisture problems. If this basement is simply a tall crawl space and is not used for storage or subject to foot traffic, cover the floor with 6-mil polyethylene sheeting followed by two inches of pea gravel. This will hold the moisture in the soil, although you'll have to be careful not to rip the plastic any time you're down there for some maintenance.

A more durable solution would be to bury the vapor barrier under two or three inches of sand and then pour a 4-inch-thick slab, the way we did in the basement of the Charlestown project. Just make sure there's enough headroom to satisfy local building codes. (You could get away with a 2-inch-thick slab if you don't plan to use the basement for living space.) Repointing any gaps and cracks in the stone walls will help to keep moisture, as well as mice, from getting in.

If you do pour a slab, you will probably have to wait a few months before you insulate because concrete releases a lot of water as it cures, and the joists overhead will need time to dry out. (You can shorten drying time by ventilating or dehumidifying the space; just wait seven days for the pour to get a good start on curing.) I'd monitor the dryness of the wood with a moisture meter until it gives a reading of 11 percent or so. At this point, it will be fine to install any type of insulation.

Chimney Brick Flakes Off

After only 30 years, the surface of my brick chimney is flaking off in spots. The existing damage isn't severe enough to warrant repair, but I'd like to prevent it from getting worse. A chimney sweep told us to install a chimney cap and to spray the brick with a commercial-grade sealer, but I was thinking about covering it with stucco instead. What do you think?

Brent Baker, Independence, Mo.

Your brick is spalling, which means that moisture is being absorbed by the porous brick, freezing, and causing portions of the face to pop off. Well-maintained stucco might prevent water from reaching the brick, but would only cover up the problem if moisture is working its way from the inside out.

FOR MORE ON CHIMNEYS TURN TO CHAPTER 5: ON AND AROUND THE ROOF

For starters, I'd take your sweep's advice and install a chimney cap to keep moisture from getting behind the brick (two options are shown below.) Also, you should have the chimney inspected by a mason. He'll take a close look at the mortar joints as well as the brick, and let you know what kind of condition they're in. If the mortar is cracked and crumbling, it will have to be chiseled out and replaced with new.

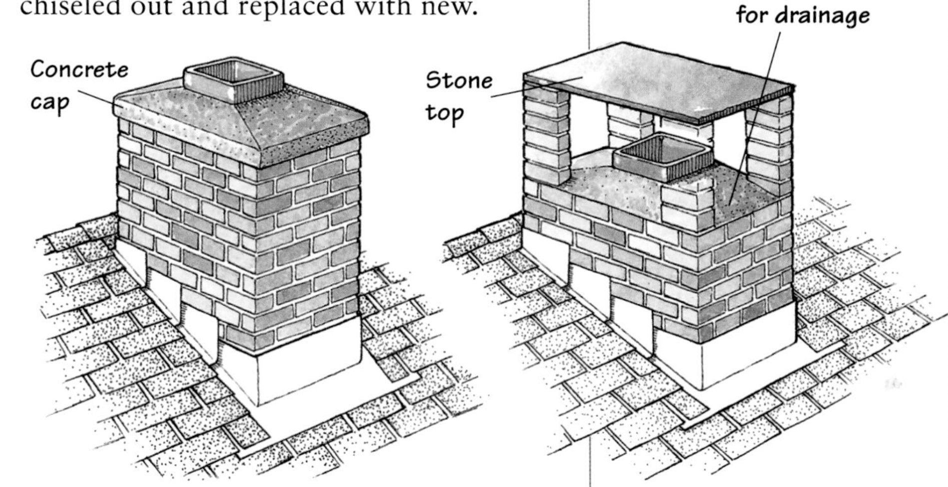

Another possible source of moisture could be your heating system. The exhaust gases of high-efficiency gas-fired furnaces contain lots of acidic water vapor, which, if routed through an unlined chimney, can cause spalling and mortar failure. Your mason can determine if this is the source of your problem when he's checking the chimney. If it is, installing a special metal flue liner (AL294-C stainless steel) should do the trick.

After you take these steps, the spalling should stop. Then you can cover your brick with stucco if you want. Just keep in mind that it will need a fair amount of maintenance in your Midwestern climate and may look out of place with the rest of the neighborhood. You can also apply a sealer to the brick, but don't expect a miracle cure. I tried sealing one of my chimneys to stop a seepage problem, and it didn't help. And mason Lenny Belliveau, who works with *This Old*

House contractor Tom Silva, tells me that you'll have to reapply it every five years or so in order to maintain its effectiveness.

Stopping Basement Seepage

You've said that only minor seepage can be stopped from inside the basement. But I've recently stopped a significant problem in my basement by drilling weep holes in the bottom course of cinder blocks and directing water to a newly installed sump pump. In addition, I coated the walls with a waterproofing masonry paint. What do you think of this combination?

Daniel J. Nieman, Rockford, Ill.

I've seen such weep holes before, where a hollow metal or plastic baseboard "dam" is cemented to the floor next to the basement walls. This dam leads any water draining out of the holes toward the sump. The dam system is okay for water that leaks in through cracks, but I don't like the idea of drain holes in a foundation. The goal, after all, is to keep water out. Even if you direct

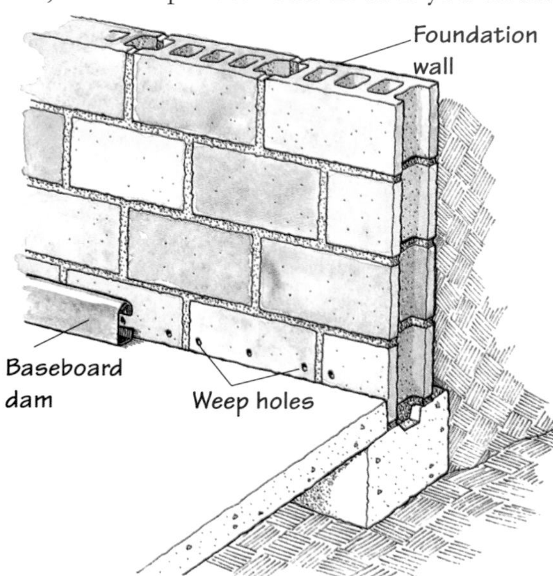

water to a sump, a little stream running alongside your basement walls will probably increase humidity levels enough to require you to use a dehumidifier. As for the "waterproofing" paint, it is formulated only to stop water from seeping through the masonry, not to completely waterproof the walls. But this part of your strategy is fine.

Crumbling Garage Slab

I have a single-car detached garage that I'd like to convert into a workshop. The structure dates to 1923, looks sound, and has a brand new roof, but the concrete floor is crumbling badly. Can I pour a new slab over the old one or will I have to tear down the building and start over?

J. Thomas-Carroll, Minneapolis, Minn.

It would be a shame to send all those new shingles to a landfill, so I'd try to save the building. A garage that's been around since '23 won't be perfect, but if the structure is sound—the walls are fairly plumb and you can sight down the roof edge without getting seasick—the foundation is probably in decent shape, and that's quite an asset.

You have a couple of alternatives for fixing the floor. If the crumbling is superficial, you can pour a self-leveling topping compound over it. These toppings can be as thin as ¼-inch and don't have to be troweled smooth. Within 12 hours, this surface will harden enough to walk on, and within a few days, you'll be able to park a table saw on it.

If the crumbling and cracking go deeper than ½-inch, you could pour a new concrete slab over the old one. It should be 2½ to 4 inches thick, so keep in mind that you'll lose some headroom and probably have to reframe and reposition all the doors. For an overlay slab like this, you'll want to attach a ½-inch-thick strip of fiberboard to the garage walls before the concrete is poured. The fiberboard, often used in sidewalk joints, provides a measure of cushioning so the new slab can move a bit, and, in those cases where the wall framing rests on the old slab, it serves as a barrier so the wood won't be buried in concrete, which will hasten rot. To get a good bond between the slabs, clean the old one thoroughly with a wire brush, vacuum, and just before the pour, dampen the surface with water and apply a concrete bonding agent.

FOR MORE ON BASEMENT REMODELING, TURN TO CHAPTER 1: GENERAL REMODELING AND REPAIRS

Your last resort would be to rent a jackhammer, break up and haul away

TAKING A BREAK *during the Milton House project, Norm pauses to assess the day's progress.*

the old slab, then hire a concrete contractor to pour a new one. He should put a polyethylene vapor barrier on the ground, cover it with an inch or two of sand (so the concrete will cure on schedule), and use steel-mesh reinforcement. A mix with a compressive strength of at least 3,500 to 4,000 psi should be sufficient. For your wintry climate, I'd recommend using air-entrained concrete, which does a better job than regular concrete of resisting freezing weather.

Pros Disagree on Settling

We are the owners of a four-story brownstone built in the late 1870s. Sometime in the 1890s, a three-story brick addition was added. The walls of the addition were attached to the original house with mortar only. It has cracked quite a bit, for reasons we discovered in the middle of our renovation: The foundation under the addition doesn't extend below the frost line, leaving it susceptible to soil movement. Apparently that was fairly common for the era, but the settling damage proves it wasn't a good idea. Our architect and our building contractor, however, are giving us mixed messages about how to solve the problem. What do you think?

Chris Danguilan, Brooklyn, N.Y.

Whenever opinions differ between a contractor and an architect regarding structural issues, there's only one person to turn to: a structural engineer. Architects and many builders can handle some structural calculations, but only a structural engineer specializes in quantifying the forces tugging at a house, so that's who should calculate a response that will counteract them. Some of the critical issues I'd expect the engineer to examine in your project would be the poor connection between the addition and the house, the bearing capacity of the soil, and the weight of the addition and its contents.

When the engineer specifies exactly what should be done, your architect and contractor can huddle up to figure out how to do it. For instance, there are ways to anchor masonry walls to each other using epoxy and rebar, the way we did at the Santa Barbara project. But nothing will keep that joint together if the addition continues to settle.

Whenever opinions differ between a contractor and an architect regarding structural issues, there's only one person to turn to.

Sinking Slab Floors

Our garage has a concrete slab floor, and the adjacent family room that's one step above it is also on a slab. Unfortunately, both floors have gradually settled since they were poured about 40 years ago. The garage is the worst; it is down about 3½ inches in one area. The family room slab has settled about ½ inch. I've heard that slabs can be raised, and I know that they can be replaced. What would you do?

Jon Ralinovsky, Oxford, Ohio

Slabs can sink if poured on improperly compacted fill or soil loaded with organic material, or if a broken water or sewer pipe washes the sub-slab fill away. Slab-jacking (we call

FOR MORE ON SLABS, TURN TO CHAPTER 1: GENERAL REMODELING AND REPAIRS

it mud-jacking around here) is a technique that calls for drilling a series of 2-inch-diameter holes through the sunken slab, then pumping quick-setting cement and sand grout (the "mud") through the holes under pressure. The pressure lifts the slab as the grout fills voids in the soil. When the grout hardens, it supports the slab in its new position and the holes are patched. You can jack almost any slab this way, including driveways, sidewalks, and patios, as long as it's in good condition. But just because you can doesn't mean that you should. The settling in your family room doesn't sound that bad to me; I'd probably leave the slab alone or top it with a layer of self-leveling floor leveling compound. Mixed to the consistency of pancake batter and poured over a floor, it hardens to a surface smooth enough to accept finish flooring.

Whether you should go with slab-jacking or demolition on the garage floor is a tough call. Slab-jacking is less disruptive, but demolishing and replacing a slab can be cheaper, particularly when there's good access for pavement breakers and trucks to haul off the debris. Your best bet is to get bids from at least four contractors and check their references. You might even want to call in an engineer for an independent evaluation. That way, all the contractors can base their bids on the same analysis.

THE FIRST *order of business at the Watertown house: replace termite-infested sills.*

Spending $5,000 on a dubious technique to prevent modest damage from a once-in-a-lifetime storm seems excessive to me.

Flooded Out

Our 50-year-old house sits on a hillside overlooking a river and has a walkout basement. The river's level is normally about 30 feet below the house, but about a month after we moved in, Hurricane Floyd hit the area and dumped over 23 inches of rain on us in 24 hours. As water seeped into our basement through cracks between the slab and the block walls, we mopped, swept, and hustled to keep the water heading toward a single floor drain. When the storm ended, we had about 3 inches of water in the basement. Now we'd like to finish the basement but want to solve our water problem first. One company quoted us a price of $5,000 to spray fiberglass onto the block walls and about 12 inches onto the floor, saying that the technique is used frequently to waterproof industrial facilities. Does this sound like a reasonable solution?

Arthur Midgette Jr., Smithfield, Va.

We'd all like to believe that our houses will protect us from everything, but when a storm like Floyd hits we're reminded of just how vulnerable they, and we, are. Granted, you spent some anxious moments in the hurricane, but it sounds like your house rode it out rather nicely thanks to that one floor drain. Spending $5,000 on a dubious technique to prevent modest damage from a once-in-a-lifetime storm seems excessive to me. You'd be better off with simpler, less expensive, and more dependable solutions, such as ensuring proper drainage around your house and painting the inner foundation walls with a cementitious paint to eliminate seepage. And no matter what, don't ever let that floor drain get clogged.

Garage Floor Always Wet

The house we bought last summer is built on bedrock and has such a severe conden-

sation problem in the garage that a thin film of standing water forms on the floor. Any tool left in the garage rusts quickly, and the water wicks up the wall between the two garage doors. Is there any product we can use to prevent this problem?

John Gemery, Norwich, Vt.

This doesn't sound like condensation to me. I'd be surprised if there was anywhere near enough humidity in your location to accumulate as standing water. More likely, your culprit is the bedrock beneath or near the slab, which is probably diverting water into the garage through hairline cracks or the joints between the slab and the foundation wall. There might even be an underground spring that's forcing water into your garage. First, try sealing up all cracks and joints with hydraulic cement. If that doesn't work, you will need to create a landscape drainage system outside that stops the water from getting underneath the slab.

Hiding Ugly Concrete

We need your advice for correcting two eyesores on our hillside home: an exposed concrete foundation wall around the entry and a concrete retaining wall at one corner of the driveway. We thought about covering the concrete with stone, but were sobered by a $13,000 bid to cover about 600 square feet of wall. Are there any other less expensive approaches we should consider?

Craig Beyer, Park City, Utah

Concrete makes a wonderful foundation, but who wants to look at it in its raw form? Around the entryway, I'd simply cover it with siding to match the house—I can't imagine why that wasn't done in the first place. The work is straightforward: just take pressure-treated wood furring strips and anchor them vertically to the concrete, 16 inches apart, using masonry screws or spring spikes. The face of the strips should be flush with the back of the existing siding. Then nail the clapboards to the strips. You should leave at least 8 inches between the bottom of the furring strips and the finish grade to protect the wood from splashing water. Plug the opening along the bottom with short lengths of furring to discourage insects and other pests from moving in. Also, be sure to prime all surfaces of the siding before installation. As for that concrete retaining wall, you might want to use gauged stone—rectangular "tiles" of a fairly consistent thickness—to keep installation costs down.

Finishing the Basement

I'm planning to finish off the interior of my basement but don't want to go to the trouble of putting up studs. Instead, I'd like to glue rigid foam insulation to the concrete walls and then glue drywall on top of it. What do you think of this plan?

Rob Hayes, Spokane, Wash.

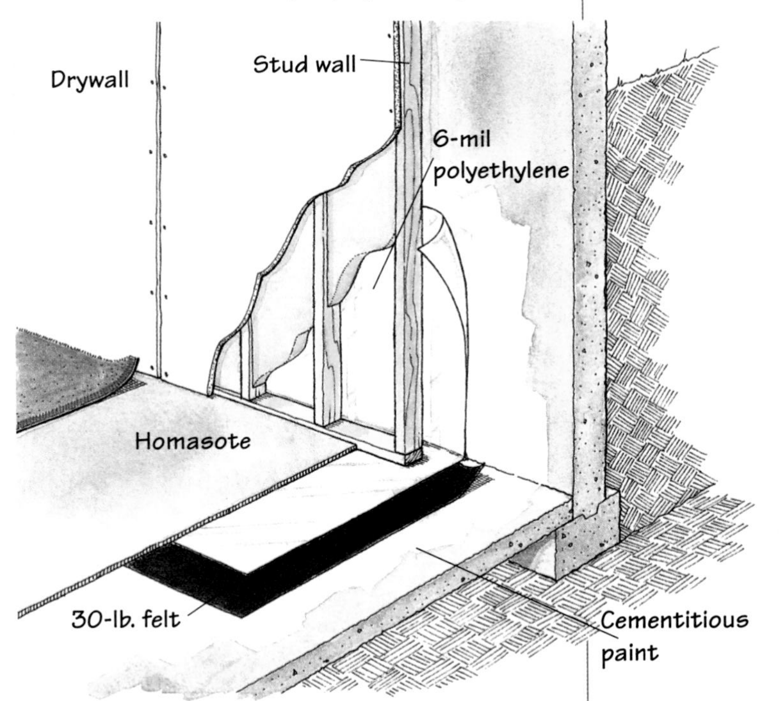

You have more faith in the holding power of adhesives than I do. Even if you get both materials to stay in place, which I doubt you can, the assembly won't be strong enough for you to mount electrical boxes or add any of the other amenities you'd likely want in a basement. To do it the right way, construct stud walls just inside the foundation walls (see drawing above). Then you can insulate, wire, and finish them as normal.

Basement Water Defense

I want to build a storage closet in my basement for off-season clothing. The basement sump pump runs continuously during heavy rainstorms and in the spring, but only sporadically the rest of the year. How would you recommend I proceed?

William J. O'Neil, Gaithersburg, Md.

I'd think twice before storing anything valuable in a basement where the first line of defense against water is an overworked sump pump. For more reliable protection, you should make sure that your gutters and downspouts are moving rainwater away from the foundation. Beyond that, you could regrade or install French drains, but these are expensive solutions, especially if you only have problems part of the year. If you do choose to rely just on a sump pump, you should make sure your unit has the capacity to handle anything that Mother Nature dishes out: A ⅓-HP submersible pump should do the job. You may want a power generator or battery bank as a backup to keep the pump running if the power goes out. Finally, to protect against dampness and mildew, run a dehumidifier in the rainy seasons. Your wardrobe will thank you.

WHAT LOOKS GOOD *from the outside may conceal rot beneath. Here's one way to find out.*

Settling of a foundation is common and can often be ignored ... if it has stopped.

Garage Floor Paint Peeling

The concrete floor of my garage is over 40 years old. I painted it with a latex porch-and-deck paint, then let it cure for over a month before driving in. But even so, the paint just peels up where the tires touch it. Can you suggest a solution?

Alphonse Miele, Yonkers, N.Y.

I think you made a mistake in your choice of paint. Even "floor & porch" paints suitable for use on concrete aren't likely to survive conditions in the "tire lane." Hot rubber lifts paint as easily as a heat gun, and the solvents, grit, water, and small stones that tires drag in do a good bit of damage, too. If you want to paint a garage floor, it's better to use a two-part, industrial-grade epoxy paint. It can be brushed, rolled, or squeegeed on. (Don't try to clean epoxy-covered applicators—you'll have to toss them once the paint starts to harden.) Paint won't stick to oily or wet concrete, so you'll have to pressure-wash the floor with detergent and water to remove any oil. Just let the concrete dry thoroughly before you put on the coating. Be warned: If moisture gets under the slab, and you don't have a vapor barrier to stop it from migrating up through the concrete, the epoxy will bubble, blister, or pop off.

Deteriorating Concrete Walls

For 40 years, I've lived with concrete turning to powder and spalling off the lower part of my basement walls. The condition is not aesthetically pleasing. I've tried various specialty paint products without success—nothing sticks. Moisture is probably the cause—but the house has good gutters and drainage. The basement isn't wet—the tools

I store there don't rust and leather goods don't mildew. Before I get started on this, I'd appreciate your comments.

Pete Landry, Mystic, Conn.

After four decades, the surface must look like a war zone. Spalling, where the surface of the concrete flakes off, can be caused by a number of things, but the peeling paint and powdering (a film of mineral salts called efflorescence) indicate without a doubt that moisture is slowly damaging your walls. Because only the lower walls are affected, my hunch is that it's coming up from under the basement floor. First, you'll need to clean off the efflorescence with a dry brush or diluted muriatic acid (wear gloves and eye protection, and rinse well). Then seal every crack or hole on the floor slab and the walls with an epoxy mortar.

In addition, lay down a bead of polyurethane sealant in all the corners and along the seam between floor and wall. To stop the spalling, I recommend applying a hydraulic cement patching compound before sealing the walls with a breathable coating such as latex paint.

Skirting a Problem

Our 1926 Sears kit-built home has 42 original double-hung windows, most with original glass. How do we repair them and make them as weatherproof as possible? Also, we have all the original longleaf pine floors, but there is no sub-flooring. We are going to stone-skirt the house, which sits 36 inches off the ground on 64 concrete piers. What is the best method of insulating and weatherproofing this work? The ground is very dry and has excellent drainage, and moisture is not a problem.

Kip and Beverly Zimmerman, Blanco, Tex.

With 42 windows to renovate, I'd say you've got plenty of work on your hands. If you want to get a book on the subject of rehabilitating windows, make sure it covers the repair of windows that have sash weights, pulleys, and old glass. Your stone skirt sounds like a good idea. Properly done, it'll make your house appear as if it's part of the landscape instead of floating above it, and it will hide the piers. Be sure to check beneath the house so you don't hide any problems that will be hard to get at later, and take care to provide adequate venting (well-screened to keep bugs and animals out). Finally, insulate between the joists with fiberglass batts or sprayed-on foam insulation, which is installed by licensed contractors. But don't buy any more R-value than necessary. You can find out how much venting and insulation you'll need by talking to a town building inspector who is familiar with local codes.

FOR MORE ON WINDOWS, TURN TO CHAPTER 4: DOORS AND WINDOWS

When to Solve Settling

My husband and I own a 1921 California bungalow. We knew it had settled, but since the house passed an inspection easily, we thought it was nothing to worry about. We've spoken to several contractors, however, and all of them tell us to fix the settling by jacking up the foundation. One mentioned that secondary problems could arise from the work. Is the settling something we should rush to correct?

Kelly Peck, Los Angeles, Calif.

Settling of a foundation is common and can often be ignored . . . if it has stopped. In older houses, it usually has. The contractor who mentioned secondary problems is right, though. Houses are like people. If you spend all afternoon in a hammock, you could pull some muscles if you leap to your feet. Your house has spent more than 75 years "getting settled," and any attempt to jack it back to its original condition may indeed cause other problems. That's why it should be done very slowly—if at all.

That Summer-Place Smell

Our 10-year-old cabin is built into the side of a hill. The basement is buried on three sides, which are cement block, but you can

walk out the front, which has siding and sliding glass doors. I smell mold, but my husband doesn't. I think we need more air circulation. He says we should just keep the basement warm, summer and winter. What do you suggest?

Judy A. Matthias, Bloomington, Minn.

Whether or not you have mold now, warmth isn't the solution. If you've got moisture, warmth won't get rid of it and may only foster mold growth. The key is plenty of air circulation to keep the humidity down. If the cabin is closed all winter and shaded, you're going to have some mildew. If only one of you smells it and the other doesn't, maybe all you have is "summer-place smell," that temporary fustiness that most of us associate with such cabins.

Crumbling Family Fireplace

In the basement of my 1857 house, moisture is damaging an inlaid-stone fireplace my father built by hand about 45 years ago. I'm baffled because I'm confident I've done everything possible to keep the basement dry. That includes installing new gutters, making sure the ground is graded properly, patching and sealing cracks and running a dehumidifier on humid summer days. The basement can be damp at times, but it's never wet. Still, the mortar in the fireplace and on the walls is starting to crumble. Outside, the chimney is faring a bit better, but I am concerned about it also. Is there some kind of modern product, maybe a spray-on or brush-on solution, that can stabilize the old mortar?

Allan Cotter, Prescott, Wis.

You may have moisture coming from the chimney, the one point of entry you haven't tended to. If so, the solution may be as simple as installing a chimney cap. Or the flashing may be failing. But I suspect moisture may not be your problem at all. It's possible that the mortar that is crumbling may not have been mixed properly to begin with. You'll probably have to chip all the loose mortar out of the joints and repoint the fireplace and chimney. As for a spray-on or brush-on solution, that's pretty much the Holy Grail of home repair. Lots of people are looking for it, but no one has found it yet.

Gas Furnace Flue Flaws

I bought a house that was once heated with coal but now has a high-efficiency gas furnace that vents—like the hot-water heater—through the original, unlined chimney. As a result, a lot of condensation is seeping into the house. Three chimney specialists have recommended lining the chimney. One wants to install a stainless-steel flue and insulate the gaps between it and the chimney wall. The second contractor proposes installing a stainless-steel flue without insulation. The third suggests a spiral-weld flexible liner that is very expensive. What do you suggest?

Anthony Cuschieri, Westwood, N.J.

High-efficiency gas furnaces generate a lot of exhaust moisture as a by-product of combustion, but because the exhaust isn't hot, I see no need for insulation. As for a liner, yes, you need one. Spiral-weld liners are expensive, but they're the easiest to install. We've used them several times on the show.

Seeping Block Foundation

I am restoring an 1860s log cabin and am stymied because I get water seepage through the cinder-block foundation every time it rains. Are there products I can use to seal the blocks?

Michael J. Smith, Montfort, Wisc.

Yes, you can seal the blocks, but doing it from the outside is the only way I know to stop anything beyond seepage, and that means major excavation work. I'd check for drainage problems first. Are the gutters and leader pipes doing a good job of carrying water away? Is the soil around the house graded to divert water? If you correct these problems, you should notice an improvement. Gutters, admittedly, don't go very

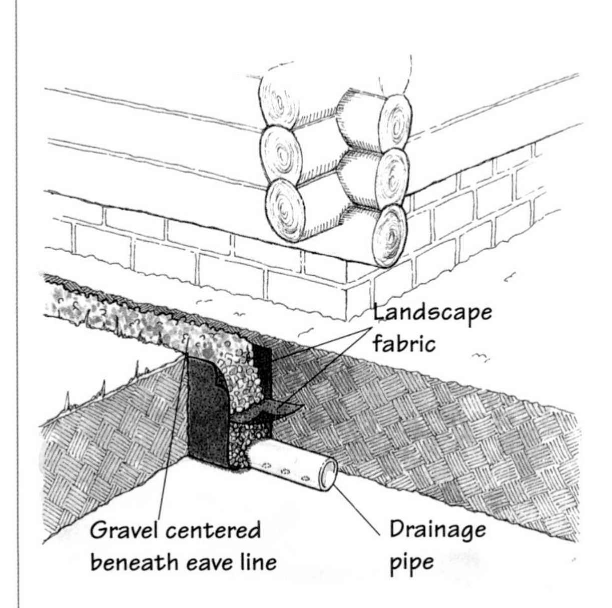

well with a log cabin, so you might consider a solution we've used on the show several times (see drawing above). Below the eaves, dig a trench that slopes to a spot at least 10 feet from the house and line it with landscaping fabric, which filters out dirt but lets water through. Then lay down a length of perforated plastic drainage pipe, with the holes facing down. Cover the pipe with washed stone (sometimes called pea gravel), more fabric, and fill the trench with any kind of freely-draining gravel. The perforated pipe will collect water and carry it away before it soaks into the ground and into your foundation.

Cold Joints Make Leaky Walls

The problem with our old farmhouse is our wet and unsightly basement. It was hand-dug, and the walls were poured one wheelbarrowful of cement at a time by the farmer who built it. The floor is bedrock, and in one corner a boulder sticks up that the farmer obviously couldn't move. My husband wants to redo the whole basement. I think we can save money by just waterproofing it. What do you think we should do?

Danielle Thompson, Hermantown, Minn.

A foundation doesn't have to be waterproof to hold a house up, but dampness can damage the wood structure. If you want a dry basement, first check that your grading slopes sufficiently to carry water away from the house. Poor grading is surprisingly common on older properties, and it's simple and relatively inexpensive to fix. If the grading is OK, the next option is to repair the foundation with hydraulic cement. Each time your farmer poured his cement, it began to cure. By the time he was able to pour another batch, the earlier one had hardened just enough so that the two batches couldn't bond properly. This is called a cold joint. The result: a cracked and leaky foundation. Chisel out the seams and then fill them with hydraulic cement.

FOR MORE ON BASEMENTS, TURN TO CHAPTER 1: GENERAL REMODELING AND REPAIRS

Settling Fireplace Cracks

Our old house is a large 100-year-old Colonial with a limestone foundation that has settled over the years. Deep cracks have gradually emerged in the brick fireplace surround, which has a center section flanked by two brick wings. Should we fill the cracks with colored grout to match the existing material?

Claudia Else, Toledo, Iowa

I'm afraid that the damage calls for more than cosmetic crack repairs. Judging by your photos and the description of the house, I'd say that the center section of the fireplace is resting on a firm masonry foundation while the cracking left wing of the surround is supported by sagging wood floor joists. A look in the basement may confirm that's what the problem is.

Hire a mason to push the wing back into place and mechanically connect it to the main portion of the fireplace, using metal reinforcing bar (rebar) embedded in the masonry with heat-resistant grout. If the job is done well, with a grout color matched to the original, you'll hardly be able to tell where the new work ends and the old begins. While this may fix the crack, you should also consider installing Lally columns under the floor joists to help support the wing. ■

A foundation doesn't have to be waterproof to hold a house up, but dampness can damage the wood structure.

CHAPTER THREE

Exterior Walls + Siding

Preserving Wood Clapboards

It's time to strip the clapboards on our 1920 Colonial down to the bare wood. I remember reading that some painters apply a wood preservative to bare wood before painting. Would you recommend this procedure?

Al Wiegman, Boston, Mass.

Absolutely. Weathering tests have shown that coating bare wood with a water-repellent preservative reduces the wood's tendency to shrink and swell. And the more stable a surface, the better it holds paint. There are water-based and solvent-based repellents; both appear to be effective. Make sure the repellent is labeled as "paintable," however. And if any lands on a painted surface, wipe it off before it dries.

Treating the wood this way is not a substitute for priming. Just be sure to allow the repellent sufficient time to dry (as specified on the can) before brushing on a primer.

Stripping Paint Off Shingles

I own a 1913 Arts and Crafts bungalow with cedar-shingle siding and roof brackets that have been painted many times. Originally, I believe, the shingles had been dipped in green stain. I'd like to strip the paint off the shingles, then stain them again. I've already stripped a few areas with a power washer because I was worried about sanding—the house surely has lead paint in some of the layers. But am I going about this the right way?

Carol Chase, Sioux City, Iowa

Power washing isn't a good way to remove paint from cedar shingles, or any other kind of wood. Not only does it damage the surface, it can drive water into the wall cavities and wash lead residues into your soil.

We've encountered many painted-shingle houses on *This Old House* and have found that there really is no cost-effective way to strip them. And since you want to stain the wood, the job will be even harder because you'll have to remove every last bit of paint.

FITTING SIDE WALL *shingles at the corners of a house calls for Norm's careful craftsmanship.*

Experience has taught us that it's easier and faster to remove the shingles and install new ones—I'd use clear R&R (resquared and rebutted) western red cedar shingles and dip them in stain before nailing them up.

You can take the paint off your roof brackets by wet-scraping them or by using a chemical paint stripper. Just take the necessary precautions to avoid contaminating yourself or the surrounding environment with lead.

Paint Prep for Rusty Nailheads

We're restoring our 1897 clapboard house, but before we paint the exterior, I'd like to know how we should handle the rusty nails on the siding. Some nails are slightly countersunk, while others are not. I've received lots of conflicting advice on this and wonder what you think.

Sandra Sorensen, Allentown, Pa.

Rust is not only unsightly, it's also bad for wood. Mild-steel nails—the sort used to secure siding when your house was built—expand as they corrode, which encourages water to seep in around their shanks. I've even seen the shanks rust away to mere slivers on houses of your vintage and older. But let's assume that your clapboards aren't that far gone. If they are securely fastened and just need some cosmetic attention, painter John Dee says that you should start off by looking closely at the nails.

If a rust stain has penetrated through paint that is soundly adhered, he says, simply spot-prime the rusty areas with a good oil-based rust-inhibitive primer. If a rusty nailhead is above the surface of the wood, he sands off the rust, sinks the nail, applies rust-inhibitive primer, putties over the hole, and spot-primes with an oil-based wood primer. For exposed nailheads below the surface of the wood, removing the rust would be horribly time-consuming. Instead, Dee uses a small brush to dab the nailhead with a red- or white-oxide primer or a rust converter. After the rust converter dries, he paints the nail and the hole with a rust-inhibitive primer, being particularly careful to seal the end

FOR MORE ON PAINTING, TURN TO CHAPTER 6: PAINTING AND FINISHING

Weathering tests have shown that coating bare wood with a water-repellent preservative reduces the wood's tendency to shrink and swell. And the more stable a surface, the better it holds paint.

Caulk is necessary for the vertical joints in siding, but keep it away from the clapboard's horizontal edges.

grain around the hole. Then he fills the hole with putty, spot-primes the putty, and paints.

When a clapboard pops loose because the nails are rusted through, you'll have to tap the old iron out of the siding and refasten it into good wood with stainless steel nails. Then just prime, putty, spot-prime, and paint as above. With stainless-steel nails, you'll never have to worry about rust again.

Repairs for Gouged Siding

Years ago, someone used a pressure washer to remove loose paint from the cedar clapboard on my house, leaving gouges as deep as 3⁄16 of an inch in many places. I tried to smooth out the mess with a belt sander, then primed the bare wood and painted it. But the gouged areas still look terrible. Before painting my house again, what kind of filler should I use to fill the gouges?

John Frenzel, Saginaw, Mich.

Filling small areas is one thing, but the damage you describe would be time-consuming to prepare, fill, and sand. And even if you did, painter John Dee doubts whether any filler would last as long as the paint. "You'd probably create a maintenance monster," he says. For gouges less than 1⁄16 of an inch deep, he and I both think that you're better off feathering the edges with 180-grit paper and a palm sander or sanding block, not a belt sander. (If the old paint has lead in it, call a lead-abatement pro.) Then prime the bare wood and paint again. I'll bet 90 percent of the people who go by your house won't even notice the damage unless they make an up-close inspection. And for those deeper gouges, Dee suggests a coat of primer, followed by a fill coat of exterior spackle. Sand it smooth, as above, and prime again. By the way, your letter is a good argument for keeping pressure washers away from people who don't know how to handle them.

Paint Removal Methods

We live in a house that was built in 1907. The siding is wood clapboard, and the paint is flaking off in many areas. I know power-washing isn't a good way to strip paint, but the alternatives—chemical stripping or hand scraping—might be more expensive than simply replacing all the siding. I'd appreciate your advice.

Paul C. Watson, Jr., Rock Hill, S.C.

I'll try to untangle this by starting with the most important fact: 1907. Unless your house has already been stripped down to bare wood, it's covered by layers of toxic lead-based paint. So you're right that pressure washing, which can gouge wood siding and blow loose paint into the air, is absolutely not the way to go. Stripping with heat or chemicals will be slow and expensive, but removing the siding—a tactic we used on the Watertown project—won't be cheap, either. I'd suggest that you get at least two bids from lead-abatement contractors for removing the paint, and another set of bids from carpenters for removing, properly disposing of, and replacing the siding. Whichever method you use, you'll still have to repaint the wood, but with new siding, I highly recommend priming all surfaces of the clapboards, including the backs, before they are nailed up.

DETERIORATING *sidewall shingles often conceal the water-damaged sheathing beneath.*

Flashing for Plywood Siding

I live in a contemporary-style house that was built in 1977, and I think I have a big problem with my plywood siding. Along the bottom edge of each sheet, the builder inserted an L-shaped piece of wood sort of like flashing with the short leg behind the ply and the long leg of the L overhanging the top edge of horizontal 1¥12 trim boards. In most places around the house, the exposed part of the L has cupped upward, so it acts like a trough to collect water every time it rains. Naturally, the L is rotting, and I've been digging out the rotted wood as I have time. That leaves a gap of about ¼ inch between the trim and the plywood. What do you suggest that I do next?

Gene Moore, Greensboro, N.C.

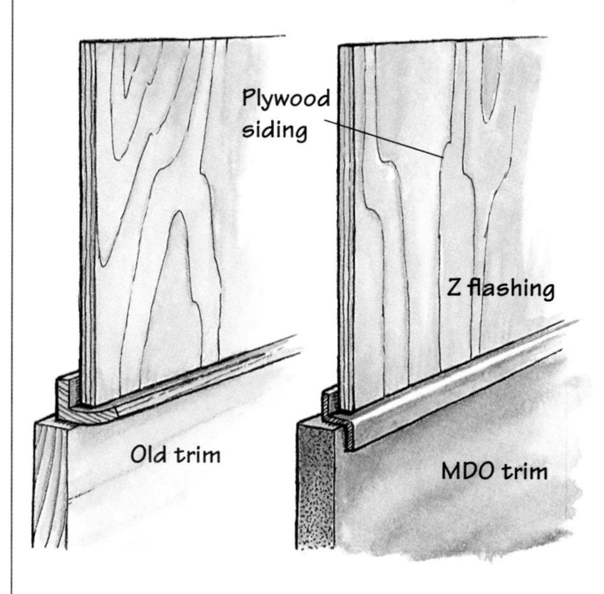

I think it was Mr. Magoo who said, "That's the most unheard of thing I've ever heard of!" and he'd probably say that a lot if he had followed your builder around. Unconventional detailing like this is just about the perfect way to destroy siding. Fortunately, there's an easy way to protect horizontal trim—metal Z-flashing— that also keeps water out of the horizontal joints between plywood (see drawing above) . One leg of the Z slips behind the siding's bottom edge, the other hangs over the siding or trim below. If you can't find any locally, a sheet-metal shop can make some up using aluminum or copper stock.

Here's what I'd do: Remove the 1¥12 trim—it's probably rotting anyway—and dig out the remnants of your L-shaped "flashing." Then I'd replace the 1¥12s with MDO (medium-density overlay) plywood or an engineered lumber product such as exterior-grade hardboard. Neither product will warp, twist, or shrink, even when used in wide dimensions. Prime all surfaces before installation, and then protect the top edges with Z-flashing.

Caulking Clapboard Siding

We've had conflicting advice from painters about whether to caulk the bottom edge of the lap siding on our 1889 Victorian. Some say caulk is the best way to keep out the rain and others say to leave it alone so the walls can breathe and release any moisture. Which is it?

Tony Barnes, Varnville, S.C.

Perhaps the painters who advocate caulking are looking for some job security. Sealing up the gaps between boards forces water vapor into the wood where it can pop off the paint. Caulk is necessary for the vertical joints in siding, but keep it away from the clapboard's horizontal edges.

Removing Oil Stain

My wife and I own a 10-year-old house that has thick "slab pine" siding left rough on the exposed side. I want to remove all three coats of oil stain and apply one that will leave the pine looking as natural as possible. Is there a way to remove all of the stain? What about sandblasting?

John P. Holtz, Three Lakes, Wisc.

I'm afraid it's too late to do much. After three coats of oil stain, you won't get back to a natural color without taking off a lot of wood. Sandblasting or power-washing will just damage it. You could try a deck-stain stripper, but with all the mess and expense that would entail, it would be easier to learn to like the color you've got.

Recurring Stains on Redwood

Our clapboards are clear, all-heart California redwood, so they should be beautiful.

THE COOL DAYS OF FALL *offer the last opportunity to square away exterior repairs.*

If only! Last fall our painter suggested power-washing and a finish of vinyl acrylic latex stain. The washing was a little too powerful—in some areas it scarred the siding—and I thought he applied the stain before the wood could dry (we'd also had a spell of heavy rains). He said not to worry, but a month later we had streaks and stains all over. We don't know how to remove them—the stains come back even after a wash-down with trisodium phosphate (TSP)—and neither, apparently, do the experts. One of them said, "If you stand far enough back you can't see the stains." What's your opinion?

Linda Baur, Sherkston, Ont., Canada

That's some expert you've got there. I'm surprised he didn't suggest wearing dark glasses. The stains are caused by "extractive bleeding," extractives being the chemicals in redwood that resist rot. Because they are water-soluble, they will leech through the finish and onto the surface when water penetrates or gets behind the siding. As you've discovered, getting rid of the stains takes more than a little TSP. To make them disappear entirely, you also need to apply latex stain-blocking primer, and put on two new finish coats of latex paint or stain (this was suggested by the California Redwood Association, which reminded me that priming the back of the siding before it's installed is the best way to prevent bleeding). I have warned before about the dangers of power-washing; even some professionals don't do it properly.

Sheathing Solution

In the near future, I plan to remove the defective strand-board siding on my house and replace it with fiber-cement clapboards. The current sheathing is a blue foamboard. Because I was told to blind-nail the new siding to solid sheathing, I plan to remove the foamboard and replace it with sheets of half-inch MDO (medium-density overlay)—I have a large supply available to me at no cost. Will it work as sheathing? Will I also need housewrap?

Robert L. Brookshire, Richmond Hill, Ga.

The MDO should be fine if you use at least 6d nails and put housewrap tape over all the joints—that way, you won't need housewrap or building paper. Fiber-cement claps should be power-nailed, but adjust the nailer so that the nail heads rest on the siding's surface, leaving room for it to expand and contract. Having said that, it might be easier to leave the blue foam in place and nail the cement boards to the studs (unless they are more than 16 inches on center); you'll save time and retain the insulating value of the foam. But check with the siding manufacturer first.

Siding With Flare

We want to strip the aluminum siding from our 1904 Shingle-style house. I took some off a long, covered porch a few years ago and found the shingles beneath to be in excellent condition. Now we want to keep going. The original builder's drawings show flared shingles where the ground-floor walls meet the foundation, and over the first- and second-floor windows. We suspect the siding men may have removed this detail to make it easier to hang the aluminum. Is it reasonable to restore it?

Tabb Schreder, Toledo, Ohio

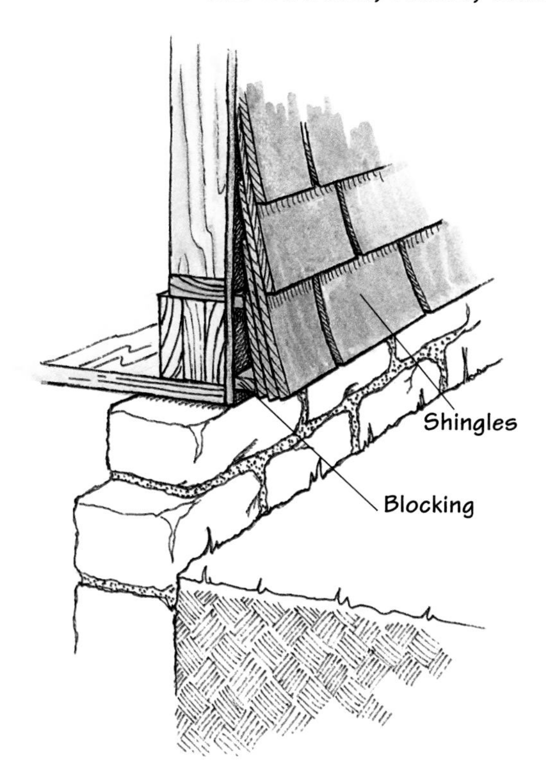

Yes, and you'll be re-creating a graceful feature that was thoughtlessly destroyed (see drawing above). This kind of work is tedious, but it's not expensive or especially difficult. Any shingler worth his salt should be able to do it, and fortunately, you have the drawings to help him get it right. The result will show nicely, right where the whole neighborhood can admire it. Can't beat that.

Choosing New Siding

I'm confused about siding my house. I've gotten prices ranging from $6,000 to $16,000. I've been told to strip off the old siding first—and also to put the new right over the old. I've been pitched on both vinyl and aluminum, on thick and thin, on foil facing out and foil facing in. And what's a fair price per square foot, anyway?

Gale Julia Hysler, Malverne, N.Y.

Let's go back to square one for just a second. Are you certain new siding is your only option? Unless your present siding is seriously deteriorated, you may need only a paint job, which will save you plenty. If you must re-side, however, get itemized bids—comparing them may explain the $10,000 spread. For example, one bid may include stripping off the old siding while another doesn't. Or the bids might specify different grades of materials. And some contractors lowball bids by including only the most necessary work, while others include such details as wrapping the soffits and covering the fascia and rake boards. As for insulation, I'm not convinced of its value, but if you install it, be sure it's the perforated type that allows for ventilation. Where you live, it's more important to keep the heat in, so put the foil face-in. By the way, don't overlook wood clapboard or shingle siding. To my eye they are a fine complement to the exterior of any house. Given all these variables, it's just not possible to produce a "fair" square-foot cost. Decide what you need and can afford, then check out your contractor. How long has he been in business? Is he insured for workmen's comp? Is he a local—someone who has to live with his clients? Investigate, think, then make up your own mind. It's the only way.

FOR MORE ON SIDING, TURN TO CHAPTER 6: PAINTING AND FINISHING

Paint Peeling on Siding

An 1893 clapboard Victorian has been in our family for five generations. It has ornate woodwork, archways, pocket doors, 10-foot oak entrance doors, and a coal-burning marble fireplace. It's on the edge of Ypsilanti, Michigan, where Preston Tucker lived while designing his innovative but unsuccessful automobile. The structure is

Unless your present siding is seriously deteriorated, you may need only a paint job, which will save you plenty. If you must re-side, however, get itemized bids.

SIDING IS *a natural two-person job. Here Norm and Tom staple building felt to the sheathing.*

sound but the roof and gutters are failing, and paint refuses to stay on the siding—it peeled less than a year after a professional paint job. I need your advice.

Roberta Bush-Taylor, Saline, Mich.

I have something of a personal interest here: My father fell head over heels for the Tucker, but never had the chance to order one. Anyway, repair the roof and gutters first—leaking water could be damaging the structure and could be part of your paint problem too. Then tackle your siding. The peeling might be due to poor surface prep (the most common cause), new paint that's incompatible with the old, or water vapor moving through the walls. Installing exhaust fans in the kitchen and bathrooms will help remove excess moisture, as will more thorough scraping, sanding, and priming before repainting. Getting back to bare wood is the best way to minimize the chance of peeling, but that leaves you with a lot of scraping. When we faced the same situation on the Watertown project, we decided it was cheaper and safer (considering the layers of lead paint) to replace all the siding.

Columns Caked with Paint

I own a lovely one-story 1905 Queen Anne in my city's historic district. Recently, I stripped the white paint off the porch columns and found a layer of black underneath. What is it and how do I get rid of it?

Elisa Trujillo, Long Beach, Calif.

It's probably a tough old coat of lead paint; get rid of it the same way you got rid of the white. Try a stripper made to penetrate multiple layers. Be sure to follow the directions exactly (many users remove the stripper too soon, before it can fully penetrate). Just remember to wear gloves, goggles, and a face-mask respirator. And if you'd rather sand off the paint than use chemicals, don't—the lead-laden dust is a significant health hazard.

Repairing Damaged Stucco

I'm stripping the siding from my 1930 foursquare house, which has aluminum everywhere except on the large front porch, where the original stucco is uncovered. The porch walls and columns need repair desperately. What should I use to repair and paint the cracks and spalling? To complicate matters, there are small pea-gravel stones embedded in the stucco, making the texture difficult to match.

David S. Overley, Janesville, Wisc.

Don't be hasty here; there's homework to be done first. Try to find out why the previous owner hung the aluminum in the first place. Maybe the "tin men" were working your street that day; maybe the owner wanted to gussy it up for a quick sale; or maybe there's ruined stucco underneath, which will have to be stripped too. You can find out what you're getting into by popping some of the siding. Once you've assessed the job, call in a pro to do the stucco work—this is not do-it-yourself stuff.

Spalled stucco will have to be excavated down to sound material, then built back up in layers, using a matching gravel aggregate. The sound stucco will have lots of holes from siding nails, but a professional can easily fill them with a color-matched "stiff mix" of stucco. According to experts at the Portland Cement Association, small areas of minor cracking are best left alone or given a skim coat of fresh stucco. Then prepare to deal with the stains which may have developed anywhere the aluminum touched the stucco. Most staining washes off—start with plain water and work up to trisodium phosphate (TSP) if necessary. Two rules: (1) Wet the stucco with plain water bottom to top, then scrub top to bottom. (2) Do not power-wash! On the other hand, if the aluminum is hiding serious damage, you'll have to go down to the sheathing and start over. Then you'll have to scrub on a cementitious paint with stiff brushes; even pros have a hard time making big repair patches blend in.

Asbestos Siding Strategies

I have asbestos shingles on the walls of my vacation house on the Jersey Shore. They're in good shape but require constant repainting, so I'd like to cover them with vinyl siding. Is that possible and, if so, how do I go about it?

Jonathan M. Boston, Philadelphia

This Old House contractor Tom Silva and I would approach this in different ways. I'd take the shingles off in order to take care of potential underlying problems such as rot and insect infestation. Unfortunately, the process can be expensive because you'd have to hire a licensed abatement contractor trained in the removal and disposal of hazardous materials. Tom, on the other hand, says you can hang vinyl siding over asbestos shingles with a roofer's nail gun that has a special setting so the nails aren't driven home. That allows the vinyl to float (expand and contract freely) in response to temperature changes. You'd still need to check to see if there is a long-forgotten original layer of siding under the asbestos. If so, the asbestos shingles must be removed. Also, be forewarned that vinyl siding added on top of shingles will project forward somewhat and make windows, doors, and eaves look recessed.

Resurfacing Siding

My 50-year-old wooden garage is structurally sound, but the paint on the clapboard siding needs to be stripped. I think it might be better to remove the siding and then plane each board smooth before replacing and repainting. Got any tips?

Bill Parilla, Park Ridge, Ill.

Which do you have more of: time or money? Taking down clapboards requires a lot of time and patience. There's almost always a lot of splitting at the nail holes. And you risk even more breakage when you strip the boards and put them up again. In the end, you might find you would've been better off simply replacing all of the siding. You can also strip the clapboards without removing them. Special siding planers are available with vacuum attachments to protect you and your neighbors from lead-paint dust. They're hardly fast, though. The manufacturers claim siding planers can clean 1 square foot every 15 seconds, but that would be on a perfect surface. In the real world, the work doesn't go nearly so fast because planers don't cope well with surface irregularities in the wood.

FOR MORE ON PAINTING, TURN TO CHAPTER 6: PAINTING AND FINISHING

Taking down clapboards requires a lot of time and patience. There's almost always a lot of splitting at the nail holes. In the end, you might find you would've been better off simply replacing all of the siding.

When moist heated air gets past inadequate insulation to the inside of the siding, it condenses and "wicks through" to destroy paintwork.

They tend to eat their way through bumps and leave bits of paint behind in the hollows. When you're finished planing, you'll still have a lot of hand-scraping to do.

Working With Steel Siding

Our 1965 house and detached garage both have sections covered with cedar siding. Almost from the start, we've had trouble keeping paint on the garage, but we've never had trouble with the house. I plan to replace the garage cedar with steel siding, which I can get in the small quantity required. The manufacturer says cutting with a saw voids the warranty because the heat generated by sawing damages the paint, and the ragged cuts encourage rust. But a professional shear and dies cost $500. Even a rental—from a place 120 miles away—will cost $25 a day. What do you advise?

Don E. Schaufelberger, Columbus, Neb.

Does your garage have heat and little or no insulation? If so, keeping the garage unheated or adding insulation could save you a lot of work. When moist heated air gets past inadequate insulation to the inside of the siding, it condenses and "wicks through" to destroy paintwork. That may be why the paint on your garage is peeling. If you do replace your cedar, the high tool costs should make you reconsider using steel. Getting a small amount of aluminum siding shouldn't be hard.

Diagnosing a Soffit Stain

We're replacing the asphalt shingles on our 23-year-old house. The aluminum fascia and soffit just below the roof are stained by either air pollution or runoff from the old shingles. We want to clean the aluminum before we replace the gutters and downspouts. But how? Once we finish cleaning up, what preventive measures can we take?

Rebecca Fresa, Bridgeport, W.V.

Your soffit shouldn't be stained by runoff because it is under the eaves. That leads me to suspect you have a leaking roof. If that's the case, your new shingles should remedy the problem. The existing stains may require a commercial house-cleaning product but, if you have any mildew, use an ammonia-based household cleaner. Either can be applied with a stiff brush or gentle power-washing, but be sure not to spray water directly into vents.

Removing Wood Shingles

The original cedar shingles on the walls of my 1925 bungalow need repair and, in some cases, replacement. I want to do some of the work myself, but I'm just a novice, and the real problem is that I can't find a professional contractor or carpenter who is willing to take on the job. What do you suggest?

John P. Humphrey, Royal Oak, Mich.

You could try to do the work yourself (see drawing below). It requires a special tool called a shingle ripper (sometimes called a shingle puller) to yank the old ones out, plus a good deal of time, even for a pro and especially for a novice. I don't want to discourage you, but I don't want you to think it's a snap. You'll learn by your mistakes, that's for sure. Before you start, I suggest you read

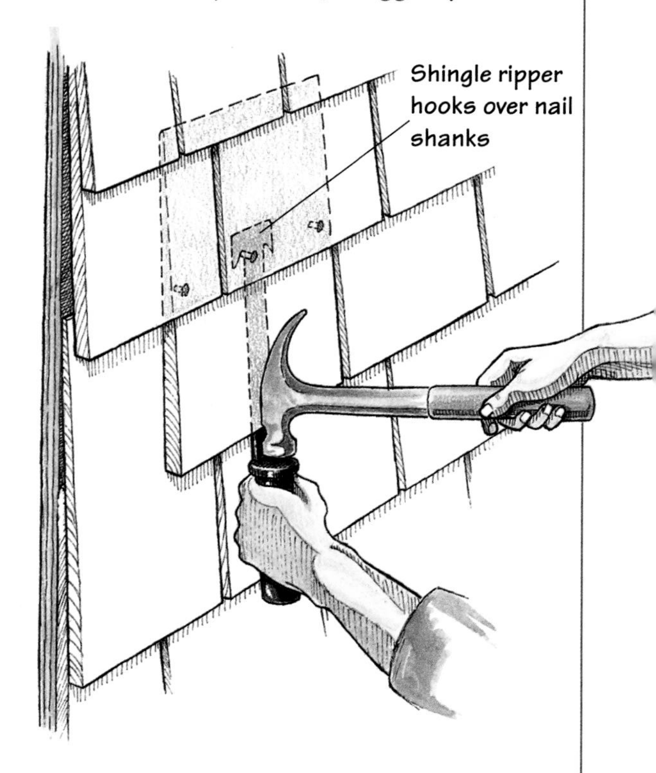

up on the subject. Be sure you can match new shingles to your old ones and, when you add the new ones, be sure to space them to match the old. Too many first-time shinglers fail to make patches blend in.

The Hazards of Power Washing

In a recent column, you said power washing can compress the fibers of wood siding and make it hard for the new paint to adhere. Is this true for stain used on rough-sawn cedar? What about grit blasting, using ground corncobs? We've been offered that recommendation, but it sounds a little harsh.

W.N. Woodward, Jr., Southbury, Conn.

If you're going to powerwash, it has to be done correctly. Never hold the nozzle too close, use too much pressure or blast water inside the structure. Also, be sure you're using the right nozzle for the job. There are various types, and lots of people, including professionals, don't appreciate how important this is. In fact, the right technique is wasted entirely if you're using the wrong nozzle. And don't use a power washer for stripping paint. This is a really bad idea. If you simply want to clean your siding before applying a new finish, gentle power-washing should be all right. But a bucket of bleach and water, applied with a stiff brush and rinsed off with a garden hose, cleans siding just as well. As for grit-blasting, you're right: It is a little harsh, and will remove some of the wood surface.

Aging Stain

My half-log house was built in 1988. A year later, I applied a coat of log oil-stain and, four years after that, I added another coat. Two sides of the house now look much darker than the other sides. Cleaning solution applied with a power washer doesn't help. Can you suggest a brush-on or spray-on cleaner to remove the existing stain? After the cleaning, I want to apply a stain—in as light a color as possible—that can be redone every two years or so. Any suggestions?

John P. Holtz, Three Lakes, Wis.

The problem isn't dirt but aging. You've got two different colors because your house has two different exposures, one sunny and one dark. So I can't give you a solution. That may not seem very satisfying, but look on the bright side: The color difference is natural. By the way, this is happening with the paint on my house, too, just as it happens to sunbathers who forget to turn over.

Replacing Failed Siding

I own a two-year-old wood-frame house with fiberboard siding, and already there are signs of damage—warping, swelling, etc. Many people in my subdivision are replacing their damaged siding with vinyl, and I've had several companies give me estimates and suggestions. One told me not to remove the old siding "because it is attached to the beams, and you could twist them and damage the drywall on the inside." Do you know if this is true? And what replacement should we choose? We've thought about masonry siding and stucco finished with a brick look.

Lori-Ann Pietruski, Jacksonville, Fla.

I can't see the point of installing new siding over old deteriorating siding, so take it off. As for twisting the beams or studs, you'd have to be extremely violent to do more than pop a few nails, so don't worry about it. But before you install new siding, add some kind of sheathing, such as exterior-grade plywood. As for your choice of replacement, keep in mind that vinyl and aluminum tend to expand and contract a lot in hot regions. Fiber-cement siding works well in your climate, and it resembles clapboard. But one thing I remember from when my grandfather moved to Florida was that the masons there were excellent, so I'd also suggest stucco. I wouldn't mimic a stone or brick look, however—I prefer it plain, showing just the texture of the stucco itself. ■

If you're going to powerwash, it has to be done correctly. Never hold the nozzle too close, use too much pressure, or blast water inside the structure. And don't use a power washer for stripping paint.

CHAPTER FOUR

Doors + Windows

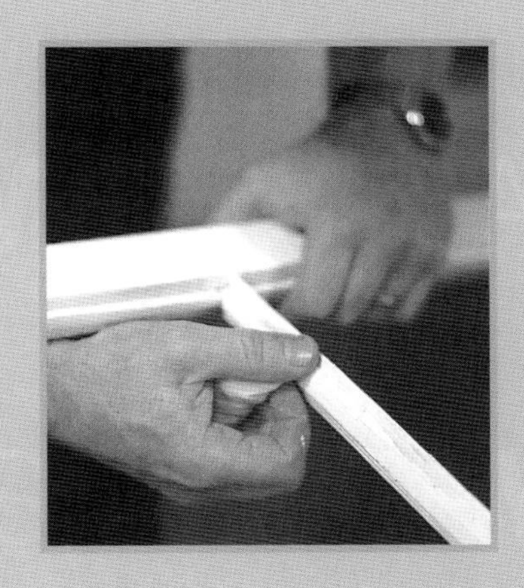

The traditional method for making mortises is time-consuming work that calls for patience and care.

MEASURE *between the jamb and a plumb bob's string and you'll know if the jamb is straight.*

Old Locks for New Doors

I'm replacing the doorknobs and locksets on 12 of the doors in my new "old house." The ones I'd like to put in are vintage mortise locks, which fit into long, deep slots cut into the edge of the door. But drilling holes and chiseling them square would take too long. What else can I do?

Frank Taylor, Humble, Tex.

The traditional method you describe for making mortises is time-consuming work that calls for patience and care. But all you need is a few common tools: a drill with an auger bit and a chisel. The hardest part is making sure each hole you drill is exactly parallel to the face of the door.

You can do the same job a lot quicker with a power lock-mortiser (sometimes called a router mortiser). It's a metal jig that clamps to the edge of the door and holds a router mounted on short tubular guides. As the router is gradually lowered and moved along the guides, a long carbide-tipped bit excavates a perfectly centered mortise. I used this ingenious rig on the doors at our

FOR MORE ON DOORS TURN TO CHAPTER 1: GENERAL REMODELING AND REPAIRS

San Francisco project and it worked great. Speed does have its price, however. The machine retails at $1,000 or so—router included. But if that's too steep, you may be able to rent one. Even with this tool, you'll still have to go in with a sharp chisel to make the mortise for the latch plate.

Be sure to measure twice—or more—before you make any holes. The door stiles have to be wide enough and thick enough to accept the door hardware. Two more things: Unless the location of the old doorknobs lines up exactly with the new hardware, you'll first have to plug the old holes and sand them flush before you cut the mortise; the same goes for the strike plates, where the locks' latches fit in the door jambs.

Of course, all this assumes that the doors are in decent shape. If the wood isn't solid, you won't have much luck cutting mortises no matter what method you use.

Thickening a Window Sill

We are renovating the exterior of an 1870 Colonial house in Maine. The original windows had a thick sill, which nicely matched the decorative trim at the top. But when we replaced some of the windows with double-glazed units, we realized that the new ones have considerably thinner sills than the old ones do. We've gone through one winter without siding because we couldn't agree on how to recreate the thickness of the original sills. But we do agree on one thing: We'll take your advice.

Paul and Jennifer Casey, Errol, N.H.

It would have been easier to do this work before the windows were installed, but you can still get the job done by fastening wood extensions to the underside of your existing sills. This may not create a perfect match with the old sills, but it will replicate their most prominent feature, their thickness (see drawing at right).

On a table saw, rip strips of a stable, rot-resistant wood such as cedar or redwood. Then rout a dripstop (a ⅛-by-⅛-inch groove) on the bottom edge of each strip to discourage water from migrating along the bottom of the sill. Attach the strips with a polyurethane adhesive and stainless-steel nails or screws. Set or countersink them slightly below the wood surface, and cover them with putty. Then fill the joint on the sill's face with epoxy, sand it smooth, and seal all the wood surfaces with an oil-based primer.

The bond that marine-grade polyurethane adhesive makes with wood is incredible. I used it to assemble the roof brackets at the Nantucket project in 1996, and Tom Silva used a fast-curing version to glue down the deck at the Billerica project in 1999.

Garage Opener Retrofit

Some time ago, I had a new garage door installed, along with a ½-hp electric door opener. That was before infrared sensors were required as a safety feature. Can I have this feature added to my existing door opener?

Margaret Pedersen, Dudley, Mass.

It's possible, but the job involves a significant reworking of the opener's motor and controls. That's no job for a novice and it won't

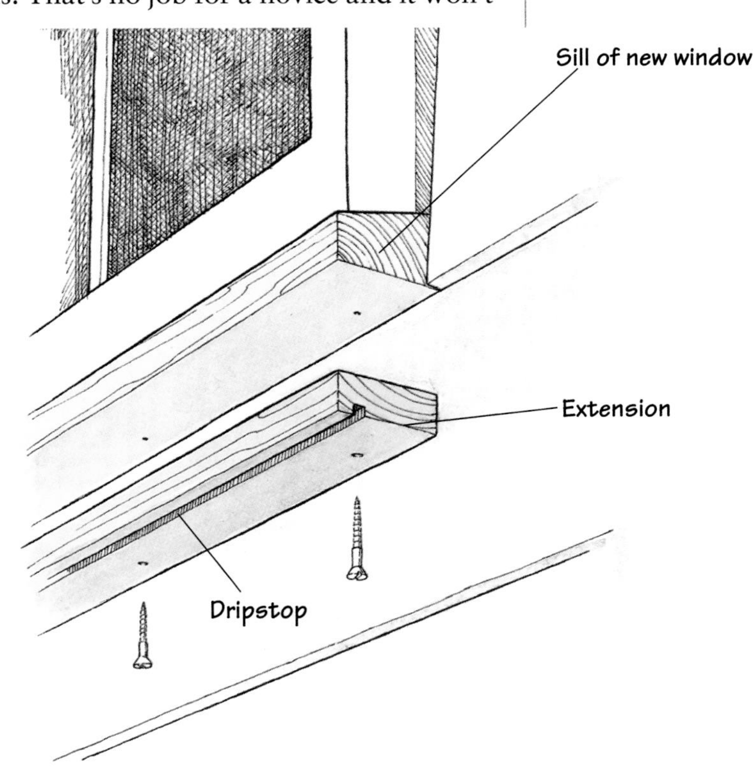

be cheap. You'll be better off replacing the existing opener with a sensor-capable unit.

I think the sensors are definitely a good idea. They prevent the door from closing on anything—object, pet, or person—that interrupts the invisible beam across the garage door opening. And as long as you keep debris or leaves from obstructing the beam, the units are trouble free.

Mystery Code on Windows

My wife and I are the proud owners of a bungalow built in 1931. When I was repainting the exterior, I noticed that the sill of every window has a Roman numeral stamped into its front edge. The numbers are sequential around the house. What is their purpose?

Doug Silvia, New Port Richey, Fla.

Back in the days before uniformly sized windows and metal-framed triple-track storm windows, storms and screens had wooden sashes sized to fit exactly within each window's casing. All three—window, storm, and screen—were given matching numbers, making it an easy matter to find which sash belonged to which window during the switch from storms to screens in the spring, and vice versa in the fall. It's a system I know well: I still have the set of metal punches used to number the windows, screens, and storms on our family cottage.

I still have the set of metal punches used to number the windows, screens, and storms on our family cottage.

Door and Window Rehab

We are starting to renovate our 1907 house in Bisbee, Arizona. It has eight exterior doors, with a transom window above each one. The door and window jambs are in fair shape, except for some deteriorating wood near the thresholds, but the doors and transom sash are looking pretty bad. Should we replace the doors and transoms, or is there some other solution?

Ken and Alice Budge, Midvale, Utah

Sure there is, if you're willing to roll up your sleeves and do something about fixing them—that's the best way to maintain the house's historic pedigree. If the doors and sash themselves are structurally sound and it's only the finish that's worn, I'd remove them, take off every piece of hardware, and then chemically strip the finish or let a commercial outfit do it. Once you're down to bare wood, fill any splits, gouges, or cracks with epoxy or glue in dutchmen (wood patches) before you repaint. As for the jambs, I'd just fix them in place by cutting out the rotted wood and fitting those areas with fresh pieces. Just be sure to brush a coat of primer over all sides of any new wood before final installation.

Shower Window Solutions

The house we recently purchased was built in 1952, and like many of its era, it has a bathroom with a tub but no shower. We want to make it a tub/shower combination, but worry about the window over it. Also, the walls around the tub are tiled, but only part way up the wall, and I think the tiles were installed over ordinary drywall. What are our options?

Don E. Schaufelberger, Columbus, Nebr.

I personally don't like the idea of a window in a shower—water will probably pool on the sill and seep into the walls, nourishing

WHEREVER BARE *wood remains from window repairs, prime it before applying glazing putty.*

FORTY-FOUR *new sash were installed at the Key West project. Single-glazing suited the climate.*

mildew and rot. If the substrate is in fact drywall, it won't last long. You'll have to strip the walls down to the studs (insulating, if necessary, while you're at it), cover them with 15-pound builders' felt, and then screw on panels of cement backer board as a substrate for the tile all the way to the ceiling. That's how tiling contractor Joe Ferrante does it. While you're at it, you could simply block up the window and tile over it. Or you could leave it in place and cover the sill and jambs in felt, backer board, and tile. Top the felt and backer board with a sloped sill of marble. Occasional water spray on the window itself probably won't be a problem, but you could drape a clear shower curtain over it or fit an inside storm pane into the window to protect its wooden parts more completely. Another approach would be to replace the window with durable glass blocks. And if there isn't an exhaust fan in the bathroom already, be sure to install one.

Leak-Free Skylights

Brushfires are commonplace out my way, so when I retired, I replaced my wood roof with concrete shingles and had a skylight put in at the same time. During one of your shows, you mentioned that a skylight added to an existing roof will eventually leak. But what about a skylight that is put in during roof replacement?

Carlos Schiebeck, Buena Park, Calif.

I'd say your chances of living leak-free are excellent. Installing a skylight after a roof tear-off gives you the chance to repair any rot or sheathing damage, and also makes it easy to flash the skylight properly with step flashing on the sides and single-piece head flashing (see drawing below). A little skylight maintenance now and then is a good idea, too. Whenever I clean gutters, I check the uphill side of the skylight and clear off accumulations of leaves, dirt, and shingle grit that can slow water down long enough to cause trouble.

FOR MORE ON FLASHING TURN TO CHAPTER 5: ON AND AROUND THE ROOF

Storm-Window Alternatives

We are renovating a 115-year-old Victorian house in central Texas, and struggling with what to do about the windows. We've spent a lot of time painting and re-glazing them, so the idea of covering them with storm windows doesn't appeal; they just seem too modern (and too "metallic"), and might hurt our chances of getting on the state registry of historic homes. Are any other options available?

Janet Leigh, Belton, Tex.

I agree with you—metal storm windows would be wrong for your house. But do you need storms at all? Far more heat is lost through gaps than through glass. I'd say your first step should be to weatherstrip the existing windows. That's what we did at the Milton project, using nylon pile weather-

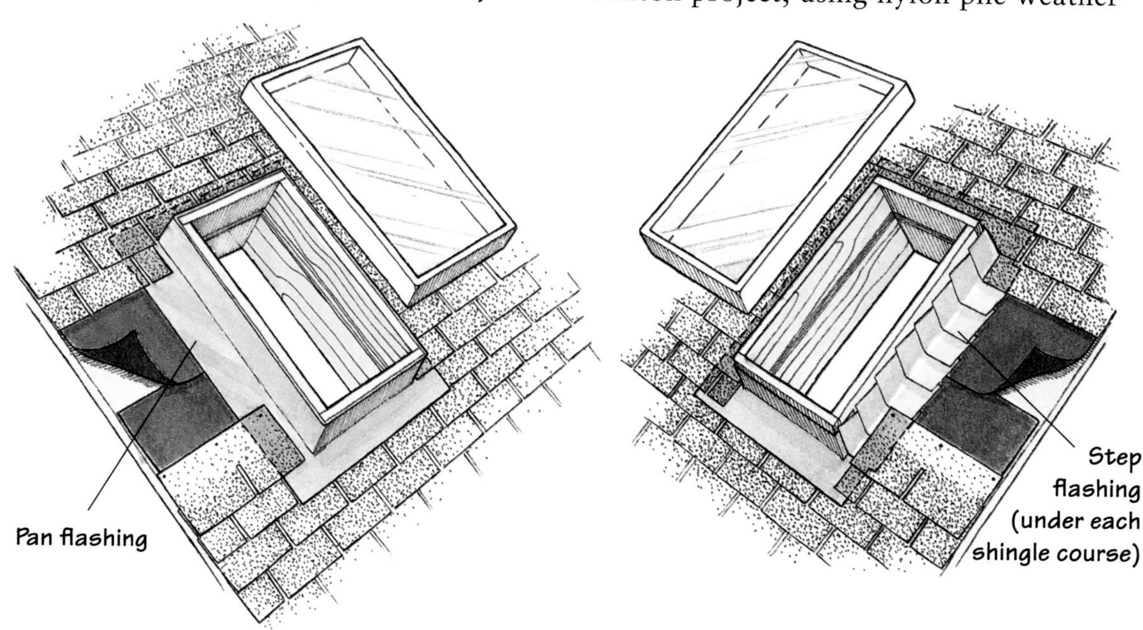

stripping. After a winter with tight windows, you might be surprised at how effective they can be in your climate.

But if pile weatherstripping doesn't quite do the trick, old-fashioned wood-framed storms are an option. They are likely to fit nicely with the house's facade and will protect your newly refurbished windows from the weather. Still, they're a maintenance headache, because you generally install them in the late fall and remove them in the spring. To avoid twice-yearly treks up a ladder with heavy sash, you can also mount storms inside, the way we did it at the Salem project. You'd maintain the exterior look of your house, and the look indoors wouldn't be that obtrusive. Just make sure the storms fit tightly against the jamb and sill to prevent condensation

BEFORE INSTALLING *the trim, be sure you've sealed and insulated gaps around the window frame.*

Far more heat is lost through gaps than through glass. I'd say your first step should be to weather-strip the existing windows.

NORM BUILT *brackets to support a portico roof, which would in turn protect a door just below.*

from accumulating on the inside surface of the primary window. And keep in mind that without outside storms to protect them from the weather, those windows will require more frequent painting and reputtying.

Insulating with foam sure beats stuffing cracks with fiberglass because foam expands to form a tight seal.

Abandoning Old Hardware

My windows have grooved sash that once accommodated spring-loaded locking mechanisms, which have since disappeared. Would it be safe to fill the grooves with pieces of poplar or alder and then apply the kind of nylon-pile weather strip you used at the project in Milton?

Thom Nash, Roseberg, Ore.

It's likely that your sash are replacements designed for a spring-balance system but installed in your friction-fit frames. In any case, the alteration you suggest is a good one, though poplar will be a little easier to work with than alder. And the same weatherstripping will suit your doors.

Spray Foam Shuts Door

I recently replaced an exterior door on my house and decided to use a can of spray foam to seal around the door and under the trim. I've seen this material used on several *This Old House* projects, but after several weeks the door stopped closing properly. After I removed the insulation, the door worked fine. Have you ever experienced this problem?

Steve McKelvey, Altus, Okla.

Insulating with foam sure beats stuffing cracks with fiberglass because foam expands to form a tight seal against drafts as well as the cold. But you're not alone in discovering that too much polyurethane foam can exert enough pressure to bend a door or window jamb, particularly if you installed the trim before the foam was fully hardened. Next time, fill only about a third of the cavity with a minimally expanding poly-foam and let it cure overnight. Then, before you install the trim, slice off any excess with a utility knife and make sure the doors close properly.

Quick Fix for Loose Locks

I have good, solid paneled doors, but the lock plates are loose because of stripped screw holes. How can I fix them?

Bill Bicksler, Clinton, Iowa

You can tighten them by stuffing the holes with glued-in bits of wooden matchsticks or shredded bronze wool (not steel, which rusts); it's an old trick that often works, at least for a while. Even better, take one screw to the hardware store and ask for the same size, only ¼-inch longer so the threads can bite into some solid wood. If you get a bigger size, and replace, say, a #6 with a #8, the heads won't fit the countersunk holes in the lock plates.

SANDING SASH *requires suitable dust protection, including a vacuum attachment.*

Sure Cure for Condensation

The single-pane windows in our 50-year-old ranch house all leak and are almost completely rotted. As we've renovated, we've replaced them with brand-name windows and have been very careful to seal them with foam and caulking. Why, then, do we get condensation on our new windows, even when we cover them with heat-shrink plastic sheeting?

Jon and Mary Graefen, Sandwich, Ill.

Sometimes it's best to tackle a problem at its source. The only practical way to reduce condensation is to increase ventilation with exhaust fans or a heat exchanger. Take other steps to minimize the creation of moisture vapor inside the house, such as using exhaust fans in the bathroom to carry off shower steam.

Splitting Door Panels

I have paneled doors in my early-1900s home. Some of the panels are split, but patching them with wood filler doesn't keep the cracks from reappearing when the house is heated during winter. What should I do?

Walter Daldrup, Avon by the Sea, N.J.

Wood wants to move when humidity levels change, and when it can't it will warp, crack, and bow. I suspect your panels have been glued, painted, or varnished into their frames, causing them to split. To free the panels, you could try to cut through the accumulated gunk with a thin knife blade, but the only sure cure would be to disassemble the doors, and that's a pretty big job. You might try instead to keep humidity levels in the house from swinging from one extreme to another.

Restringing Sash Weights

We need your advice about how we can repair the double-hung windows on our 1935 house in Tennessee. The ropes on the sash weights have all broken and must be replaced.

The Comptons, Coral Gables, Fla.

The steps are simple. Remove the side stops, the lower sash, the two parting beads

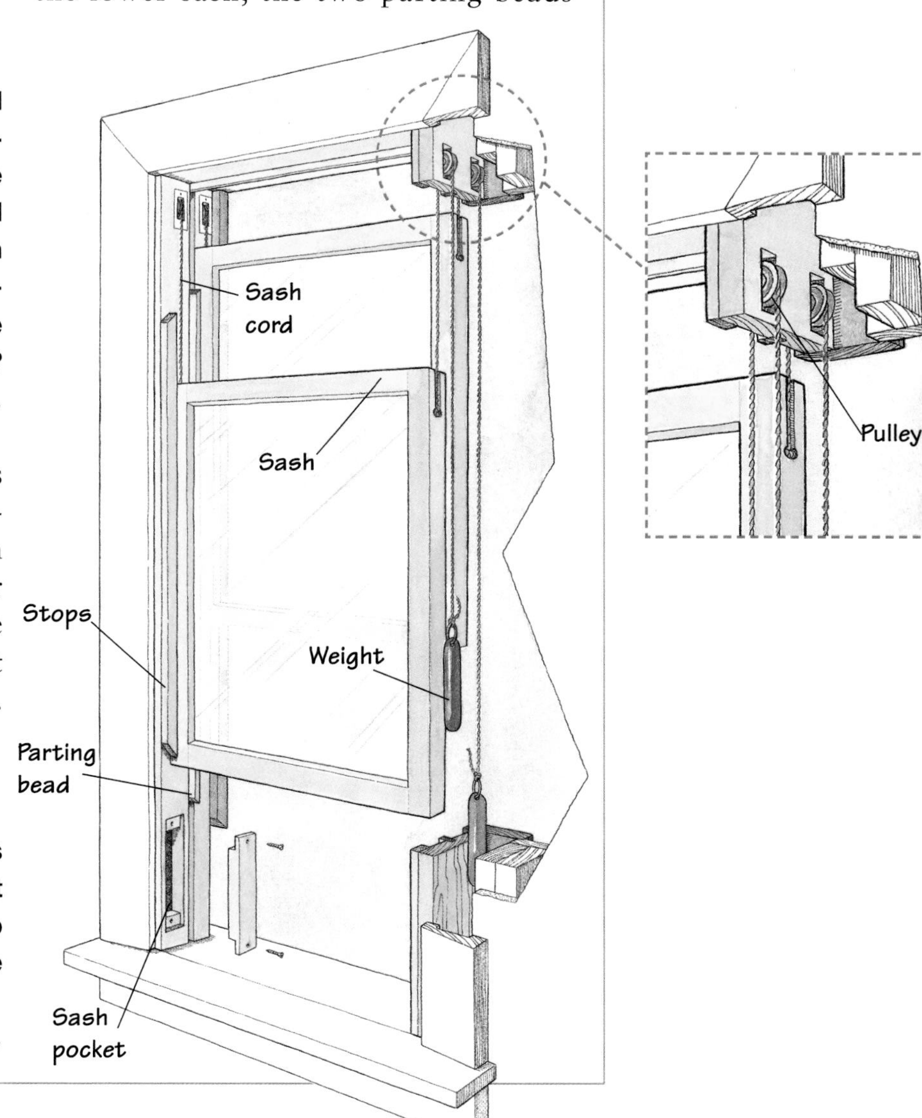

(which hold the sash in place), and then the upper sash. Next, open the sash pockets at the bottom of the frame, feed new cord or chain over the pulleys and attach it to the weights. Put everything back in reverse order. Then proceed, triumphantly, to the next window.

Double-Glazed Dogs

I have three salvaged double-glazed and double-hung windows with 12 lights above and 12 below. The outside panes are fastened with glazier's points and putty while those on the inside are held in place with thin strips of wood nailed to the muntins. How can I keep condensation from accumulating between the panes? Up here in Vermont's Northeast Kingdom, that would block my view for much of the year and contribute to deterioration of the sash.

David Ferch, Groton, Vt.

You're battling nature here and you're going to lose. You'll never be able to seal the space between the exterior and interior panes thoroughly, so moisture will always be a problem. One partial solution is to install new window sash with sealed insulated glass. But high humidity levels could still cause condensation buildup on the indoor side of the windows.

Screen Cleaning

Do you know of any way to clean old metal window screens? I have about a dozen, which I believe might be made of aluminum. Over the years, they have become so badly oxidized that I can no longer see through them.

Phil Pontier, Dover, N.H.

I won't say it can't be done, but if your screens are so corroded that you can't see through them, they probably aren't worth cleaning. Aluminum cleaners available at hardware stores might work, but the screening will probably fall apart. So use the cleaner to salvage the frames, and install new aluminum or fiberglass mesh.

No-shim Jamb Solution

Can you recommend a simple, no-nonsense way to set door and window jambs? I'm looking for something that eliminates the usual—and endless—need for shimming.

D. Deschamp, Grand Junction, Colo.

Yes, there is an easy and effective solution: jamb-adjustment screws. They consist of a long central screw that fastens to the frame. The screw rotates within a short threaded sleeve that connects to the jamb.

Once the device is fully seated, the central screw can be backed out, pushing the jamb into position. Jamb-adjustment screws are a relatively recent innovation, and they are still sold primarily at lumberyards and specialty hardware stores rather than home centers.

Wrong Choice for Out Door

Our house was built in 1966 by a former high school shop teacher and as a result has very nice birch woodwork throughout—except for two of our exterior back doors. Both are hollow-core interior doors. With only storm doors as weather protection, their veneer is cracking. Three years ago I repaired the bulging veneer by gluing it down, but now it's bulging again. Someone suggested using exterior wood filler, and I recall that a two-part product was used to repair exterior trim on the Nantucket project. If there is a solution, I'd sure like to hear about it.

Jeannette Reed, Tyrone, Pa.

They're called interior doors for a reason: this type of door should never be installed on an exterior wall. I think yours have gone as far as they can, and I don't recommend wasting more time on a couple of worn-out and relatively inexpensive items. Besides, they're a security hazard. Why would you guard your home with doors that can be destroyed with little more than a swift kick? Install exterior-grade doors and locksets, and do what you can to match the existing doors.

INSIDE *measurements take practice at estimating just where the tape measure ends.*

Double-Hung Sash Slips

The windows in our 1962 house are giving us trouble. Most won't stay up. Some are hard to raise. And nearly all of them leak. But we don't believe they're so far gone that they have to be junked. I have the time to do some work, and I'm handy with tools, so please tell me what to do.

John T. Cary, Jr., Vernon, Conn.

One common type of window from that era features a sash that easily pops out for cleaning. On one side, spring-loaded bars in the sash match grooves in the frame; on the other, aluminum ribs in the frame fit into grooves in the sash. After cleaning both sides, adjust the springs with a screwdriver so the sash will stay up but still move easily. It's a fussy job, tricky to get right the first time. If you have spring-balanced sash, you can easily replace worn parts with inexpensive new ones. The hard part is removing the stops: vertical molding strips forming part of the channel in which the sash slide up and down or covering the edge of the balance. Slip a thin putty knife between the stop and the frame; then gently loosen them, inch by inch, to avoid breakage

Why would you guard your home with doors that can be destroyed with little more than a swift kick?

A JOINT EFFORT, *the door for the Milton House wine cellar was built from 1x4 tongue-and-groove cedar boards over a spruce frame.*

and chipped paintwork. And while you're at it, you might as well weatherstrip the top, bottom, and meeting rails.

Fix for Stuck Door

The door of our master bath sometimes sticks at the top but opens and closes freely when we have rain. This usually happens in spring or fall. Drywall above the door is split on both sides of the frame. I marked the farthest point of the split five or six years ago, and it hasn't moved past that mark. This is the only door in the house that's affected. I'm baffled. Is the problem in the foundation or within the door framing?

David C. Faler, Grandview, Mo.

I like a fellow who doesn't rush into things. Since you don't seem to be in a big hurry, I suggest that you wait for a sunny day and take a block plane to the door. Give it a few licks, and then wait for a rainy day to see whether it needs a few more. That should keep the door from sticking, but it doesn't explain the mystery: Doors usually stick when it's damp, and yours is doing the opposite. Still, I really wouldn't worry about the door frame or the foundation. After you're sure the door swings freely in any weather, fix the drywall.

Owner-Built Windows

I'm an aspiring timber-framer, and I'm curious whether I can build my own windows and frames to fit the irregular and large expanses between timbers. What kinds of wood are typically used? What about double-pane windows?

Jared Rusten, San Jose, Calif.

Every homemade window I've seen has eventually failed. Building windows and window frames is an engineering as well as a millwork challenge. Doing it yourself is definitely not a way to save either time or money. ■

STICKING DOORS *may be fixed by tightening the hinges. If not, planing one edge may help. Proceed carefully to avoid removing too much.*

Give it a few licks, and then wait for a rainy day to see if it needs a few more.

CHAPTER FIVE

On + Around The Roof

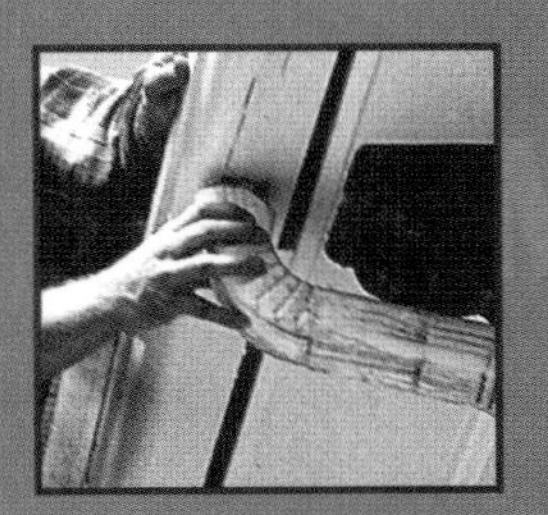

I have to admit that I'm partial to the look of a wood roof. If properly installed and maintained, wood shingles can last quite a long time.

Flat Roofs That Don't Leak

My wife and I are living happily in a 1952 Frank Lloyd Wright Usonian house with 4,000 square feet of flat roof that will soon have to be replaced. One contractor recommends removing the old tar-and-gravel roof down to the decking and replacing it with a 4-ply tar-and-gravel roof similar to the old one. A second roofer recommends a rubber membrane roof with decorative gravel spread over the top. We're getting different stories on insulation, too. Right now, there are about 3 inches of fiberglass tucked into the rafter bays, but we'd like to add more. Can you steer us through these decisions?

Jim Hardin, St. Marys City, Md.

VICTORIAN ROOF BRACKETS *were Norm's addition to the entrance of the Nantucket project.*

Wright was fond of flat roofs because their low profile emphasized horizontal lines and helped the house blend in with the landscape. Unfortunately, leaks are also rather fond of flat roofs, so you'll want to find a roofing contractor who has experience with them and won't cut corners. Strike off your list any roofer who just wants to cover the existing roofing. The old roof should be removed first so the sheathing can be inspected and repaired (if necessary) and so the flashing can be replaced, preferably with copper.

Restoration perfectionists might argue for another tar-and-gravel roof, also called a built-up roof. It consists of layers of heavy roofing felt stuck to each other with hot asphalt, then covered with pea gravel to protect it from UV radiation. Wright, however, was an innovator, and if he were still with us, I'd bet he would cover his flat roofs with a synthetic rubber membrane.

These single-ply roofs use a layer of gray-black EPDM (ethylene propylene diene monomer) just 45 or 60 mils thick. In residential work the rolls are often glued down with a special type of contact cement. This is no job for the weekend roofer; installing EPDM calls for meticulous craftsmanship. But the result is a continuous, flexible, UV-stable membrane that shouldn't leak for at least 15 years; that's 5 to 7 years more than a built-up roof. And it can be patched and repaired indefinitely. That's why a gravel topping is a bad idea—it would interfere with inspection and repair and may actually damage the roofing. *This Old House* contractor Tom Silva, who had a 60-mil EPDM membrane applied over the roof deck at the show's Charlestown project, says that it's especially important to secure the membrane's edges so that the wind can't pull it up and suck moisture underneath. If you can't find a local contractor who's experienced with EPDM, don't hesitate to look outside the area, especially among companies that work on commercial roofs. This product is well worth your effort.

FOR MORE ON SHINGLES, TURN TO CHAPTER 12: PORCHES, PATIOS, AND DECKS

As for insulation, both single-ply and built-up roofs can be placed over rigid boards of foam insulation laid on top of the sheathing. Check with your local building code to see what the board's R-value should be for your climate.

Diverting Roof Runoff

My wife and I recently purchased a two-bedroom Cape, and one of the first things we had to replace was the brick front steps, which appear to have been damaged by water dripping off the roof. Our mason was Lenny Belliveau, who has also done a lot of

work for *This Old House*, and he stressed the importance of keeping water off the new masonry. We wanted to install gutters, but our roofer said he has to hang them from metal straps attached to the roofing. He said the moldings just below the roofline prevent any other solution. We'd like to avoid the unsightly straps. Are there other options?

Stephen Dator, Acton, Mass.

What Lenny's afraid of here is that water pouring or dripping off the edge of the roof will eventually damage the mortar. Gutters could prevent this type of damage, but I'm not sure that gutters are the best-looking solution here, anyway, regardless of how they are hung. (And straps would be the only way to hang them in your case.) Instead, I'd outfit the roof with a diverter, an inverted V that channels water away from the eaves and to either side of the steps (see drawing below). You've probably seen them on old houses in the area. If you choose one that blends in with the color of your roof, a diverter shouldn't be obtrusive at all.

This Old House contractor Tom Silva likes to make them out of a drip edge, the preformed metal flashing that is used under shingles along the edges of a roof. Tom flips a piece upside down so that its 8-inch side sits against the roof and its 1-inch side points up. Halfway from either end, he cuts through the 8-inch side only and bends the piece at that point to form the V. Then he gently lifts the corner of each shingle and slips the long leg of the flashing underneath. Two or three nails tucked under overlapping shingles secure each side of the diverter to the roof. To prevent leaks, Tom dabs roofing cement over the nailheads and secures the underside of each loose shingle with another dab. As with any roof flashing, it needs to be kept free of debris.

Neither a diverter nor a gutter will keep your steps from icing up in the winter. When that happens, you need to resist the urge to spread de-icing salts, which eat into mortar, or to chip away at the surface with a shovel, which will damage the hard face of the brick. Building a roof over the steps would be the best way to protect your steps—I've seen this done on a lot of Capes, too—but that's a much more involved and expensive solution.

Looking for Lifetime Shingles

I'm the fifth generation to live at our family's 1844 Victorian farmhouse. I know that it originally had a wood shake roof, and that replacing the existing asphalt shingles with wood would be historically correct. But I'm interested in longer-lasting materials. What do you think of using slate on this house?

Clinton Wirtz, Battle Creek, Mich.

Slate certainly is a great material and would easily last for another four or five generations of Wirtzes. But it's also expensive, not to mention heavy, which is hard on a roof that wasn't designed to bear it. Have you considered built-up asphalt or fiberglass shingles? They are sometimes called architectural shingles; their extra thickness adds shadow lines to the roof, making them look more like slate or wood shingles than like standard asphalt.

I have to admit, however, that I'm partial to the look of a wood roof. It will be more expensive than asphalt, but a lot less than slate. And if properly installed and maintained, wood shingles can last quite a long time.

To get the most life out of a new wood roof, start with clear, vertical-grain red-cedar shingles, known as No. 1 Blue Labels because of their distinctive packaging. The label should also indicate that the shingles were made to standards set by the Cedar Shake and Shingle Bureau. Get the extra-thick ones, those with a ⅝-inch-thick butt edge instead of ⅜-inch. They last longer and I think they look better—they're what I have on my house. Shingles need air circulation underneath them to prevent cupping and rot, so install them over skip sheathing (a grid of spaced boards) or a special nylon mesh called Cedar Breather. Fasten them with stainless-steel ring-shank nails—I wouldn't put on a wood roof without them.

Cedar shingles don't have the longevity of slate (20 to 25 years is average), but if you take care of them—have a roofer sweep or blow off debris twice a year and spray on a water-repellent wood preservative every five years—your grandchildren could be the ones who buy the next roof.

Solving Gutter Sag

Over the years, the aluminum gutters on my garage have sagged so much that the spot where the downspout connects is no longer at the lowest point. The gutters are made of 10-foot lengths, soldered together, and are held to the roof with straps that fit up under the first course of shingles. Minnesota snow and ice probably contribute to this problem. What's the best way to get my gutters draining in the right direction again?

Mark Powell, Edina, Minn.

You may have a bigger problem than Minnesota winters (is that possible?) if your gutters are a sign that your roof is sagging. Any number of things could cause this—rot in the rafters, improper rafter spans, a settling foundation, or a rotting mudsill. Get up on a ladder and sight along the edge of your roof at the eave. You'll be able to see whether the roof is sagging. If it is, call a contractor to diagnose and correct the underlying problem.

Get up on a ladder and sight along the edge of your roof at the eave. You'll be able to see whether the roof is sagging. If it is, call a contractor to diagnose and correct the underlying problem.

If your eave is straight, all you have to do is remove and reposition the gutters. But your gutters hang from straps fastened to the roof sheathing; you'll have to pry off the first course of shingles to get at the straps. Wait until cool weather for this chore; it will be easier to break the sealing strips that hold the courses in place. Once you've taken the gutter off, establish where its highest spot should be. If it has two downspouts, the high spot should be approximately midway between them. If it only has one downspout, the high spot will be at the opposite end. At this point, you want the outermost edge of the gutter to be ¼-inch lower than the edge of the roof pitch. In other words, if you rest a straightedge on the roof, it shouldn't touch the gutter. Otherwise, every snow pile that slid off the roof would slam into the gutter's lip.

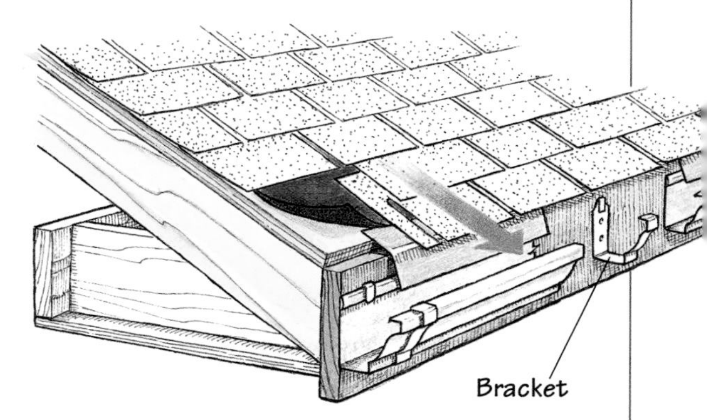

Gutters should pitch at least 1 inch every 16 feet. To get the right pitch, start at the gutter's high spot and use a level to draw a line 4 feet long on the fascia (the board that covers the ends of the rafters). At the end closest to the downspout, make a mark ¼ inch below the line; then draw a new line between the mark and the high spot. This shows the slope your gutters should follow.

You'll find this job will go a lot faster if instead of using straps you hang the gutters from brackets. Screw them to the fascia along the pitch line at every rafter tail, then just drop the gutter into place. With straps, it's always a struggle to hold the gutter in proper relation to the pitch line as you try to screw them to the roof. Finally, you'll need to anchor the outer lip of the gutter back to the fascia, either with a bracket strap or a gutter screw and ferrule. With the amount of snow and ice you probably get, the traditional gutter-spike-and-ferrule setup may not be strong enough to hold.

FOR MORE ON DRAINAGE, TURN TO CHAPTER 2: MASONRY, CONCRETE AND FOUNDATIONS

By the way, that stuff holding your gutter lengths together is probably a butyl gutter sealant; aluminum can't be soldered. You'll need to touch up the sealant because the stress of moving gutters around will probably pop a couple of seams. Follow the instructions on the sealant package for application.

LOW-SLOPE *porch roofs are prone to water damage at the eaves as well as around flashing.*

The Role of Roofing Felt

As I watch new houses being built, I question the logic of some of the construction practices. The roofers, for example, put down roofing felt using many, many staples. Doesn't that just put holes in what should be a water barrier?

David Domin, Strongsville, Ohio

Don't worry about the staples; the felt is going to get punctured even more by the roofing nails. The purpose of felt—a heavy, asphalt-impregnated paper—isn't to waterproof. It protects the sheathing from sunlight and water until the shingles are installed, keeps asphalt shingles from sticking to the roof sheathing, and offers a modest defense against any water that might someday get past the shingles.

Lightning Protection Advice

When I remodeled some years ago, I installed a wood stove with a 30-foot metal chimney. I'm wondering whether I should add some kind of lightning protection, and if so, how to do it.

Bernard Veuthey, Washington, D.C.

A metal chimney makes you a little more attractive target for lightning, but not a lot. Experts at the Lightning Protection Institute say that if lightning zeroes in on your house, you will probably get hit whether you have a chimney or not. To allay your concerns, they suggest that you hire a UL-listed lightning contractor to install a protection system. The minimum setup will have lightning rods, also called air terminals, mounted on either end of a house ridge within 2 feet of the ends and no more than 20 feet apart. Any chimney that sticks out above the ridge line should have its own terminal. A braided, 17-gauge copper cable connects the terminals with ground rods: 8-foot-long metal bars driven 10 feet into earth. You'll need at least two of them.

Even Slate Wears Out

We have the original slate roof on our 150-year-old house, which has Yankee gutters. We'd like to keep it, but roofing experts don't think we should, pointing to water damage and rotting rafters near the gutters, and the many broken or cracked slates that have been tarred over. Can't we just change the gutters and repair the slate?

Nancy Clemente, Staten Island, N.Y.

I can see why the experts you talked to favored replacement: The underlying structure is rotting and the slates themselves are in poor shape (150 years is a long time for any roofing material to survive). Any time more than 25 percent of the slates have to be replaced, you're better off getting a new roof. You ought to consider using slate again, if you can afford it. It will certainly complement the look of the house better than asphalt shingles, and you'll be passing on a legacy that should last at least another hundred years.

Fixing Failed Flashing

The roofing shingles on our 50-year-old house were replaced most recently in 1994. They still look good, but now whenever the snow melts, the roof leaks into the room next to the attached garage. We investigated and found that there was no flashing between the side of the house and the garage roof. Is there a way to prevent any further leakage without tearing off all the garage roofing?

David Calus, address withheld

I'd be very surprised if the flashing is actually missing. It's possible that in the last reshingling, your roofer simply covered up the old flashing, which has now failed. You won't need to rip off the entire roof to fix this problem—just the old flashing and the shingles 12 to 36 inches from the wall. I've found that most asphalt shingles are best removed in cool weather when it's easy to break the seal under the tabs. Replace the shingles starting at the lowest point, where roof and wall meet, and work your way up along this sloping intersection, adding new step flashing to every course (see drawing below). This flashing, which consists of sheet metal rectangles bent into an L, should go 4 inches up the side wall, 4 inches out over the roof, and cover just that part of the shingle that will be overlapped by the next course.

In addition, each piece of flashing should overlap the other by at least 2 inches; the siding should overlap the flashing by the same amount. (If you have shingle siding, some may have to be removed in order to slip the flashing into place.) Although step flashing is slow to install, there's no better way to waterproof the sloped joint where a vertical surface meets the roof.

Slate Roof Repairs

We've just bought a 1940s house with a slate roof that needs some new slates and a few minor leak repairs. My husband has put roofs on homes before but has never worked with slate, and we're not sure what steps to take. How do you replace slates? Should we repair in patches or plan on doing the entire roof over the summer?

Holly Prokop, Easton, Penn.

Repairing a slate roof requires more skill than repairing wood or composition shingles, and because slate is slippery, the job is a lot riskier. My advice is to hire a professional slater to do the patching. A novice could botch the job so badly that you'd end up needing a new roof.

Antenna Removal Cautions

Our house is topped by a large, ugly TV antenna that we no longer need. Does it at least offer us some protection by serving as a lightning rod? And assuming I don't fall off the roof, is it safe for me to remove the antenna?

Michael A. Spielman, Kensington, Md.

Assuming you don't fall off the roof? Michael, please don't assume any such thing. Call in pros

CLEANING GUTTERS *regularly can improve the life of roof shingles as well as the house paint.*

for this job; the experts who take antennas down are the same people who put them up, so check the phone book. If the arrival of cable has put local antenna guys out of business, try construction or demolition contractors. They'll have the skills, the gear, and, most important, the insurance for this job. Just make sure they do a thorough job of sealing every mounting hole, including those for the guy wires. And don't count on getting any lightning protection from an antenna. Experts at the National Lightning Safety Institute, say that there's a strong likelihood that even a disconnected antenna will lead lightning to your electrical system. They recommend removing the antenna and using surge protectors to safeguard expensive household appliances against lightning. Put one at the main circuit-breaker panel, one at each secondary panel, and, for good measure, one plug-in model at each TV, computer, and stereo system. These protectors are rated in joules; the more joules, the better the protection.

Roof Shingle Choices

Our house has a cedar-shingle roof that's 12 years old and ready for replacement. Should we use red or white cedar? We're also considering asphalt or fiberglass shingles, or even clay tiles.

Jim Thrasher, North Easton, Mass.

I can't see a properly installed cedar roof failing in just 12 years, unless the builder nailed the shingles over plywood sheathing and didn't leave an air space to ventilate their undersides. For replacement roofing, you can use Western red cedar, Alaskan yellow cedar, or redwood. White cedar shingles are suitable only for sidewalls. Sure, you can look at other materials, but I'd forget clay tile. It may last the better part of a century, but it's rarely seen in New England, costly, and so heavy that your rafters may not be able to handle the additional weight.

Maintaining a Cedar Roof

Our house dates to somewhere between 1785 and 1800, and about seven years ago we put on new cedar roofing. How should we maintain it? We've asked six or seven roofers and have not gotten the same answer twice. One says to just clean the roof with a hose; others recommend sealants.

Michele and Tom Weisz, Wilton, Conn.

I was pretty much intending to ignore the wood shingles on my roof, except to clean off leaves and other debris, until I checked with *This Old House* contractor Tom Silva. He said that spraying a cedar roof periodically with cedar roof treatment product will add years of life to the shingles. It can even flatten out old shingles that have begun to curl. It's not an annual task, he says—every five years or so is probably fine. According to Marty Obando, a technical consultant for the Red Cedar Shingle & Shake Bureau and a longtime roofer, there's another way to tell if your cedar roof is ready for treatment. If the shingles maintain their grayish color when they're wet, he says, there's no reason to treat them. But if you notice a slightly greenish color, it's time for the spray.

FOR MORE ON WOOD SHINGLES, TURN TO CHAPTER 3: EXTERIOR WALLS

Various products can be used on a roof, but never

Although step flashing is slow to install, there's no better way to waterproof the sloped joint where a vertical surface meets the roof.

SIDING AND TRIM *are common casualties of improperly maintained gutters and flashing.*

use a waterproofer, a sealant, or a plasticizer. They seal the outside surfaces of the shingles, says Obando, but if moisture does wick into the wood, as it will eventually, a sealant prevents it from getting out. Trapping moisture in the wood is exactly the wrong thing to have happen. Instead, have the roof sprayed with a water repellant wood-preservative that contains a UV inhibitor. Read the list of ingredients on the can—if you see copper or zinc napthenates, you probably have the right stuff. If the label doesn't specifically note that the product is intended for use on cedar roofs, however, keep looking. Tom has had good results using linseed oil to seal cedar roofs, but he's been looking for something better after reading reports that under some circumstances, linseed oil may attract carpenter ants and other insects.

Whatever you use on your roof, this is absolutely not a do-it-yourself project—I can't overemphasize that. A roof is slippery enough without the lubrication of protective liquids, so leave this work to a roofing professional.

Weathering Wood Shingles

My century-old house is weathering badly on the south and west sides, where many shingles are dried-out, warped, and cracked. The shingles on my barn, however, are in fine shape. The main difference seems to be that the house is painted and the barn isn't. Should I repaint the house or replace the house shingles?

Malcolm Ray, Canton, Maine

Your barn shingles are behaving just like roof shingles: when they get wet, they can dry out evenly. Painted shingles can't always do this. Your barn's shingles are fine partly because they haven't suffered from years of the central heating cycling on and off, which drives moisture through the walls and into the shingles' unpainted backsides. The best solution for your house, I'm afraid, is a complete reshingling on the weathered sides; piecemeal replacement doesn't make sense when more than 25 percent are broken and warping. Leaving shingles unpainted saves a lot of time, money, and maintenance, and I prefer the look—especially near the shore, where white cedar and Alaska yellow cedar turn a pretty silver-gray. But if you paint, dip-prime first, or buy them pre-primed: Shingles last much longer when all sides are coated.

Asphalt Shingle Advantages

I'm looking for a roofing material that is not much more expensive than asphalt shingles but will last a lot longer. I've considered various new and non-traditional products, including sprayed-on coverings, but nothing seems to suit my needs. I hope you have some suggestions that I haven't heard of yet.

James D. Parrent, Essexville, Mich.

Actually, I don't, but that shouldn't bother you. Let's back up here a minute and look at your needs: low cost, long life, easy availability, no maintenance and—one you didn't mention—simple, fast installation. It seems to me that asphalt shingles, which you dismiss out of hand, are just the ticket. Surely 15 to 25 years—their usual life span—is enough. And remember two very important things: Until a new product is proven, (1) all the manufacturer's promises are just promises, and (2) you're the guinea pig.

Finding Steel Tile Roofing

We're currently renovating a 100-year-old brick bungalow with a stamped-steel "tile" roof. It doesn't leak, but a chimney was removed, and a small overhang was reroofed with asphalt shingles. We've searched everywhere for replacement pieces, but no luck. We want to put on a metal roof but can't find instructions and have to do it ourselves because of the cost.

Anna Zager, St. Mary, Neb.

If the roof isn't leaking, and all you need is enough pieces to replace the missing ones, it won't hurt to keep looking. Hit the Internet, contact preservation societies and everyone in your area who has the same kind of roof. Another alternative—one that was used at *This Old House's* project in Key West, Florida—is to steal pieces from the back of the house to patch holes in the front, although there we had a new addition to hide the deed. If you have to reroof, forget about standing-seam sheet metal—it isn't a job for amateurs. But there are interlocking metal shingles that might be just the ticket. Contact the Metal Building Alliance for a list of manufacturers. Should you decide to go up on your roof—and I don't encourage you—be sure to have a safe place to stand, a safety line, a harness, and insurance. Roofers pay higher rates than anyone else for workman's comp. There's a reason for that.

Wood-Shingle Sheathing

I've heard that cedar shingles for roofs should always be installed over skip sheathing. But then why is cedar siding fastened directly to solid sheathing?

John Stephen Carey, Melbourne, Fla.

The reason is simple: After prolonged rain, cedar roof shingles will be soaked all the way through. If the shingles are nailed to solid sheathing, they will dry unevenly and curl at the edges because no air flows underneath them. The solution is to nail the shingles to skip sheathing, narrow wooden strips laid across the rafters, with spaces between each board.

Replicating Traditional Gutters

I have a late-19th-century Queen Anne house. Photos taken before 1917 show no gutters hanging from the soffit. Instead, there is some sort of trough built on the roof about a foot from the edge. At first I thought the trough might be built into the roof, but that would require notches in the rafters. I've already checked in the attic, and the rafters I can see show no sign of having been notched, patched, or replaced. This, therefore, was a surface installation and, since I'm replacing part of the old slate roof anyway, I'd like to do a faithful restoration and bring back the trough. Any advice?

Robin C. Hovis, Millersburg, Ohio

The trough design could be a local variation on traditional gutters. If so, your public library or historical society might have more information about it. One thing to keep in mind is that this design might have disappeared because it didn't work well. In a location prone to icing and roof dams, for example, it would probably cause trouble. On the other hand, maybe this trough gutter was just too expensive for ordinary folks, as trying to replicate it certainly would be today.

Switching to Metal

In winter, the roof of our vacation cottage on the Olympic Peninsula gets so little sun and so much rain that the moss grows thick on our composition shingles. We're tired of scraping it off every summer and would like to switch to a metal roof. Can we simply clean the roof and install the metal over it, or must we strip off the shingles first?

John Marrs, Lake Sutherland, WA

I think the metal roof is an excellent idea, although it doesn't mean that you'll be moss

Remember two very important things: Until a new product is proven, (1) all the manufacturer's promises are just promises, and (2) you're the guinea pig.

free. And I'd take the shingles off first. Whenever I change to new material, I like to start on a clean surface. That way I also get to see what's underneath. I don't like to take the chance of covering up an existing problem.

Estimating Roofing Materials

I'm going to replace the roof on a small garage. Is there a way to figure out how many shingles I'll need?

Lawrence Smith, Cedar Rapids, Iowa

Roofing materials are sold by the square, a unit that's equivalent to 100 square feet. All you do is measure your roof and divide its square footage by 100. Then add a little for waste. For a straightforward gable roof with no valleys, the waste factor would total about 10 percent.

Leaky Roof Valley

I have a house with a slate roof, and one of the valleys seems to be leaking. How do I repair it? Do I need to remove the entire valley, or can I just slip pieces of new sheet metal over the old valley?

Michael Timmer, Akron, Ohio

I dumped this in the lap of Joe Jenkins, a roofer for 30 years and the author of *The Slate Roof Bible*. He says slipping new metal over old is a slick trick but a bad plan and eventually will result in more leakage. A real repair involves taking off enough slates—about 18 inches on each side—so the old valley can be removed and a new one installed. This is a routine job, but it still requires a skilled roofer. Another trick some contractors use is simply to tar the valley and hope for the best. That's only a short-term solution. Your best bet is to find a qualified person to do a permanent job.

What you're looking for is that old favorite, the quick fix. My advice: Don't do it.

Recoat Asphalt Shingles?

I live in the house my grandparents built in 1941. So far, the roof doesn't leak, but in some areas rust has bled down from a TV antenna. And other areas, especially valleys, are beginning to show wear—the grit has come off. Can I paint the roof or coat it with something to make it look new again? Can I add grit to replace what has come off over the years?

Brad Mazanek, Alma, Ill.

A GOOD ROOF *protects the entire house, but depends on solid walls and a good foundation.*

Roofing grit is used as a UV block to protect the underlying material in asphalt and other shingles. If the grit has come off, that means portions of your roof are unprotected and deteriorating. I don't know of a way to apply more grit, and attempts to remove rust stains probably would inflict more damage to the shingles. I'd say you have a new roof in your future. And I recommend you strip off the old roof beforehand so you can inspect the sheathing for rot or other damage. Even though reroofing over one existing layer of roofing is generally allowed by building codes, I prefer not to.

Rotting Roof Supports

The front stoop of my Victorian is sheltered by a small canopy, which is supported by brackets and beginning to collapse. I remember a show when you installed steel posts and provided a finished look by splitting wooden columns and using them to conceal the posts. How do I go about doing the same thing?

Rose Lightfoot, Brooklyn, N.Y.

What you're looking for is that old favorite, the quick fix. My advice: Don't do it. First, your canopy is collapsing because of rot caused by leakage in the canopy where it's tied into the wall of your house. That's where the repair has to take place. Just propping up the canopy will only let things get worse. The rot could spread into the walls if it hasn't already. And installing posts will result in a clumsy, belt-and-suspenders look unless you also remove the brackets. The right way to tackle this job is to repair the canopy so the brackets can do the job they were designed for.

Insulating Exposed Rafters

Our old stone farmhouse has a slate roof that is nailed to lath rather than sheathing, and there is no roofing felt beneath. As a result, water, snow, and pine needles blow into the attic. What's the best way to weatherproof the attic? What insulation will provide the greatest R-value but still be thin enough to allow our handsome old rafters to be exposed?

Frank J. Vargish III, Lancaster, Pa.

It's a mistake to assume that "blow-ins" are the price you pay for a slate roof: You simply have a leaky roof. Get it fixed. As for insulation, you'll get maximum R-value by covering the rafters. Exposing the rafters makes for a much harder job. Here's how to do it. Panels of 2-inch rigid polyisocyanurate foam will provide an R-value of about 14, which is relatively low. If your rafter bays permit you to add more, do so. To install the foam, you first nail eave-to-ridge cleats (1-by-1-inch strips) to each rafter just under the roof. That will ensure ventilation by keeping the foam from contacting the underside of the roof. The rafters won't be perfectly square and parallel, so you'll need to do some finicky fitting with a utility knife and, with canned foam, fill the gaps. That's not such a big deal. But a finished look—and probably your local fire code—will require covering the foam panels with drywall. That may alter your devotion to your handsome old rafters.

Restoring Copper Details

The top of the cornice at my parents' 19th-century Italianate house is made of copper that has been painted many times. I would like to remove the paint and bring the copper back to its natural color. What can I use to keep it that way?

Jeff Sommer, Jersey City, N.J.

My expertise is in wood not metal, but I can at least get you started. To begin with, removing the paint may involve dangerous chemicals, so consult with a restoration contractor. But don't even think about making copper penny-bright. You'd spend the rest of your life trying—and failing—to keep it that way. When the Statue of Liberty underwent a multimillion-dollar restoration a decade ago, her copper skin was left alone. There's a reason Lady Liberty is still green.

Don't even think about making copper penny-bright. You'd spend the rest of your life trying—and failing—to keep it that way. There's a reason Lady Liberty is still green

Destructive Bees

During spring and summer the last two or three years, large black carpenter bees have attacked fascia boards on my house. They bore perfect vertical holes up through the bottom edge of ¾-inch fascia, eventually digging tunnels as long as 4 inches. Can I prevent this before damage becomes visible?

Dennis Abraham, Bridgeton, Mo.

Carpenter bees can cause considerable cosmetic damage, digging tunnels about ½ inch in diameter. They rarely threaten a building's structural integrity with deep burrowing, as termites and carpenter ants do, but their tunnels invite rot and other problems. Consult an exterminator to get rid of the bees and their eggs, which will otherwise hatch a new generation of tunnelers. You may also need to replace the damaged wood with pre-primed lumber. Paint discourages these bees, but if you leave even a tiny area uncovered, they will find it. Bees and other insects need water and seek it out, so I suspect the root of your trouble is moisture. You should check carefully around the fascia boards for leaks or other sources of dampness that may have created an attractive microenvironment for the bees. ■

CHAPTER SIX

ASK **NORM**

Painting + Finishing

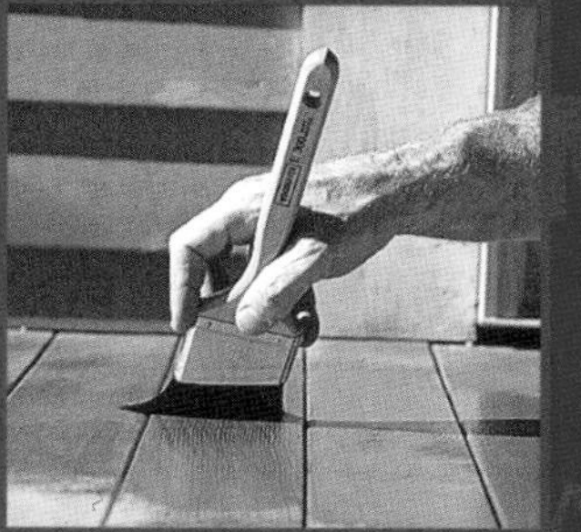

What Is Paint?

Could you please explain the difference between paint and opaque stain and why one is chosen over the other?

Greg Cote, Grandby, Conn.

I've always assumed that opaque stain (also called solid-color stain) was just thinner than paint—containing fewer solids—and would therefore breathe better, but because I don't have a degree in paintological art and science, I called painter John Dee, who has done a lot of work with *This Old House*. He agrees that opaque stain is thinner and breathes better, but there's more to it than that. Dee says the thinness of opaque stain allows the texture of wood, but not the grain, to show through. That makes it excellent for shingles. He also says that stain "goes on like a breeze," but that a high-quality acrylic paint lasts longer. I have both finishes on my house, and my experience is that the stain lasts five to six years and the acrylic, seven to eight. When it's time for a new coat for either, I recommend light sanding to roughen the surface just enough so that the new finish has something to grab onto. Any areas of bare wood should, of course, be primed.

Stain goes on like a breeze, but a high-quality acrylic paint lasts longer.

Painting Over Varnish

We think woodwork painted a simple semi-gloss white will look best in our Queen Anne house, but we're feeling a bit guilty about covering wood that a previous owner clearly spent a lot of time stripping and varnishing. Is there a way to protect the varnish when we paint over it so that eventual removal of the paint would be a practical proposition? What would the Victorians have done?

William and Ellen Turpin, Rutledge, Pa.

Don't feel guilty. If someone comes along later and wants to go back to a clear finish, the underlying coats of varnish will make

BARE WOOD *outdoors invites rot and insect attack, and suffers from exposure to the sun.*

stripping the paint much easier than if it were applied to bare wood. Just be sure to sand the varnish lightly—enough to give it some "tooth"—so the paint will stick. Keep in mind that the mania for showing wood grain everywhere is relatively modern; the Victorians painted some trim and left other parts natural. I've done the same in my house to show off both paint and varnish.

Paint-Stripping Caution

I'm repainting our shingled Dutch Colonial, one section per year. I burn off the thick, cracked paint; then sand and apply a good oil-based primer, which dries for five to seven days and then gets two finish coats of latex. What do you think of this approach?

Bill Bicksler, Clinton, Iowa

I want to urge you to be really careful about stripping paint. If there's lead paint on your house, I wouldn't heat-strip it because that might vaporize it and become more of a threat to your health. Heat stripping presents a fire hazard, too. You might consider a chemical stripper (one of the safer ones that doesn't contain methylene chloride), although that gets messy and expensive. Or you could hire a lead-abatement pro and let him take care of the stripping and cleanup.

Bathroom Paint Oozes Muck

After we stripped the wallpaper in our three 20-year-old bathrooms, we removed the glue, sanded the walls, and applied two coats of oil-based paint followed by two coats of latex enamel. Two of our bathrooms are fine, but the third oozes a mysterious substance that runs down the wall every time we take a shower. It's yellow and looks like tree sap, though it's easily removed with a little scrubbing. What's going on?

Kim Scott, Grand Rapids, Mich.

The first thing I thought of when I read your letter was *The Amityville Horror*. Then I thought to check out the Web site of the Paint

Quality Institute, and sure enough, there was the answer. The "tree sap" you describe is probably the surfactants (their word, not mine) found in all latex paints. These chemicals sometimes leach to the surface when moisture condenses on the paint, which happens when you take a shower. They say the stuff is harmless; just wipe it away with a wet cloth. If it comes back later, wipe it some more. After a few more scrub-downs, it should be gone for good. To avoid this problem the next time you paint, wait a couple of days for it to dry before taking a shower.

Black Stains on New Beams

The glue-laminated beams we're using for the addition to our house are handsome enough that we want to show them off by using a clear finish instead of painting them. But they arrived with black strap marks that we can't get off—even using an oxalic-acid wood cleaner and a sander. What will work?

Laurie Yeager, Durango, Colo.

The marks come from the metal shipping band applied at the factory. The beams probably got wet somewhere along the way, and that turned ordinary, easily removed strap marks into stains that went pretty deep into the wood. Sometimes the straps actually dig into the wood (see drawing below),

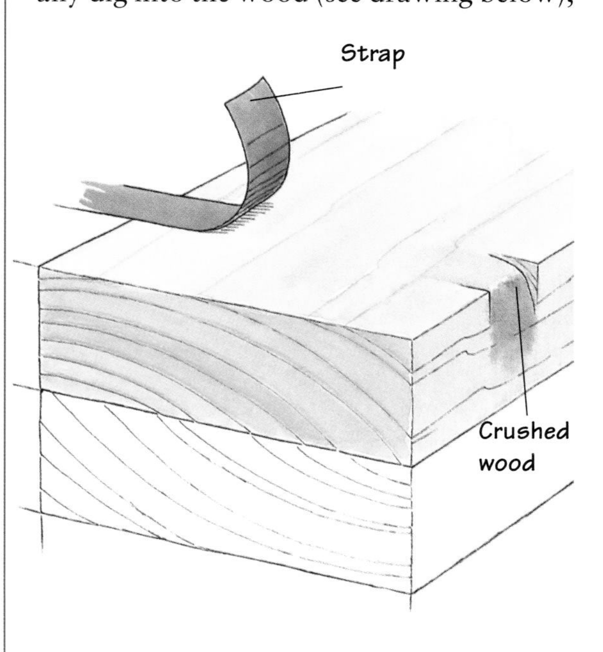

which is something to watch for when picking out stock at a lumber yard. But if you feel you've reached the limit with sanding and cleaning, your alternative is to find some kind of decorative way to camouflage the stains: a stenciled design, for example. In any event, others can benefit from your experience. Laminated beams are usually painted or hidden. So unless the factory is alerted ahead of time that you want to leave the beams exposed, no special care will be taken to keep them from being marked or stained when they are shipped to you. By the way, glulams are graded by various appearance characteristics, not by strength.

FOR MORE ON LUMBER TURN TO CHAPTER 11: WORKING WITH WOOD

Recipe for Whitewash

Years ago, when I lived on a ranch in California, an old-timer gave me a recipe for making whitewash. Every spring we'd mix up a batch in a 5-gallon bucket, break out the brushes, and paint all the fence posts, sheds, and anything else that needed to look clean and fresh. It was very inexpensive—less than 75 cents per gallon. Now I'd like to make some again but I no longer have the recipe. Can you help?

Sheila Coburn, Westminster, Calif.

Whitewash was popular in an era when people had more time than money, but still wanted something to spruce up fences and outbuildings. I don't know much more about it, except that Tom Sawyer had pretty good luck with the stuff. But it turns out that Rory Brennan, a plaster craftsman who has worked on some of the show's projects, is a great fan of whitewash. He explained that it's actually a masonry product made of lime (burned limestone) and water. The material is fire-resistant and strong, and when applied to a masonry surface, it bonds to form a tough, weather-resistant coating. Each additional layer added over the years increases its protective ability. But Brennan also says that whitewash is brittle and doesn't flex with wood movement. That's why other sub-

PAINT PROBLEMS *on sash may be caused by condensation dripping down the glass.*

stances are sometimes added to improve its performance. Salt, for example, makes the surface harder, while casein (milk protein) makes it more durable. Because of its high pH, whitewash is toxic to mold and mildew. But whitewash's highly alkaline nature also means that the wet mix will burn skin: Always wear eye protection and rubber gloves when mixing or applying it. And keep a bottle of vinegar nearby as a clean-up solution and emergency neutralizer.

Brennan's recipe for whitewash starts with safety precautions. First, coat your hands and face with petroleum jelly, and put on goggles, gloves, and clothing to cover as much skin as possible. Then, in a garbage pail, mix 50 pounds of hydrated lime with 6 gallons of water. Cover the mixture with a thin film of water, put on the lid, and let it sit overnight. The next day, you'll have creamy lime putty. Water down the putty to the consistency of half-and-half, and you'll have whitewash.

Make sure the surface you're coating is clean and free of paint, or whitewash won't stick to it. The surface has to be damp, too, or else the whitewash will turn to dust. Apply the mix in an overlapping figure-8 pattern, using a wide masonry brush of tampico bristles, a vegetable fiber. Wait 30 to 60 minutes between coats, and apply a new one as soon as the moisture sheen dissipates; you don't want the surface to dry out. Three or four base coats is usually sufficient. Once the sheen has left the last coat, you can burnish the surface by stroking a clean, dry brush in circular patterns. Burnishing seals and smoothes the surface and makes it even more water-resistant, but for sheds and fence posts this step may be overkill. Just slap on a fresh coat of whitewash every year to keep them looking good.

Mix 50 pounds of hydrated lime with 6 gallons of water. Cover the mixture with a thin film of water, put on the lid, and let it sit overnight.

To get an idea of what you're dealing with, look inside, where the wood won't have any finish at all.

TO FIND ROT, *gently probe outdoor locations where a vertical surface meets a horizontal one.*

Refinishing a Cedar Chest

I want to restore a cedar chest. It has a dark, Mediterranean-style finish, so I'm not sure what I should use to strip it. And what do you suggest I use for the new finish?

Kimberly West, Pinellas Park, Fla.

Cedar chests can be tricky. Many are made of inferior cedar—scraps, really, that show a lot of knots—and white sapwood. The poor quality of such wood may be disguised by a dark finish but would show up glaringly with a clear finish. To get an idea of what you're dealing with, look inside, where the wood won't have any finish at all. Then, if the finish isn't damaged, consider cleaning with mineral spirits or refurbishing with a kit available from paint stores and home centers. You should avoid refinishing if you can. First, you'll have a hard time cleaning out the grooves. Also, the stain that has penetrated the wood won't come out.

Reviving Dull Finishes

I bought an antique mirror with a wooden frame that I think is mahogany. The frame is about 2 inches wide and has some carving at the top, but the wood looks dull. How can I bring it to a nice, glossy finish?

Felice Mikelberg, Redbank, N.J.

A kind of mahogany called "plum pudding" often looks dull; it has a rich red color but doesn't show much grain. Even if you have fine, furniture-grade Honduran mahogany, there's a good chance the finish is simply dirty and will clean up nicely if scrubbed with mineral spirits. It's a petroleum by-product, so check the label for safety precautions. Mineral spirits is a favorite with furniture pros, who usually try cleaning first if the finish isn't actually damaged. When it comes to cleaning the carving, you'll quickly discover why you should never throw away old toothbrushes.

What's Under the Paneling?

Our older house was built when paneling was popular, and that makes our living room and dining room very dark despite nice-size windows. We want to replace the paneling with drywall someday, but in the meantime we'd like to brighten up the rooms with paint. What kind of paint would adhere well to wood paneling?

Pat Johnson, Granby, Colo.

Any product made for wood will work on wood paneling. A light scuffing with fine sandpaper will provide a little tooth to grip the primer. But first find out what's beneath the paneling (see drawing above). Removing the cover of an electrical outlet should tell you (be sure to cut power to the circuit first, just to be on the safe side). It could be drywall or even plaster, needing only a little patching here and there. Your house may be a fashion victim—there was a rage for do-it-yourself paneling in the '60s—so you may be in luck. If the paneling was applied with small nails or brads, it will be easy to remove. But if adhesive was used, the wall behind may be ruined.

FOR MORE ON WIRING TURN TO CHAPTER 10: ELECTRICAL AND PLUMBING

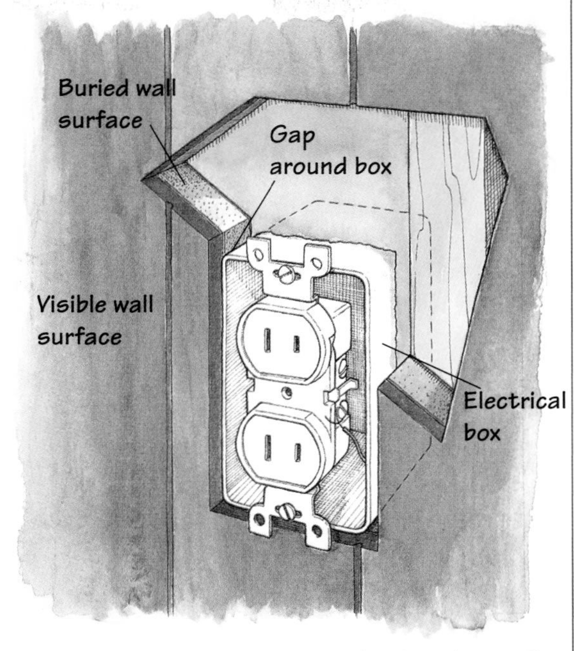

By the way, the same technique can also be used to determine what sort of insulation might be in the walls.

Preparing a House for Paint

I have a classic 1950s house of wood with brick detail in front, and it is in desperate need of a paint job. The paint is coming off in big flakes that reveal bare wood. One painter suggests using a pressure washer to remove the flaking paint, then scraping a little to even out the finish. A second painter

PROTRUDING TRIM *(or anything else that slows water down) is a potential incubator for rot.*

wants to wash the house with a cleaner, let it dry, then scrape and sand the old paint, using putty to feather the edges of the flaked areas. Both approaches sound reasonable, but which is better?

Melissa C. Aspell, Birmingham, Ala.

I've heard that line before: "Oh, we'll just power-wash the paint off and then paint it." Using a power washer to remove paint bothers me for several reasons. You're not going to get the loose paint off unless you angle the spray just right. And if the pressure is too high, you'll almost sandblast the wood, compressing the fibers and making it harder for the new paint to adhere. Worse, there's the risk of water getting behind the siding. And finally, you'll be blasting little chips of paint all over the place, making cleanup a headache.

Instead, scrape off loose paint and sand areas as needed to even out the finish. Then clean the siding with liquid siding cleaner, a coarse scrub brush, and a hose. This is the safest way to clean paint that's still well-adhered, and it's the technique I use on my house. You can get the cleaner at any home center. Just mix it according to instructions on the label.

FOR MORE ON PRESSURE WASHING TURN TO CHAPTER 3: EXTERIOR WALLS AND SIDING

STRUCTURAL PROBLEMS *revealed when "sighting" the lines of an old house may identify areas where water can get behind a painted finish.*

Stripping Paint Off Brick

My home has a brick fireplace that the previous owners inexplicably coated with several layers of latex paint. I've tried wire brushes and muriatic acid, but paint remains embedded in the pores of the brick. I may try sandblasting next. Any ideas?

Daniel Rolla, New York, N.Y.

This question comes up so often that hundreds of basement geniuses must be working on it, and they still haven't found a solution. I don't know anyone who has gotten every little speck of paint off brick. Sandblasting ruins it. Maybe the room will look good by candlelight.

I don't know anyone who has gotten every little speck of paint off brick. Sandblasting ruins it.

Furniture Refinishing Basics

My late father left behind an antique jelly cupboard that's going to be a lot of work for this novice to strip, repair, and repaint, but I'm willing to try. Any suggestions?

Jean SmilingCoyote, Chicago, Ill.

Refinishing destroys much of the value of antiques, so consult an expert to find out what you have. If the cupboard is simply old, rather than antique, light sanding and feathering the edges where it's chipped may be all the preparation you need before repainting. "Old" paint usually means lead paint, so make sure you wear a dust mask and work outside with the cupboard on a disposable plastic sheet, and use wet sponge-type sandpaper or a sander attached to a vacuum with a HEPA (high-efficiency particulate air) filter. Stripping is rarely necessary unless you want to show the wood grain. If that's your aim, check a hardware or paint store for an ecologically friendly stripper, and follow the directions on the label.

Matching Old Finishes

You've duplicated so much old pine furniture that I'm sure you have also been able to duplicate the old-time finishes. So how about sharing your secrets?

Cal Ditch, Sun City, Calif.

In the early years of *The New Yankee Workshop*, I used off-the-shelf pine from the local lumberyard and wanted to make it look old, but nothing worked. I tried commercial finishes. I tried making my own. Still, I just couldn't get the look I wanted. In recent years, I started using recycled lumber. That is the main secret. Older pine grew more slowly than new pine does—look at the growth rings, and you'll see how close they are—and was seasoned slowly, too. I also started using a stain-polyurethane mix, a product I had once vowed never to use because it can't be removed without sanding down to bare wood. But when I tried it on old pine, either straight from the can or in mixes of various shades, I discovered it was easy to apply and gave exactly the look I wanted. Still, it's important to experiment on pieces of scrap wood first, to be sure of getting a pleasing finish.

Finish for Butcher Block

My husband and I installed a butcher block counter, and it turned black from splashed water around the sink. We scraped the butcher block clean and lacquered it, but now everything sticks to the lacquer—even the rubber feet of our food processor. What should we do?

Susan Wilder, New Smyrna Beach, Fla.

Butcher block is easy to like but hard to live with because it requires a lot of maintenance. You can remove the lacquer and apply light mineral oil periodically, remembering never to let water stand on the surface. Or you could build up a tough epoxy coating followed by spar varnish, a finish that people in the boating industry use to protect wood from moisture and ultraviolet light. Of course, then you'll have a boat look, gleaming and glossy, not the raw-wood butcher block that most people prefer.

Cleaning Brass and Copper

How do I get old tarnished brass to polish up properly—so it has a warm glow instead of a tacky, brilliant gleam?

Pia Davis, Shady, N.Y.

Reddish brass, which is high in copper, tends to give a warm glow while yellowish, low-copper brass naturally buffs to a high house-proud gleam. There's not much you can do about the gleam except avoid using metal polishes containing fine abrasives, which produce a higher shine. Or you could try an old-fashioned cleaning method. Mix ordinary table salt and warm white vinegar, then apply the solution with a rag (see drawing below). This will often clean copper almost instantly and leave a soft satin glow. With brass, prolonged soaking may be necessary. One note of caution: The salt-vinegar mix is acidic, so you'll need full-face protection, rubber gloves, adequate ventilation, and running water for rinsing. ■

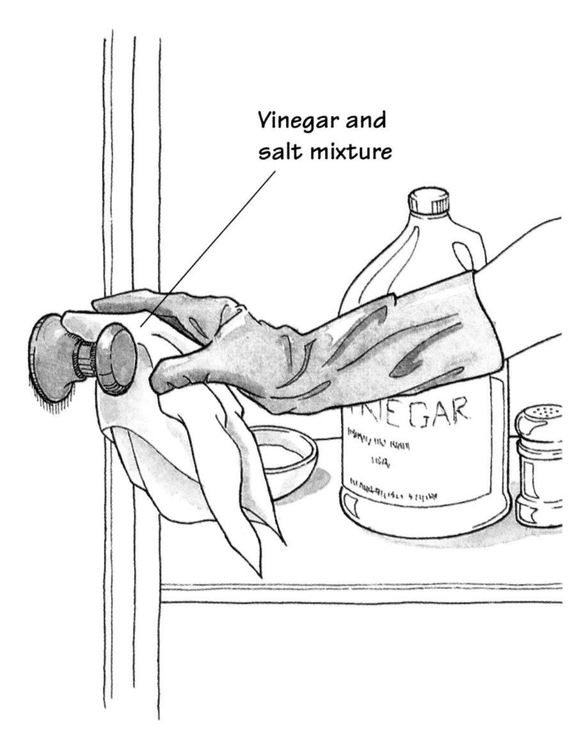

CHAPTER SEVEN

Interior Floors, Walls + Ceilings

New Tiles Over Old

I'm about to move into a new house, but my contractor installed the wrong color of wall tile in the shower stall. I'd like to have him replace it with the color I originally asked for, but my mother-in-law is concerned that removing the old tile and retiling will damage the wall. What do you think?

Eileen Russ Heltzer, Fort Lee, N.J.

Never bet against a mother-in-law, even if you think she's wrong. But in this case, she isn't. Tile setter Joe Ferrante, who does a lot of work for the show, says it's very unlikely that the existing tile can be removed without damaging the substrate it's adhered to.

You have two options: Rip out everything down to the studs and start over, or tile over the existing surface, a technique known in the industry as T.O.T. (tile over tile). If you go the less expensive T.O.T route, Ferrante recommends scuffing up the tile surface with 80-grit sandpaper and leveling it with a coat of thinset adhesive. Then the new tiles can be installed as you normally would, capping any exposed edges with matching trim tiles. Ferrante has used this method several times with good results. This technique does increase the thickness of the walls slightly, which has repercussions at the faucet valve. With any luck, you can just reattach the escutcheons or plate over the new tile, but then again, you may have to replumb and reset the valve. To check whether this will be necessary, take a few sample tiles and try to reassemble the valve handle and escutcheon over them.

Just one more thing: Before you start correcting this problem yourself, talk to your contractor. A good one should correct his mistakes, and this sounds like a pretty serious mistake to me.

A CIRCULAR SAW *guided by an oversize square yields accurate crosscuts on panel wainscoting.*

Paint Prep for Plaster

The walls of our 80-year-old house are covered with plaster and multiple layers of old wallpaper, but our redecorating plans call for painted walls. How should we prepare the plaster surfaces for painting after we remove the paper? And what type of paint would you recommend?

Ben Soldo, Palestine, Ohio

The answer depends on the condition of the walls, and you won't know that until you get the paper off. Cracked or crumbling plaster must be repaired before you paint, and if the damage is extensive, you might want to consult a professional plasterer or drywall contractor. But let's hope for the best here and assume that the plaster is in good shape.

To prepare walls for paint, I rely on painting contractor John Dee for advice. He suggests filling a pump sprayer with 5 ounces of wallpaper stripper diluted with a gallon of water, wetting down the wall, then scraping off the paper—and as much paste as you can—with a 3- or 4-inch scraper blade. When the paper is gone, spray the walls again with the stripper solution, scrape off more paste residue with a broad taping knife (the kind used on drywall) and then immediately wipe the walls down with a large wet sponge. Rinse it frequently in clean water and keep wiping until no paste remains. Give the walls 24 to 48 hours to dry before painting.

Dee recommends rolling on a primer-sealer as the first coat over plaster. Doing this evens out the porosity of the surface so the finish coat will have an even sheen. It also creates a barrier to slow the passage of water vapor through the walls, and provides a surface to which paint can readily adhere. On very old walls, a primer-sealer also helps to bind plaster particles to each other, hardening the surface. Dee thinks that oil-based primers generally do all of these things better than latex primers. Also, you can use either oil or latex topcoats over an oil-based primer. Latex eggshell finish paints are the most popular choice for walls because they're more easily cleaned than flat paints and more forgiving of imperfections than glossy ones.

Pesky Ceiling Leaks

We have a leak in our bathroom ceiling, but we can't seem to find where the water is coming from. We had new roofing put on but that hasn't solved the problem. Now we're running out of ideas. Can you help?

Ida Mae McMillan, Pana, Ill.

The problem with water is that it seldom follows a direct path from its entry point to the spot where you notice the damage. Wait for the next rainstorm and go up in the attic with a flashlight to see if you can trace its trail back to the source. The most common trouble spots are around roof flashing, so take a close look around any plumbing vent stacks and chimneys, and along roof valleys and any place a gable or dormer wall meets a roof. If you can't find an actual trickle of water, see if you can find its calling card: irregular coffee-colored stains or black patches of mildew on the underside of the sheathing or on the rafters.

Because it's so difficult to track down the source of a leak, *This Old House* contractor Tom Silva never reroofs over existing shingles, even though building codes allow the practice. He prefers to strip off the existing shingles just so he can inspect flashing and sheathing, and replace it if necessary. He says it costs more initially to do it this way, but it's cheaper in the long run.

But as proof of how sneaky leaks can be, a *This Old House* reader wrote and told us that he traced a leak in his bathroom ceiling to a horizontal length of vent pipe that ran above the ceiling. Apparently water entering the vent collected in the pipe and dribbled out onto the ceiling through a crack in one of the pipe joints. Unusual, yes, but it just goes to show how sneaky leaks can be.

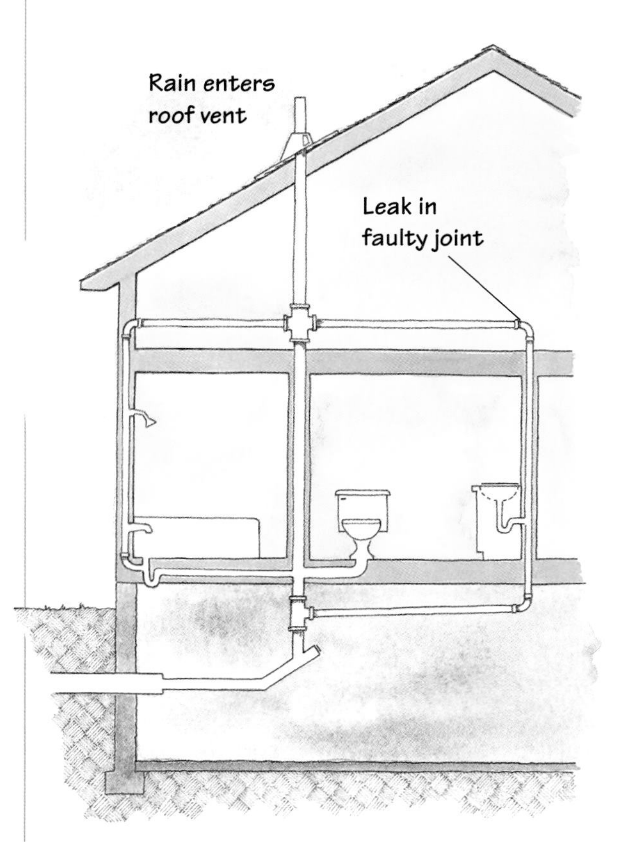

The problem with water is that it seldom follows a direct path from its entry point to the spot where you notice the damage.

Popcorn Ceiling Secrets

On the ceilings of our house, we have a textured "popcorn" surface which is cracking as the drywall tape underneath comes loose. This is happening around the edges of most rooms, but in some cases the tape is coming loose in the middle of a ceiling. What is the best method of repairing this problem?

Roger Draper, Greeneville, Tenn.

If the damage were limited to one room, I'd figure that a leak had soaked the drywall enough to loosen the tape. But because other rooms are involved, I suspect either a flaw in the original installation, such as joint compound being applied too thin, or too much humidity inside the house. Unfortunately, once they're damaged, textured ceilings can be tricky to repair. Also, ceilings put up before 1980 may contain asbestos and should not be disturbed. If that's the case here, skip ahead to the last paragraph.

The original surface was probably sprayed on using a special hopper gun attached to an airless sprayer pump. If you have a lot of repairs or patches bigger than 2 square feet, I'd hire a pro to redo your ceiling with the same equipment; matching it by hand won't be easy. For small areas, however, even an imperfect match will probably look a lot better than what you see now, so here's what to do.

Peel off the loose tape, then butter the area with joint compound and press new tape into it. After it dries, brush on a coat of oil-based primer. Now for the artistic part. Lay on another coat of compound and push perlite texturing additive into the wet surface with your hands, doing your best to mimic the surrounding texture. Perlite is a lightweight silicate derived from volcanic rock, and looks something like coarse salt. Use a granule size that approximates the texture you're trying to match. When the patch dries, it will surely be a different color from the surrounding ceiling, but don't grab your paintbrush. You're not supposed to paint popcorn; the paint prevents it from absorbing smoke and dust and will probably peel off in a few years anyway. To equalize color variations, clean the rest of the ceiling with an oxidizing cleaner made for the purpose.

If you're still not happy with the results, or you have a ceiling that was installed when asbestos was still being used, bury the problem under a new layer of 3/8-inch drywall. I'll be the first to admit that drywalling a ceiling isn't much fun, but at least you'll end up with a fresh, problem-free surface. Crown molding installed around the perimeter will conceal the ceiling/wall joint. And this time, paint the ceiling; save the popcorn for the movies.

I'll be the first to admit that drywalling a ceiling isn't much fun, but at least you'll end up with a fresh, problem-free surface.

A CRACK'S *width determines its repair. Cracks less than 1/16 inch wide can be caulked or spackled.*

Repairing Nail Pops

I know that a lot of builders these days install drywall using screws, but my home dates to an era when nails were the most common fasteners. Unfortunately, there are nail pops throughout the house, in varying degrees of severity. As I remodel each room, I sand down the bumps so that they're flush with the wall surface, but no matter what sandpaper I use, it soon gets clogged with paint. This work is getting pretty tedious. Can you offer any time-saving solutions?

Peter J. Tinnesz, Trumbull, Conn.

My first piece of advice is to stop sanding—that's no way to repair a nail pop. Instead, push on the drywall to hold it against the stud, and then drive a drywall screw 1½ inches above and below the popped nail. Now give the nail a whack to drive it tight again. (If the head is exposed, pull the nail out.) Use joint compound to fill the depressions created by the screws as well as the damage created by the nail pop—two coats of compound usually does the trick (just let the first dry before adding the second). You'll find that sanding unpainted joint compound smooth is a lot easier than sanding drywall bumps. If you have a lot of pops to repair, use a silicon carbide sanding screen. The open weave of the material eliminates clogging entirely.

The reason nails pop in the first place is often due to lumber shrinkage. That creates a space between the drywall and framing, so that the nails push out if any pressure is put on the drywall. Ring-shank drywall nails hold better than smooth-shank, but nothing beats drywall screws for holding power.

Solution for Uneven Grout

We recently had ceramic tile installed above our bathroom vanities. The tile is fine, but the grout has high spots and low spots. Is there anything we can do to correct this? I think it looks terrible.

Karl Guenther, Saint Johns, Penn.

The grout that fills the gaps between tile is like icing on a cake—it can make everything else look bad if it's done poorly. This particular problem is a good example of what can happen if you don't inspect a job when the contractor is through. If the two of you had been standing there, you could have pointed out the problems and had him fix them right then. Now you've got to chase after him.

If you aren't able to get him to make repairs, here's how you can make them. According to tilesetter Joe Ferrante, the best way to even out the high spots in wall grout is to rub them with very fine (000) steel wool, which won't scratch the tile's glaze as sandpaper or a nylon scouring pad might. Wear rubber gloves to protect your hands from the steel wool.

As for the low spots, you should be able to touch them up with fresh grout. Dampen the area with water, then use your finger or a spatula to spread grout over the low spots. Wait until it dries to the touch, then wipe any excess off the tiles. Finally, seal the area with whatever grout sealant you put on originally. I wouldn't be suggesting this if the grout had been in place for years—the color difference between old and new would be too obvious—but because your job was completed recently, this remedy shouldn't be a problem. With any luck, your tilesetter left you with some extra grout after the original installation. If not, try to find out which brand and color of grout he used so that the repairs will match.

Tricks for Matching Old Tile

We want to expand the tiled area of our bathroom walls (we're putting in a shower) but can't find tiles that match the originals. These are 4-inch-square tiles marked "102-6" on the back. Is that a code number that can help us identify the manufacturer?

Clinton and Ann Philson, Atkinson, Nebr.

Unfortunately, it's probably just a code the manufacturer used to identify a specific production run. Even if you were able to find the manufacturer, the company may not be able to provide an exact match; colors and sizes differ slightly from one lot to another. So

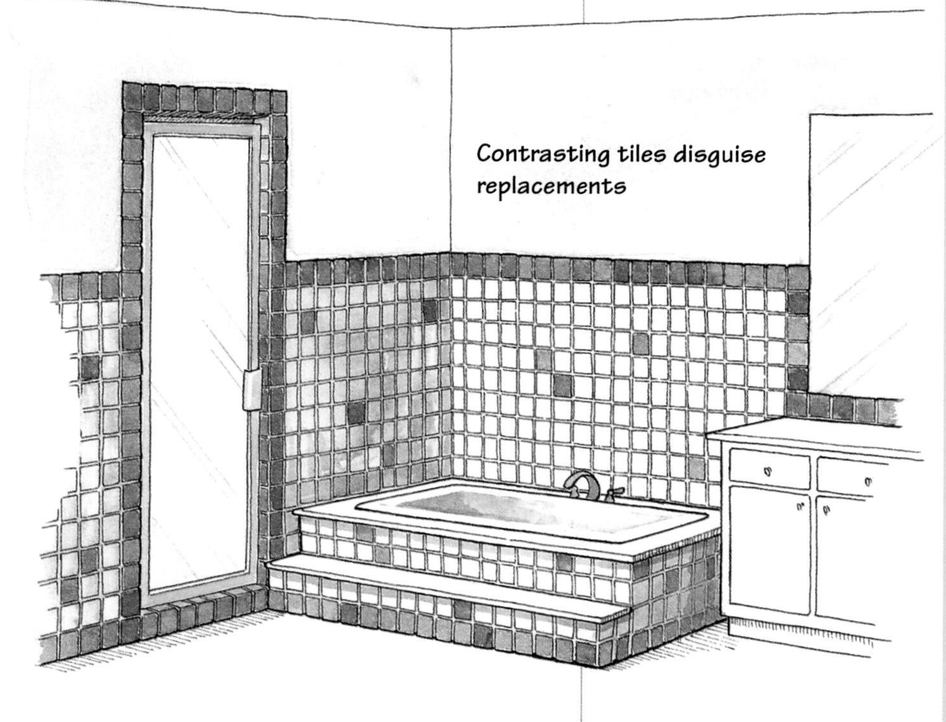
Contrasting tiles disguise replacements

STRAIGHT *walls and flat ceilings are easy to achieve due to the uniformity of engineered lumber.*

what to do? You could "stretch" the existing tiles by mixing new tiles with the old (see drawing, previous page; start new tiles at a corner to minimize the apparent color change; or rip out the old stuff and start fresh—whatever suits your budget and taste.

Stained Wood Ceilings

Although the leaks that caused the stains on our wood ceiling were repaired long ago, the spots remain. Before I surrender and paint over the discoloration, I'd appreciate any suggestions you may have.

James E. Foy, North Hollywood, Calif.

A deck cleaner might get rid of them, but working overhead with potentially nasty chemicals is not my idea of fun. It's also work that calls for a full complement of safety equipment. Sanding may remove some of the spots, but you'll probably end up having to sand everything—beams and ceiling—to even out the look, and that's not a very appealing prospect, either. Brushing a dark stain into the wood may disguise the water damage, but you'll have a tough time getting uniform coverage. So painting would seem to be the simplest solution. And if you still want to see some wood in its natural state, sand just the beams—a far less onerous task—and then paint the boards in between. You'll end up with an attractive ceiling that will reflect more light and therefore brighten up the room.

FOR MORE ON PAINTING TURN TO CHAPTER 6: PAINTING AND FINISHING

Fire-Resistant Drywall

Why don't builders use ⅝-inch fire-code drywall throughout the entire house? I'd certainly pay a premium over standard drywall to have a more fire-resistant structure.

Steve Miller, Sylvan Lake, Mich.

The ⅝-inch, "fire-code" drywall (called Type X) increases a wall's fire rating to a minimum of 1 hour, from the 30-minute rating for standard ½-inch drywall. And it's not just thickness that makes the difference. Type X has a denser core and contains glass fibers that keep it from crumbling in the heat. But because Type X is slightly more expensive, it's rarely used in residential construction except where the building code requires it—on walls separating an attached garage from the house, for example, and around the boiler in multiple-family dwellings. If you're willing to shell out the extra dough, you certainly could use Type X throughout a house, yet it won't necessarily be dramatically safer. You'd also have to close off all the other pathways for fire to travel—open doorways, non-fire-rated doors, walls without fire blocking—and that could get costly. Type X does have another virtue that is often overlooked: it dampens sound transmission through the walls. Do you have teenagers?

Silencing Squeaky Floors

When we bought our house two years ago, we were told that it had hardwood floors under the carpet. Recently, we decided to tear up the carpet and refinish the floors. To our surprise, we discovered many large nails in the walking areas of the floor, making it look like it has the chicken pox. Do you have any suggestions on how to fix this problem?

Margaret Petras, South Euclid, Ohio

Carpet sure is great at concealing the sins of previous owners, isn't it? I can't imagine anyone face-nailing a hardwood floor because they liked the look, so I'd bet the nails are a clumsy attempt to stop the floor from squeaking. I wish I could say, "Remove the nails, refinish the floor, and you'll be all set." Unfortunately, if you did that your floor would still be peppered with nail holes (or the putty used to fill them) and you'd have taken many years off its life. The way I see it, you have only two options here: rip up the damaged flooring and put down new, or hide the mess under new carpeting.

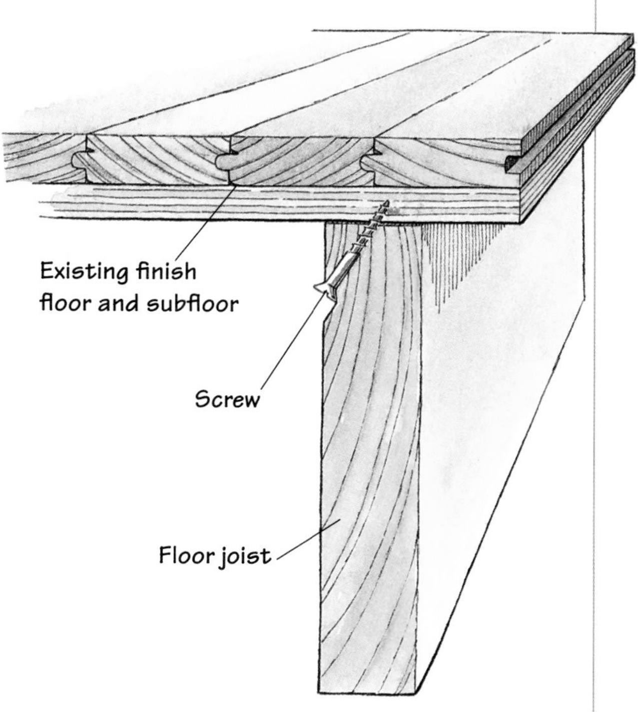

Whichever route you take, you'll first want to silence those squeaks. Basically, that means pulling the flooring tight to the subfloor, and the subfloor tight to the joists (see drawing above). If laying a new floor is in your budget, then make sure that the subfloor is screwed and, if possible, glued (with construction adhesive) securely to the joists before the new floor is laid. If you plan to put down new carpeting instead, then go into the basement, locate the squeak, and drive short screws up through the subfloor and into the bottom of the finish flooring. To stop a squeaking subfloor, drive longer screws at an angle through the tops of the joists (see drawing above). But if you can't get to the underside of the floor, drive screws through the top of the flooring and into the joists, countersinking the holes. Cover the screw heads with wood filler or wood plugs

Carpet sure is great at concealing the sins of previous owners, isn't it?

sanded flush. It's not the most attractive solution, but at least no one will see the screws.

Cure for Bouncy Floors

Our 6-year-old daughter often sits with us as we watch what you're making each week, and says, "Norm can fix anything." I hope she's right. When our house was built in 1998, we wanted a large family room in our basement, without any posts in the middle of the room. We were assured that 20-foot-long, 14-inch-deep wood I-joists set on 16-inch centers would provide ample support to the floor above. They don't. There's a noticeable bounce to the surface, even when our daughter walks across the floor. The basement isn't finished yet, so we still have access to the floor structure. What should we do?

Jill Sherret, Cranbrook, British Columbia

First off, let me assure you that your floor is probably strong enough; you shouldn't worry about it suddenly collapsing. What you are noticing is its lack of stiffness. No material used to support a floor, whether it's sawn lumber, engineered lumber, or steel, is stiff enough to completely eliminate the flexing that happens when a "live load," such as your daughter, walks or skips across it. Building codes allow floor joists to deflect within a certain range. But when joists have to span a long distance, the flexing becomes noticeable. That's why I'm a believer in going beyond the basic code requirements to get the stiffness I want. That may mean using deeper joists, putting them closer together, or both.

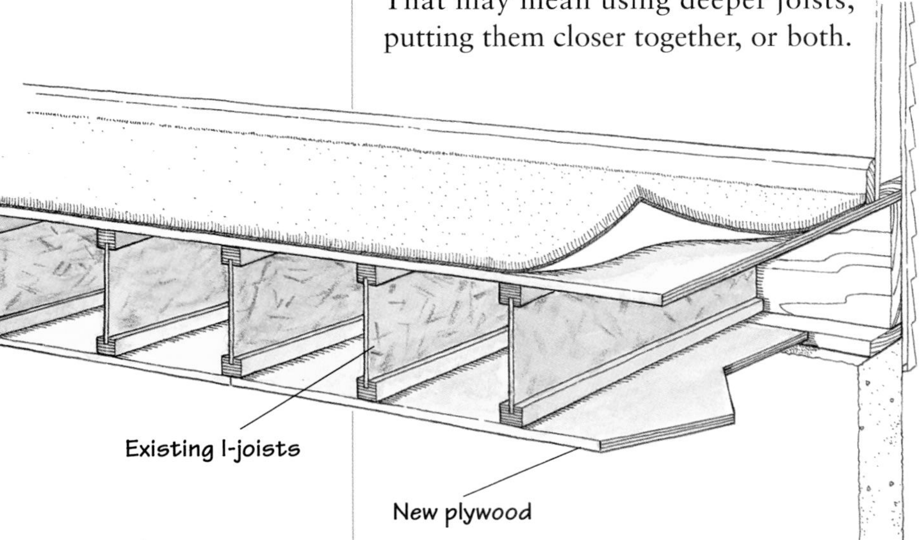

The subfloor also plays a part in floor stiffness, which is why I recommend using screws and construction adhesive to attach it to the joists.

To firm up your floors now, you could try to add joists between the existing ones, though that isn't always practical or possible. Fitting pieces of 2× blocking or crossbracing between the joists should help, or you could fasten lengths of 1×4 wood strapping to the underside of the joists. Space straps 16 inches on center perpendicular to the joists, and nail or screw each strap where it crosses a joist. But an even more effective method for stiffening an I-joist floor is the approach taken by Tom Silva. He glues and screws sheets of ½-inch plywood to the underside of the joists, in effect forming a ceiling (see drawing below). This may seem a drastic solution, but he's used it several times and says it's quite effective. Of course, the most effective way to stiffen any floor would be to reduce the joists' span, but you know what that means: You'd have to put a beam and support posts in your family room.

Plaster Ceiling Repairs

Well, we've fixed our roof, but how do we repair our bathroom ceiling, which was ruined by leaks? So much plaster has fallen you can see the wood lath. Can we nail drywall directly to the lath?

Annette Perry, Union, N.H.

No, you can't, but you can fasten through it. Drive extra-long drywall screws (I don't recommend nails) through the lath and into the joists above. That will give you a solid new ceiling. By the way, you should use ⅝-inch drywall on ceilings and lay it perpendicular to the joists.

Cracks in Wood Paneling

Last summer I painted my old bead board walls and ceilings. Then I turned on my new heat pump, and now all the paint is cracking along the seams between the boards. What should I do?

M.D. Randall, Elberton, Ga.

EXCESS ADHESIVE *should be removed from tiles before it dries; otherwise cleanup will be tough.*

The "cracks" were always there—they are the seams between the individual bead board strips, which allow the wood to expand and contract with changing humidity. The paint film merely broke along the cracks when the wood shrank. What to do now? The easiest option is to do nothing—in time you'll forget all about them. If that doesn't suit you, lay a bead of paintable caulk in the cracks so it lies just below the surface of the boards. That way, when the seams close with the next change of weather, the caulk won't be pushed up into a visible rib between boards. Then you can touch up the seams with paint.

Canvas-Covered Plaster

My old house was built by my great-uncle sometime around 1906 or 1910, and it has canvas-covered plaster walls and ceilings. They have been painted over many times through the years, and no maintenance has been done since the 1970s. Now it's time. The paint in some areas looks like alligator hide; there are some large cracks under the canvas; and there are places where the canvas is pulling away from the plaster. My family and I want to do something, but we're not sure just what. Naturally, we are getting lots of free advice ranging from spackle-and-forget to sandblast with dry grit.

Dorothy E. Pittman, Carrollton, Ga.

Frankly, I'd be inclined to get in there with a wallpaper steamer and pull all the stuff off. That would make patching the cracks simple and leave you with a nice, paintable surface. But plaster craftsman Rory Brennan has a different approach. He's a conservationist at heart, and suggests using wheat paste to glue the canvas back in place. He points out that, around the turn of the last century, canvas was used not only to cover plaster cracks but also as a decorative surface—a "canvas" so to speak— for ordinary paint and, occasionally, for intricate artwork. Something of that sort could lie beneath the layers of paint on your canvas, which could add to your house's value if uncovered and restored.

Around the turn of the last century, canvas was used not only to cover plaster cracks but also as a decorative surface.

Cracked Ceiling Solution

The bedroom of our 60-year-old Georgian looks a bit too rustic. Paint on the plaster ceiling is cracking and flaking in large sections, some as big as 3 by 5 inches. First, what could be causing this? I can't find any evidence of moisture buildup. Second, what do you consider the best method of removing old layers of paint from plaster?

Stephen Brown, Chicago, Ill.

If moisture isn't the problem, you may have a buildup of paint layers that aren't adhering well to each other. I'd recommend laying up $\frac{3}{8}$-inch blueboard and plastering over it. I checked with painting contractor John Dee, and he agrees. Chemical-stripping such a large area would be an awful job, he says. It's also messy, and the workers are at risk from nasty fumes. After the stripper is applied, it must be scraped off and then neutralized by flooding the area with denatured alcohol and wiping it down—several times.

In most circumstances, my advice is quite simple: Don't remove a floor unless there's absolutely no alternative.

Shower Curtain vs. Door

Paint on the wall along the back of my bathtub is bubbling and cracking. The trouble starts at the baseboard, which has separated from the drywall. The grout and ceramic tiles of the shower wall aren't leaking, but water seems to be getting behind the baseboard and under the quarter-round floor molding. There's also a lot of mildew. Would replacing the shower curtain with shower doors help?

Brent J. Bartholomew, Kokomo, Ind.

Shower doors will indeed help, because it seems a lot of water is getting past the curtain. You'll still have to repair the damage already done. Whatever lies behind your baseboard and beneath your molding might keep you busy with repairs for some time.

Reusing Old Wood Floors

I have a farmhouse that's over 200 years old and still has the original random-width pumpkin-pine floors. Downstairs, however, they've been covered with maple-strip flooring, which I'd like to remove so I can refinish the pine underneath. Is this possible, and if so, will I be able to reuse the maple anywhere?

Jena Rae, Millington, N.J.

When you think about how much abuse a wood floor gets, it's not surprising that so many people ask me about how to revive them. In most circumstances, my advice is quite simple: Don't remove a floor unless there's absolutely no alternative. The underside of your pine planks might look great, but remember that the top side has experienced at least 100 years of wear. And I'll bet it's worn beyond the point where sanding and refinishing could erase the damage. That's probably why the pine was covered over in the first place.

Even if you did remove the maple flooring—the chances of reusing it are next to none, by the way— you'd have to go back and add filler pieces that extend the bottoms of all the doors, which probably were trimmed when they installed the maple. I won't even talk about all the nail holes you'd need to hide, unless it's a very rustic look you're after. As I've said before, sometimes the most valuable renovation skill is knowing when to leave well enough alone.

One Cause of Sloped Floors

As a home inspector, I find that the floors in homes over 50 years old are rarely level. But why do the second-story floors so often slope downward toward the chimney?

David Biggerstaff, Catlin, Ill.

In many old houses, it's not uncommon to find the end of a floor beam resting in a pocket in the side of a chimney. So when the chimney settles, as most usually do, it takes the floor framing with it. Even if the masonry hasn't moved a millimeter since the day it was built, the floor still might slope toward a chimney if joists in contact with the damp stone or brick have rotted.

You can thank the building codes for putting an end to this practice; framing now has to be at least 2 inches away from the chimney, and about the only thing you'll notice when the chimney settles is that the hearth drops a bit.

FOR MORE ON STRUCTURAL REPAIRS TURN TO CHAPTER 1: GENERAL REMODELING AND REPAIRS

Mill-It Yourself Flooring

I'm planning to take 1-inch-thick pieces of white oak salvaged from pallets and turn them into the flooring for my attic. I'll cut grooves into the edges of the boards and glue in oak "tongues" on one side. Since I'm after a rugged nautical look, I'll screw and plug the ends of each board and toenail through the tongues. Do you see any problems with using this approach? I was wondering, as well, why commercially manufactured wood flooring has two grooves in the bottom. Should I add them to my boards?

John Marinovich, Boonton, N.J.

REMOVING *walls and ceilings calls for a "cat's paw" nail remover coaxed along by a hammer.*

I hope you like your floors rustic, because that's exactly what you're going to get from short pallet pieces. But I think it's great to get more life out of old wood that would otherwise end up in a landfill. And if you have the time, I don't see any problems with your approach, as long as you take certain precautions. Keep the wood under cover as long as you can so it can air-dry before you start milling. Flooring manufacturers prefer to mill their stock when its moisture content drops below 10 percent. This way, your jointed edges will likely stay nice and straight. I think the milling will go faster if you simply cut real tongues and grooves on a router table or shaper using the bits or cutters specifically designed for that purpose. Just don't forget to run a metal detector over the wood before you cut. An embedded nail will instantly turn an expensive saw blade, router bit, or shaper cutter into a useless hunk of metal. Finally, be sure to lay the flooring on a stiff subfloor—¾-inch plywood would be good. Toenailing in addition to screwing and plugging is a good idea.

You don't really need the bottom grooves, however. According to folks at the National Oak Flooring Manufacturers' Association, the grooves (called "hollow backs") on the underside of commercially milled wood flooring reduce shipping weight and show installers which side goes down. (Floorboards are thicker above the tongue than below, so a floor that was accidentally installed upside down would wear through faster than one laid properly.) The grooves also encourage air circulation between the floor and the subfloor. In case you're wondering, two grooves is the standard configuration, but some boards might have three and some only one.

Sealing Slate

The previous owner installed a slate floor in the foyer, but he didn't clean off all the grout residue before he sealed the stone. What can I do to make this floor look more presentable?

Jim Hallas, Janesville, Wisc.

Before you can get at the grout, you'll have to remove the sealer; tiling contractor Joe Ferrante recommends a bond stripper, available at tile suppliers. They also sell non-acidic grout-haze removers, to use once the sealer is off, but Ferrante says scrubbing the stone with an abrasive pad and white vinegar should do the job just as well. After the haze is gone, seal your slate again; Ferrante favors acrylic sealers with penetrating oil-based solvents. Whatever you use, I'd say the same thing I would about floor finishes: Buy the best product you can afford. This is no place to cut corners.

Correcting Bowed Floors

We've lived in our 1912 Arts and Crafts house for 25 years. Recently, I've noticed

that the floor at the center of the house is bowing upward. What's going on?

Vicki Flickinger, Burrton, Kans.

I can almost bet that your house has a rotten or termite-infested mudsill, the timber that rests on the foundation and supports one end of the floor joists. (We seem to find deteriorated mudsills in almost every *This Old House* project.) The floor is probably bowing because a support beam in the center of your house is holding the floor at its original level while the exterior walls are crushing the punky sill. The result: Your joists are bending like a teeter-totter with a sumo wrestler in each seat. The situation gets worse when the damage extends into the floor and rim joists. If you go into the basement and poke at the wood with a screwdriver, you'll probably see what I'm talking about.

To correct the immediate problem, you'll have to replace all the rotten wood. To prevent future problems, make sure the new mudsill is pressure-treated and at least 8 inches above the finish grade, which should be sloped away from the house to encourage water to drain away (see drawing below). On the other hand, if you find the sills are intact, the only other explanation for the bowing is that the foundation itself is sinking. To correct that problem, you'll need to call a structural engineer or a foundation contractor.

FOR MORE ON FLOOR REPAIRS TURN TO CHAPTER 1: GENERAL REMODELING AND REPAIRS

Asbestos in Resilient Flooring

We recently bought my husband's old family home which was built back in the '50s—apparently by enthusiastic amateurs. I say that because practically nothing in the house is of standard size. All the doorways are much too short, for example, and the ceilings are 7 feet 3 inches high! But it's the flooring that's giving me fits just now. Some sort of tar has the linoleum stuck really hard to the concrete slab. The linoleum comes off in layers, leaving one layer and the tar behind, and when I follow up with a scraper, cement comes up with the tar. I've tried commercial solvents, but all they seem to do is smear the stuff around.

Maggie Dean, McIntyre, Ga.

Before you proceed any further, consider this: Much of the vinyl and linoleum flooring made before 1985 contained asbestos, and there's no way for you to know if yours does just by looking at it. To be safe, contact a certified asbestos abatement contractor and let a pro do the removal. In many cases, it's actually best just to bury the suspect material under new floor sheathing and/or flooring. That eliminates the risks of ripping it up.

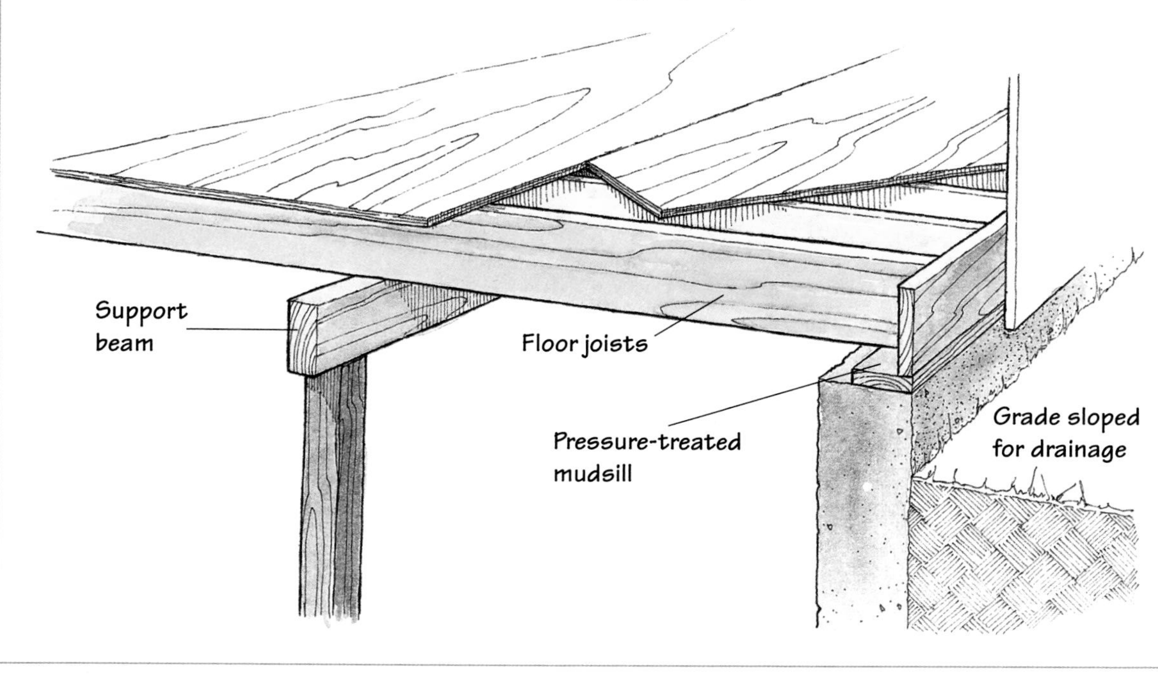

ROTTEN SILLS *are a common old-house malady. Every bit of punky wood must be replaced.*

Reviving a Wood Floor Finish

The urethane finish on my apartment's wood floor is about 15 years old and still looks very good, except in the kitchen/dining area. I thought of roughing up the whole floor with a buffer rather than sanding it down to bare wood, but it seems a shame to screen the areas that still look fine. Could I screen and then refinish just the worn area?

William A. Marsano, New York, N.Y.

It's no surprise that your floor is looking a little ragged in the kitchen. This is the busiest room in a house, and the target of myriad spills, stains, and subsequent mop-ups. I think you're correct in not trying to sand the entire floor Even a careful, professional sanding removes some of the wood surface and reduces the floor's life. Screening a floor with a buffer simply scours off a bit of the finish, preparing it for a new coat. But spot-screening a floor is tricky business. For one thing, blending the new finish into the old isn't easy. Also, some floor finishes tend to yellow over time, so an adjacent area of new finish may be obvious. So you should screen the entire floor with a 120-grit abrasive and refinish with two coats of polyurethane. You'll have to move all your furniture, but you'll get better results. Before screening, give the floor a thorough cleaning with turpentine to remove any wax, grease,

Even a careful, professional sanding removes some of the wood surface and reduces the floor's life.

and dirt. After screening, vacuum and wipe up every speck of dust before you recoat the floor.

New Color for Old Grout

We put down off-white tile and matching grout in the kitchen of our old house. To protect the grout, we put on a sealer, which we renew every six months, and we even take our shoes off at the door. Well, the grout is showing dirt. Is there any way to stain or color it so you can't see the dirt?

Susan Tedder, Eliot, Maine

There's nothing like "mud season" in Maine to foul up grout on a floor. But don't throw in the towel yet. Tiling contractor Joe Ferrante tells me that before you can change the grout's color, you have to remove the sealant. Call the manufacturer to find out the best way to do that, then find a grout stain you like (brown or gray is good for hiding dirt) and apply two coats. After that, you shouldn't need a sealant. Just make sure that all those shoes stay at the door.

Concealing Mortar Patches

I recently patched some of the mortar joints in an indoor flagstone floor, but the repaired areas are very distinct from the original joints, and I don't think that looks very good. What can I do to make the mortar blend in?

Jim Pileggi, Ambler, Pa.

You could experiment with mortar stains, but I think you'd be asking for trouble because the color will probably still be inconsistent. You could replace all the old mortar with new, but that's an awful lot of work. I'd try cleaning the old joints first with muriatic acid to see if they can blend a little better. Otherwise, try a little patience; the patched joints will gradually gain some patina and match the older ones.

Flood-Soaked Paneling

The ground floor of my home is tongue-and-groove oak. It is rather stained because I'm within 30 feet of a tidal river, and during spring tides the southwest winds raised the river to slightly above floor level. (There's no basement, only a 6-inch ventilation space.) How do I get rid of the stains?

D.M. Warner, Vancouver, B.C.

Some of the stains might be removed by bleaching, a job best left to the pros; others might be sanded out. The black spots that remain, from wet oak reacting with the iron in the nails, may never come out. A more important project is to keep the water from coming back. You can't lower the river, so you'd better raise the floor by jacking your house up above the high tide mark. While you're at it, check the framing for rot.

You can't lower the river, so you'd better raise the floor by jacking your house up above the high tide mark.

Expansion Gap Stands Out

We built a house with a main room that's half–living room, with a floating wood floor, and half–kitchen/dining room, which is tiled. Both floors look wonderful, except there's a ¼-inch expansion gap where they meet. What can we do to make the gap less obvious?

Terry C. Anschutz, Sturgeon Bay, Wisc.

Detailing the meeting of two dissimilar materials is always touchy. The way I see it, you have two choices: You can take up the floating floor and re-lay it so it butts up against the tile, but you'll have to leave room for expansion on the opposite side. Or you can leave the floor as it is and fill the gap with a bead of color-matched silicone caulk. Just be sure it's below the level of the floor, not flush with it. Otherwise the caulk will push up above the surface when the floor expands.

Yankee Thrift

I've seen episodes of *This Old House* showing beautiful old floors with high-quality wood surrounding a patch of

WHEN ONE *nail is located, a spirit level can be used to plot the probable location of the stud.*

cheaper stuff meant to be covered by an area rug. Now I'm looking to install a prefinished manufactured floor and I wonder whether I can do the same thing beneath my area rug. After all, can't we have good old Yankee ingenuity in the new century?

Lawrence Loewy, Coram, N.Y.

Yes, we can. All it takes is a layer of plywood installed exactly where the rug will go. Keep two things in mind, however. Your approach limits decorating options,so it may affect the resale value of your house- And as with any floating floor, you must leave an expansion gap around the perimeter of the room.

Waxing Wood Floors

I've read about carnauba-rich wax being used on a hardwood floor. Can you tell me a little more about it? Does it make the floors slippery?

Dean Taylor, Cuyahoga Falls, Ohio

Carnauba, a hard wax that comes from the leaves of a Brazilian palm tree, is added to the paste waxes that shine and protect bars, bowling alleys and boat hulls as well as floors. It yellows in time. (You've heard, I presume, of the dreaded "waxy yellow buildup.") A non-yellowing alternative is microcrystalline wax, a petroleum by-product. It's expensive, but a very little goes a long way. All waxes must be reapplied, buffed, and stripped periodically, but a floor will last practically forever if given such care. Any wax makes floors slippery, so put antiskid pads under area rugs and avoid running in stocking feet.

Gaps in Hardwood Flooring

I've just purchased my first house. It's in the Victorian style, built in 1905. The hardwood floors still have a pretty good finish on them, but they have quite a few separations between the boards. Is there anything I can do about that, without pulling up the old wood or covering it with new?

Carol Douglas, Yale, Mich.

Your floors have been expanding and contracting for nearly a century and will continue to do so. That's the nature of wood floors, so don't worry about them.

Dogs and Wood Floors

I have a dog and don't want any smells to soak into my pine and oak floors. Should I apply a polyurethane finish?

Melissa Abernathy, Hoboken, N.J.

First things first: Housebreak your dog—I've had personal experience here. If you really want to know what will strip polyurethane, dog urine is it. And a wood floor is a series of cracks, so the urine will seep down into them and do even more damage. You may be able to avoid refinishing if you wipe up puddles quickly and clean the floor often.

Eliminating Subfloor Bumps

I'm building a house with subflooring of tongue-and-groove plywood. It's mostly 1⅛ inches thick, but there are slight differences in thickness—not much, but too great to sand out. I'd like to use some sort of self-leveling bedding material that will allow me to lay vinyl tile and carpeting. Do you know of anything that would provide a suitable base?

Thomas W. Alsobrook, Wellston, Okla.

If the differences in thickness are truly slight, don't worry where you're laying carpet. Any good padding should serve as a sufficient base. As for the other areas, you could pour a gypsum-based floor leveling compound over the entire floor, but most vinyl-floor installers simply erase inconsistencies with a trowel. They spread just enough floor patching material to even out the bumps and fill in small depressions. The resulting floor isn't perfectly flat, but you'll never know it.

Wood Floors in the Kitchen?

My grandmother is remodeling her kitchen and wants an engineered wood floor. Personally, I think she will be better off if she uses solid wood. What do you think?

Chris Grinch, Bellefontaine, Ohio

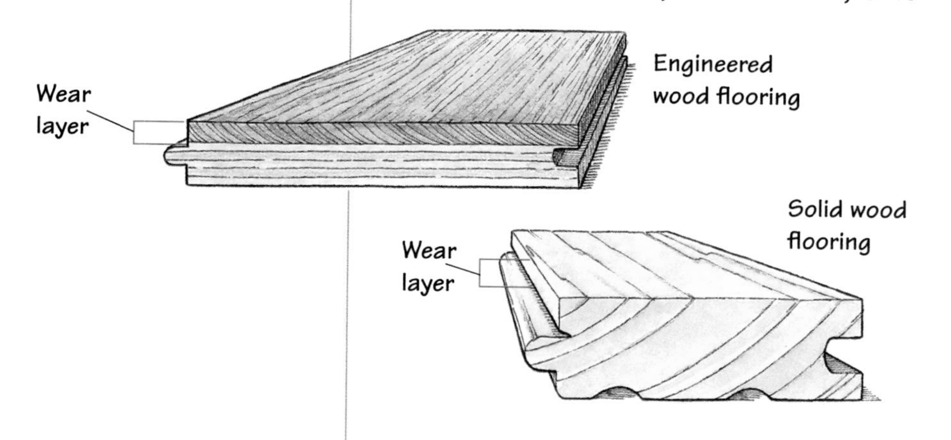

An engineered wood floor (see drawing below) consists of layers of wood veneer topped with a somewhat thicker layer of solid wood. Depending on the thickness of the wear layer (the solid wood above the tongue of a floor board), they can't always be refinished as often as solid wood, but how much wear and tear is your grandmother likely to cause? Just be sure that the floor she installs in her kitchen has a moisture-cured urethane finish or is prefinished with a high-tech acrylic, which can stand up to all the normal kitchen spills. One of the advantages of an engineered wood floor over solid wood is that it is very stable, and cracks between the boards are far less likely to open up with the seasons. That's good news in a room where spilled liquids are likely.

Reusing Wide Flooring Planks

I have a 1790 Cape Cod house in the middle of cranberry country, and I need to repair some of the joists. What's the best way to remove the old wide-plank floorboards so I can reinstall them later? What tool can I use that will pull out the nails, with the least amount of damage?

F. Scott Seitz, Carver, Mass.

A magic wand. It's not easy to remove and reinstall wood flooring, but it can be done. Actually, you'll need a hammer, either a nail set or a punch and some pry bars for this finicky work. To get the first board up, just drive the nails all the way through the wood. That will give you access to the ends of other boards, which you can pry up gently and carefully, bit by bit. Prying from the ends is harder work than prying along the sides, but you're less likely to split the boards. Be prepared for some breakage, though. I can't think of a single such job where we haven't damaged at least a few planks. Invariably, we run out of not only luck but also patience as lower-back pain begins to set in. Sometimes damaged boards can be glued or saved by trimming off broken edges. Still, if you rip up floors in four rooms, you'll be lucky to have enough usable boards for three. If the job involves just one room, you'll undoubtedly come up short. You might take some boards from closets. Or you can try staining new or salvaged wood, but you'll never get a perfect match. The trick is to put the replacement boards in spots where they can be hidden by furniture and go unnoticed.

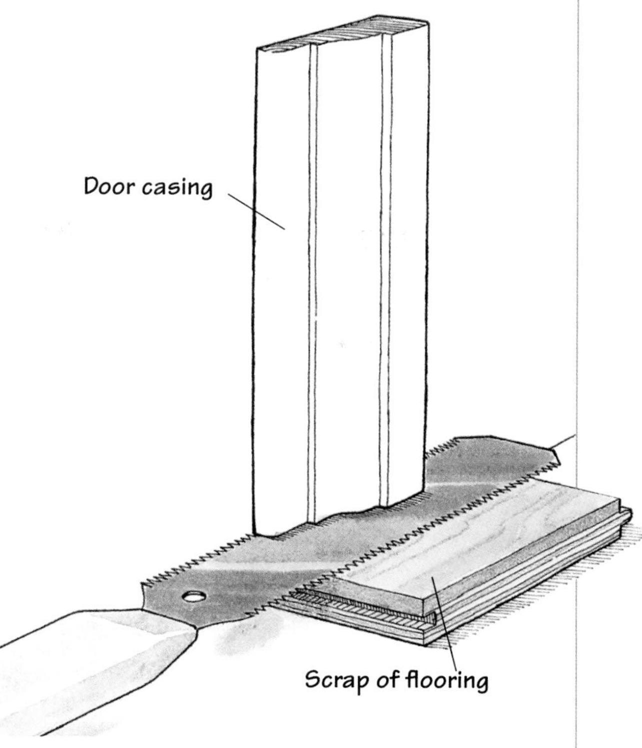

End-Grain Block Flooring

In our 1870 farmhouse, two dogs and one child add up to a need for durable but low-cost flooring. What do you think of the idea of using end-grain blocks laid as if they were tiles? We have an old barn beam we can cut up.

Patricia Johnston, Medford Lakes, N.J.

End-grain blocks make terrific indoor flooring—they're beautiful and extremely durable. An old barn beam, assuming it's been kept dry, will yield excellent blocks because they'll be completely seasoned and won't shrink. Douglas fir and yellow pine are good choices, cut no less than 1½ inches thick, so you'll need to be sure you can raise your floor that much on a retrofit. The blocks should be cut accurately to avoid unnecessary sanding of end grain, a slow task. Let the blocks acclimatize before installation by storing them for five days in the room where they'll be used. Butt the blocks edge to edge in flexible bedding compound spread on ¾-inch plywood subfloor. You can use existing subfloor if it's sound, but be sure to renail it; and if it's made of boards, install ½-inch plywood underlayment over the top. Flooring contractor Jeff Hosking recommends that you protect the block flooring with tung oil or three coats of shellac, maintaining either finish with wax. Or you can use wax alone.

Flooring Over Concrete

The lower level of our raised ranch has a concrete floor. We want to cover it with ceramic tile, and carpeting or parquet. Do we need to put down plywood first, and what about the existing moldings?

John Argiro, Norwell, Mass.

If there are no signs of moisture or mildew on the slab, it's probably safe to add new flooring without putting down a layer of plywood. Ceramic tile can be installed directly on the concrete with thin-set mortar. For carpeting, coat the floor with a concrete sealer. For wood, I suggest you use a floating system. Put down a suitable foam pad, and then add laminated flooring that glues to itself, edge to edge. Because all wood floors move, leave a little expansion space at the baseboards and cover it with molding. Door casings have to be cut so the flooring can slide just under them (see drawing above). Baseboard radiators should have a 1¼-inch or 1½-inch airspace between the finished floor and the bottom of the front cover.

Because all wood floors move, leave a little expansion space at the baseboards and cover it with molding.

Stripping Crown Molding

My house has high-ceilinged rooms with crown moldings that appear to be in good condition but have been covered with layers of paint over the years. I'd like to strip them down to bare wood. Is it possible to

NEW PARTITION *walls are assembled on the floor and then tilted into place. But be sure to frame them an inch shorter in height, or else each one will hit the ceiling as you tip it up. Once a wall is plumb, secure it with nails driven upwards through wood shims.*

remove the moldings, or should I strip them in place?

Carol Douglas, Yale, Mich.

It's hard enough putting crown moldings up, let alone taking them down, and you might in the process damage them and the walls. You'd be better off stripping the moldings in place. Get an environmentally friendly chemical stripper, and then prepare yourself for a long, miserable job.

Floor Sanding vs. Screening

My wife and I are restoring a circa 1870s Victorian house in upstate New York. Our floors are random-width tongue-and-groove knotty pine, 15⁄16 inch thick, laid on true 2-by-9-inch joists on 16-inch centers. We want to refinish the pine as finish flooring, but we're worried that sanding will leave us with too little thickness. There is no subflooring at all.

Robert Weber, Hancock, N.Y.

You should never sand a floor to less than a 3⁄4-inch thickness if there is no subfloor beneath it. And unless you want the look of a brand-new floor, think twice before sanding anyway. Sanding removes the old finish but also erases the patina and the little nicks and dings that give floors character. At the *T.O.H.* project house in Milton, Massachusetts, we retained the visible history of the wide-plank pine floors by giving them a light screening instead of a sanding. Screening is done with a machine like a floor polisher and a coarse pad something like a green synthetic pot-scrubber. It removes dirt and wax buildup but doesn't remove wood or even all of the finish. Instead, it roughens the surface just enough to give it the tooth to hold a new coat of finish.

Tiling Over Vinyl Flooring

We want to redo our bathroom floor, replacing the ½-inch underlayment and vinyl tile with ceramic tile laid on cement backer board. The new floor would be level with the hall carpeting. But contractors we've talked to want to tile right on top of the existing vinyl. That will raise the floor ½ inch and require a molding strip to meet the hall carpeting. What do you suggest?

Bob Cummings, Hartland, Wisc.

I'd go with your original idea. The booby trap if you tile right on top of the vinyl is that you'll also have to raise or at least extend the flange for the toilet, which could be quite a job. Another reason for taking the old floor out is to make sure there's no hidden damage beneath it. Old bathrooms often have rotting subfloors from years of seepage or condensation around the toilet and tub areas.

Tile Floor Replacement

Our family moved into a wonderful 1929 Arts and Crafts home a year ago, and we are trying to decide what to do about the flooring in the kitchen and bath. The original ceramic tiles have cracked because of settling. Once the floor is leveled, would you use tiles, wood (all our other floors are maple) or period-look linoleum? We want a floor appropriate to the period.

Karol Eggers, Yankton, S. Dak.

The big question is: What's under the tiles? Your floor was probably a "mud job" laid in a bed of mortar about 1½ inches thick. That's a high-quality technique still used today. The bad news is that the structure of the floor was inadequate or the bed of mortar cracked when the house settled, and now the mortar will all have to come out. The floor frame should be made structurally sound and flat, though not necessarily level. Then you have a number of options. The simplest is a wood floor; it will match your other floors and can be installed over a ¾-inch plywood subfloor. I'd think oak would be the most appropriate wood for an Arts and Crafts house, particularly quarter-sawn oak.

If you're going to use wood flooring in a kitchen or bath, however, you better maintain it because these are the wettest areas of the house. Do what you can to prevent water and other liquids from spilling on the floor and mop up spills right away. Bathrooms are particularly tough locations for floors, and linoleum will probably last longer than a wood floor.

FOR MORE ON REMOVING TILE TURN TO CHAPTER 10: ELECTRICAL AND PLUMBING

If you go with tiles, you can either start with a mud job or put down the plywood, followed by a layer of cement board. Linoleum was pushed off the market by vinyls, but now it's making a comeback, and at least two manufacturers supply it. To install it, you again start with the plywood subfloor, but this time you add the underlayment (¼-inch void-free plywood) on top. Then you'll have to fill the underlayment's seams so they won't show through the linoleum.

Floor-Finish Caution

Three years ago we refinished our Douglas fir floors. We sanded to bare wood and applied mahogany oil-based stain, then added three coats of a water-based finish. The results were beautiful. But not for long. Soon we noticed that drops of water left whitish marks. That's a problem, what with the rain we have in Oregon. You can't just walk behind people with a rag, wiping up after their every step. So we're starting over, but not before we hear from you.

David and Mary Plank, Silverton, Oreg.

I'm surprised you put a water-based finish over an oil-based stain. That's not to say it can't be done, but the oil stain requires a great deal of cure time first. Where floors are subject to a lot of water, you want the toughest protection you can find. I'd prefer an oil-based polyurethane finish over an oil-based stain. Oil-modified polyurethane might also be all right, but keep in mind that the stuff is extremely toxic. I've seen guys who applied it and were barely able to stand up afterward, so this is a job for professionals who know what safety precautions to take. Finally, remember that some spotting is inevitable if water is allowed to dry on a wood floor, no matter what is used to protect it. ■

Old bathrooms often have rotting subfloors from years of seepage or condensation around the toilet and tub areas.

CHAPTER EIGHT

Heating, Cooling + Ventilation

Removing Attic Insulation

The previous owner of our house installed blown-in insulation in the attic, but all that billowy material prevents us from putting the valuable space to good use. What is the best way to remove all the insulation so that we can replace it with something more compact?

Pamela Perkins, Callender, Iowa

Assuming you want to use the attic only for storage, not as a living space, I think you'll be better off leaving the insulation in place, rather than removing it. Scooping it out would be a dirty, difficult job, and the only more compact replacement with the same R-value is spray-on polyurethane foam, which will be expensive. If there's enough headroom, I'd recommend building a platform over the existing blown-in insulation. But if headroom isn't sufficient, leave the attic, and its insulation, alone.

Venting a Dryer Indoors

What are the benefits and disadvantages of venting a dryer inside the house? I see heat-recovery kits in many home stores, and the packaging always touts the savings in energy costs. I remember from my childhood that a friend's mom had an indoor dryer vent, and it seemed to warm up the house quite nicely. But surely there has to be a catch or two to this system.

Peter Tinnesz, Trumbull, Conn.

I bet your friend's dad put a nylon stocking over the end of the dryer vent to catch the lint, too. That's what we had when I was growing up, but my mom used a clothesline most of the time, so the dryer never added much heat to the house. When she got older and started using the dryer more, my dad installed a vent to the outside to control the humidity.

And that's the catch with indoor venting. Although it seems shameful to dump a dryer's heat outdoors, it's worse to exhaust all that water vapor indoors. Even in old,

Although it seems shameful to dump a dryer's heat outdoors, it's worse to exhaust all that water vapor indoors.

drafty houses, too much moisture can cause severe problems when it condenses on windows and in wall cavities and fosters the growth of rot, mildew, and mold. So I think it's always best just to run the dryer exhaust outside. (If you have a gas dryer, you have no choice—it must be vented outdoors.) If you want to save energy, don't dry the clothes more than necessary. Or do what my mom did and use a clothesline.

Preventing Mold and Mildew

My husband and my father built a log house from a kit in 1990, and ever since we've had a lot of problems related to dampness, especially when the temperature falls below 40 degrees. We get mold and mildew on our outside walls and in our closets and cabinets. If furniture is up against a wall, we get mold there, too. Many of our clothes have been ruined and our windows are rotting. I've known others with log houses from the same company who have similar troubles, but the company has gone out of business. Do you have any suggestions?

Sheila Sipple, Mileses, N.Y.

I guess we know why that company isn't in business anymore. It's possible the logs were green (not seasoned enough) when you built the house, but even green logs dry out eventually. Maybe moisture is getting into the house from another source, such as a damp basement or crawl space. Putting splash blocks under down spouts and grading the land next to the foundation will direct rainwater away from the foundation. If you have a block foundation, a coat of cementitious paint will eliminate minor water seepage. Turn off humidifiers if you're using any, then make sure other sources of excess humidity, like dryers, stoves, and bathrooms, are well vented.

FOR MORE ON MILDEW TURN TO CHAPTER 3: EXTERIOR WALLS AND SIDING

ONCE SECURED, *radiant-heat tubing for the Milton workshop was covered with concrete.*

This Old House plumbing and heating consultant Richard Trethewey tells me that the ultimate solution may be a heat recovery ventilator, which is used in the winter to bring in dry outside air and exhaust moist inside air with minimal heat loss. They are expensive and require ductwork, but given the extent of your problems, such a device may be worthwhile.

Fix for Cold Brick

I live in a brick house that was built in 1957, and this old home is awfully drafty and uncomfortable in the winter. Even the walls are cold. My brother told me that the windows are part of the problem, but new ones were installed only about 15 years ago. What can I do?

Maria K. Tolgyesi, Norridge, Ill.

It's entirely possible that your walls do need insulation, but I wouldn't jump into that job before you take your brother's advice and check your windows. It isn't difficult or expensive to replace most window weather stripping (except for interlocking metal weather stripping). In fact, it's about the most cost-effective home repair I can think of. But if the draftiness persists after the new weather stripping is in place, then insulate the walls.

There are two ways to insulate brick, depending on how the wall was originally constructed (see drawing below). In a brick veneer wall, the brick is like siding: It isn't structural, and there's a standard wood-framed wall behind it. After the framed wall is sheathed, bricks are laid in a single layer outside. Metal ties, which are embedded in the mortar and nailed to the sheathing, connect the brick to the framing; that leaves a 1-inch ventilation gap between the two. If this is how your house was built, you should leave this gap clear and have a contractor blow insulation into each stud-wall cavity from the inside of the house.

A brick cavity wall, on the other hand, is actually two parallel walls of brick, called wythes, separated by an airspace anywhere from 2 inches to 4½ inches wide. If this is the type of wall you have, hire a contractor to inject a slow-curing low-density urethane foam into the cavity. (Low-density foam lets water vapor move

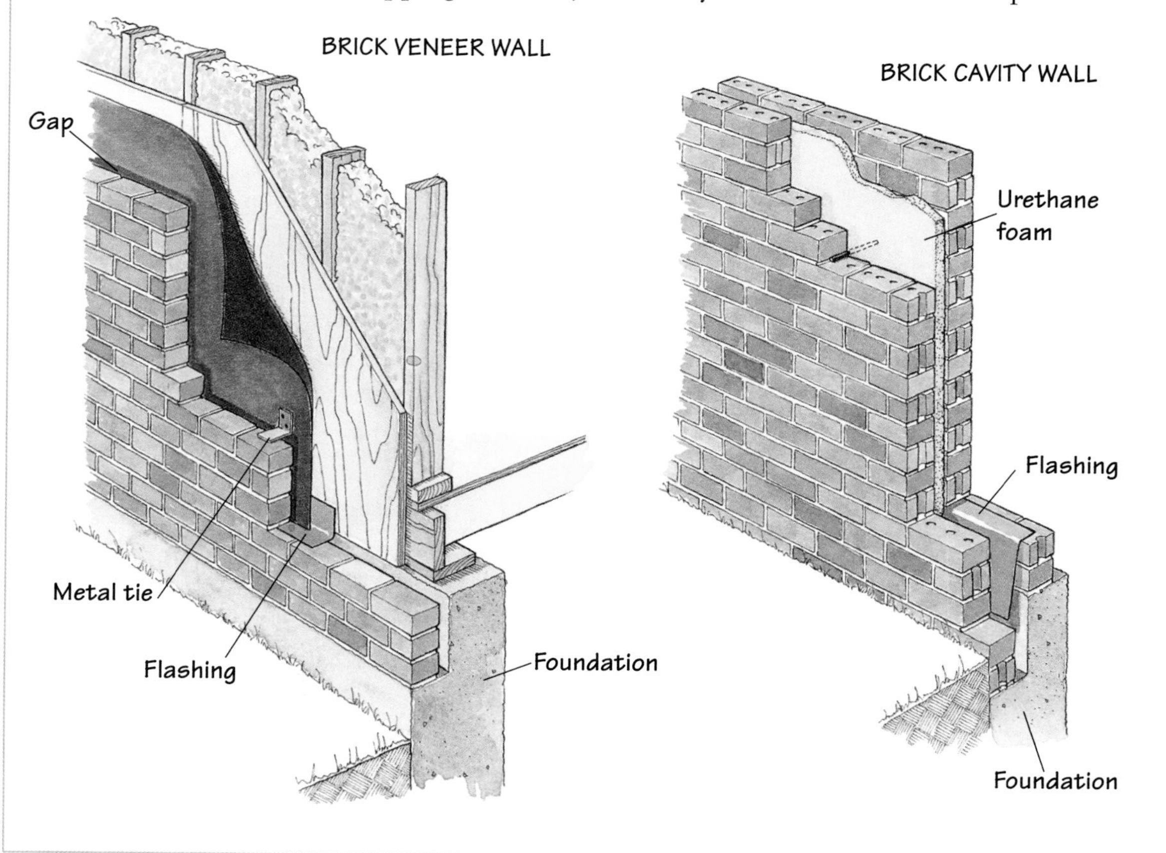

through the wall rather than being trapped inside it.) First, he will probably drill a series of holes into the exterior mortar joints (not the brick) about halfway up the wall, and another series of holes near the top of the wall. Then he'll shoot the foam through the lower holes, and when it expands out of the upper ones, he knows that the cavity in that part of the wall is full. After he's done, a mason can easily patch the holes in the mortar.

Whichever insulation you use, have an independent energy auditor take an infrared thermogram of your walls after they're filled to make sure there aren't any gaps in the insulation coverage.

Maintaining Proper Humidity

I have a humidifier on the furnace and also own a portable dehumidifier. What time of the year should I switch from one unit to the other, and is there anything else I should know about the changeover? Also, would the use of a ceiling fan help to decrease the humidity inside my house?

Gerald Semrau, Roseville, Mich.

The time to think about humidifying is in the fall, after you turn on your furnace. Waiting until you notice the dryness isn't good for you or your wood furniture. Once you turn off the furnace in the spring, you probably won't have to turn on the dehumidifier until late June or so, depending on the weather. By the way, whenever you turn off your furnace, don't forget to close the water valve leading to your humidifier, then drain its reservoir and clean it with white vinegar to remove any mineral buildup. If you let water sit in the reservoir all summer, you'll provide a breeding ground for mildew and bacteria to grow.

To get the best performance out of your dehumidifier, gently dust off the unit's intake fins using a vacuum cleaner with the soft-brush attachment. You should do this once or twice during the season. Working together, these appliances should be able to keep the inside humidity level at a comfortable 35–40 percent all year round.

Ceiling fans, by the way, won't change the humidity level in your house one bit. Their job is to keep air circulating—that's what makes you feel more comfortable when the weather is warm.

Radiant Barrier Hurts Shingles?

I've read a number of suggestions about using foil or some other heat-reflective material on the underside of roof decking to keep the attic cooler. However, I'm concerned that reflecting the heat upward might make the asphalt shingles hotter and reduce their life expectancy.

Fred Wengel, Saluda, N.C.

Radiant barriers—those under-the-roof foils that keep a house cooler by reflecting the sun's heat—generate a lot of questions like yours. According to the Florida Solar Energy Center, radiant barriers do increase shingle temperatures, but only by 2 to 5 degrees Fahrenheit. Shingles are made to take the heat in the warmest parts of the country, where a roof can approach 170 degrees in the summer. So the additional heat load caused by a radiant barrier is hardly significant, particularly if the roof deck is properly ventilated with soffit vents at the eaves and a ridge vent at the peak. More to the point, adding a radiant barrier might not be cost-effective in your relatively mild climate: The benefit you gain from reflecting the heat away in the summer will be lost in the winter, when you want to capture the sun's heat. Check with your state energy department and see what they recommend.

FOR MORE ON SHINGLES TURN TO CHAPTER 5: ON AND AROUND THE ROOF

Problems With Dry Air

I live in a home that has forced-air heating. The air gets very dry in the house during the winter, so I'm thinking about installing a

The time to think about humidifying is in the fall. Waiting until you notice the dryness isn't good for you or your wood furniture.

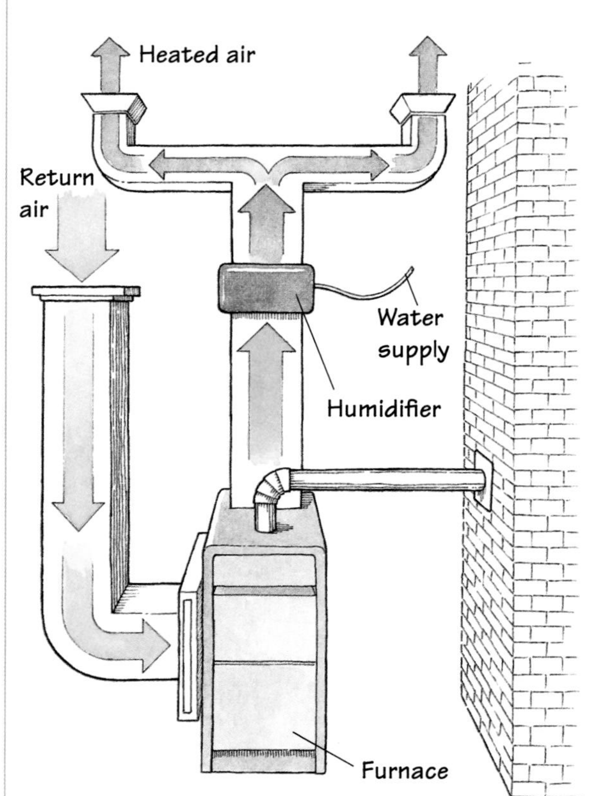

humidifier on the furnace. What are the advantages and disadvantages of such a system, and are some better than others?

Fred Beneri, Douglaston, N.Y.

On matters such as these, I defer to *This Old House*'s heating and cooling expert, Richard Trethewey. He says that humidity—the amount of moisture in the air—has a huge impact on people's comfort. A relative humidity of 35 to 40 percent is considered ideal, but any time you heat or cool the air inside a house, you change humidity levels as well. The air passing through a forced-air furnace is heated to as much as 500 degrees Fahrenheit, so it's no wonder that the air feels bone dry after the furnace has been operating for a few weeks. Portable humidifiers in individual rooms can replace some of the moisture baked out by the furnace, but to humidify the whole house, says Richard, you'll have to attach a humidifier to the furnace's hot-air supply duct (see drawing above). Furnace-based humidifiers work well, but they can turn into a maintenance headache if the house's water supply contains lots of dissolved minerals, which collect on the humidifier when the water vaporizes.

If not cleaned regularly with white vinegar throughout the heating season, the unit will eventually cake up and fail. Once that happens, there's not much you can do except replace it. To avoid such an outcome, check the mineral content of your water with a local testing service; it may have to be treated.

Humidity—the amount of moisture in the air—has a huge impact on people's comfort.

Adding Central Air

We have a two-story, five-bedroom house in Stockbridge, Massachusetts, that dates to 1872. It's heated with a hot-water baseboard system. Can we add central air-conditioning?

Barbara Pape, New York, N.Y.

Sure, but it might not be easy and it probably won't be cheap. The problem is that standard central-air systems require a blower and a system of ducts to distribute the cooled air throughout the house, and a hot-water baseboard system has neither of these. That means, in addition to the air conditioner's condenser (mounted outside the house), you'll have to install an air handler (containing a blower and air filter) somewhere inside the house, and some sort of ducting throughout the house for supply and return air. If the ducts can be routed from the attic to the first floor through closets, you can get by with a single condenser outside and an air handler in the attic. But if there's no path for the ductwork, you might need separate systems for the first and second floors.

Richard Trethewey says that there are two other systems better suited to cooling old houses: the ductless mini-split, or high-velocity forced air. With a mini-split, refrigerant and drain lines run from a small condenser outside the house to three or four compact air-handler units that fit entirely within a wall. These units are quieter and have greater capacity than a window-mounted air conditioner, but they're best suited for cooling individual rooms. To air-

ONE HIGHLIGHT *of 1993's Belmont project was the removal of asbestos siding. But energy improvments included insulating exterior walls and installing insulating glass in the old window sash.*

condition an entire house, you'll want to consider a high-velocity system, which has a network of 2-inch flexible ducts that are easily snaked through ceilings and floors. High-velocity units, like the one the show installed in the Salem project, are more expensive than regular forced air but not more than two or three mini-splits.

Incidentally, winter is a very good time to start thinking about installing central air-conditioning. If you wait until spring to make phone calls and get bids, you might find that installers are completely booked through the summer and beyond.

Crawl-Space Ventilation

In my 1955 brick house, mold is abundant in closets and on some walls. Covering the windows with plastic sheeting hasn't helped. The house sits on a 2-foot crawl space, which is vented about every 8 feet. No water gets in there, but the space is cool and damp year-round. Two large oaks in the front yard keep the house shaded. What do you suggest?

Pamela King, Alexandria, La.

The window sheeting is making things worse by trapping moisture in a space that's already too damp. But you could use plastic in the crawl space to keep ground moisture from working its way into your house. Cover the dirt with 6-mil plastic sheets overlapped at least six inches, then cover them with a couple inches of sand (see drawing above). You didn't say how big those vents are, but in any case, make sure they're never obstructed.

Vent-Free Heaters Safe?

I have a five-room brick bungalow that I'd like to heat with vent-free propane units in each room. It will enable me to avoid the expense of installing flues and let me heat only the room I am in at any given time. I don't know much about propane, though. I've not been able to determine what would be required to maintain a temperature of 70°F to 72°F either, and I'm not clear about managing air exchange.

Karen Cooper, Chicago, Ill.

There's no national consensus regarding the safety of vent-free gas or propane fireplaces. Because these flueless fireplaces exhaust pollutants such as carbon dioxide, carbon monoxide, nitrous oxides, and copious amounts of water vapor directly into living spaces, the industry recommends that they be used no more than four hours per day. And that rules them out as a primary heat source. If you want to heat with a gas fireplace, Richard Trethewey strongly urges you to install direct-vent units, which have flues to the outside.

Wood Floors Sweat

My wife and I live in the same 80-year-old home I grew up in. We used to cool the downstairs—all 1,500 square feet of it—with a 3-ton air conditioner. Then, about two years ago, we built a 300-square-foot addition. When the existing air conditioner couldn't adequately cool the extra space, we added a 2-ton unit. All the ducts run through a crawl space beneath the floor. At the same time, we had additional insulation blown into the attic and then replaced the sagging insulation that had been put in under the floor years earlier.

Our problems began that summer. The pine flooring in the living and dining rooms began to sweat, especially under the furniture, and dark stains appeared in those wet spots. An energy-efficiency expert from the extension service at Louisiana State University advised us to cover the bare dirt in the crawl space with a plastic vapor barrier, which we did. Thinking we had solved the problem, we sanded and refinished the floors, but the

problem reappeared the following summer. Could it be that our house is too tight for Louisiana weather?

Wesley R. King, Denham Springs, La.

When he heard your question, Richard Trethewey had an idea about what was going on. He said it's much like what happens when you leave a cold glass of lemonade outdoors on a warm summer day. Beads of water—condensation—form on the glass, which makes the glass look like it's sweating. He thinks the same process is at work in your house. Chances are good that the AC ducts running below your floors are leaking cold air so badly—one may even be disconnected—that the crawl space is getting cooler than the house. When moist air in the room hits the relatively cold floors, they sweat, regardless of the new floor insulation. And Richard says that the problem will be worse wherever the air circulation is poorest, such as under the furniture.

He also thinks that your system is oversize; you have enough cooling capacity for a 3,000-square-foot house. (The rule of thumb Richard suggested is that 1 ton will cool 600 square feet.) A properly sized system actually helps dehumidify a house, but yours is cooling everything so quickly that it shuts off before it has a chance to squeeze moisture out of the inside air.

So your first order of business will be to seal those ducts. Richard cautions against using duct tape, though, because even the good stuff will peel in humid weather. Instead, use a sheet-metal mastic with aluminized tape. Then make sure the ducts are swaddled in insulation. In really warm, moist climates like yours, push for as much R-value as you can—R-4 at the minimum; R-6 would be better.

Unfortunately, says Richard, there's no way to fix the humidity-control problems that happen with oversize systems. The only thing he can suggest is to add room dehumidifiers or go back to cooling with just your 3-ton unit.

FOR MORE ON WOOD FLOORS TURN TO CHAPTER 7: INTERIOR FLOORS, WALLS, AND CEILINGS

Radiant Ceilings Are Real

My girlfriend insists that she has radiant heating in the ceiling of her 1960s condo unit, but I've built houses for years and have never heard of such a thing—have you? Also, I've noticed that the caulking between the crown molding and the ceiling is badly cracked. Is there a particular caulk I can use to fix this?

Steve Orton, Seattle, Wash.

First of all, your girlfriend is correct: They've been making radiant panels to attach to home ceilings since the '30s. They are fast to install, allow each room to be controlled by separate thermostats, and don't need radiators or vents. I can remember my father working in the '60s on a new house that had a radiant ceiling system. A crew strung resistance wires across rock lath (an old-fashioned plaster substrate that replaced wood lath), then plastered over the wiring. We don't see many heated ceilings around here these days because electricity is expensive. (In your region, however, electricity is a relatively cheap heat source, because much of it comes from dams.) Also, some people find that their feet get cold in rooms with radiant ceilings, particularly when they're sitting at a table or desk that "shades" the heat.

Now I bet you'll understand why the joint above the crown molding is cracking: The heat is causing the wood trim to shrink. Don't try to nail it in place; you might put a nail through one of the wires. About the only thing you can do about it is caulk with a paintable silicone sealant and hope that it keeps up with the movement. I'd install it in the summer when the ceiling won't have been in heating mode for a while.

Insulating a Vaulted Shop

Our two-car garage does double duty as a woodworking shop. I finished the walls with insulation and drywall, and installed an insulated garage door. I'd also like to insulate the concrete-tile roof but don't

Chances are good that the AC ducts running below your floors are leaking cold air so badly that the crawl space is getting cooler than the house.

The only way I know to retrofit insulation without ripping off siding or plaster is to blow it in.

want to put in a ceiling. I was thinking about installing rigid foam insulation board between the rafters, against the underside of the sheathing, and wondered if I need to leave an air space for ventilation. An added benefit of the white insulation boards would be that they'd reflect light and make the shop brighter. What do you think?

Mike Bishop, Moreno Valley, Calif.

I think I have some good news for you, and some bad. First, the good news: You don't need to leave an air space between the insulation and sheathing. The primary reason for this gap is to carry off moisture, but I doubt a garage/shop will generate enough to worry about. The other reason to leave a gap is to prevent heat from building up and damaging shingles, but this shouldn't be a problem with your concrete roof tiles. The bad news is that building codes require foam insulation on the interior of a building to be covered by a nonflammable surface, such as drywall. So there goes your reflective surface. Check with your local building inspector to see how he interprets the codes in your case, and prepare yourself for some heavy lifting.

Radiant Barrier Suitable?

My house here on Long Island has an unheated attic that was originally insulated with R-19 fiberglass blankets. I added another layer of R-25 blankets, but I wonder if it would be worthwhile to staple a radiant barrier to the rafters as well. Would this be a cost-effective improvement?

M. Ackert, Manhasset, N.Y.

If you lived in a hot climate, I'd say yes. But you don't need radiant barriers where you live, or anywhere else that requires the heat to be on for more months than the air-conditioning. This barrier, which is simply a layer of aluminum foil attached to the underside of rafters, prevents heat from radiating into the attic, which would force the air conditioner to work harder. For example, I've read that a radiant barrier in the attic can reduce cooling costs by as much as 12 percent in the Southeast U.S. But Michael Lamb, of the U.S. Department of Energy, tells me you'd be wasting your time—and your money—to install such a barrier in Manhasset. With R-44 in your attic, you should have plenty of insulation; Lamb says Long Island is on the border between the R-38 and the R-49 zones.

Retrofitting Insulation

My 1879 house is in a historic area near North Carolina's Outer Banks. The local historical society won't permit blown-in cellulose or foam insulation. Do I have other alternatives that won't require removing the clapboards outside or the plaster inside? I need help—my heating/cooling runs close to $450 a month.

Shirley Stokes, Washington, N.C.

The only way I know to retrofit insulation without ripping off siding or plaster is to blow it in. There are materials besides foam and cellulose that can be blown in—rock wool, cotton, and Air-Krete come to mind—but if these are acceptable, the others ought to be as well. I've never heard of a historical society that tried to control the inside of a house, let alone the inside of its walls. Could there be a misunderstanding here? If not, maybe the society is exceeding its authority a little.

Radiator Book Storage

I want to construct a built-in bookcase in the space above a radiator, but I'm not sure of the clearance required for safety and I don't want to have every fire chief in the city looking for me. What's the correct clearance?

Brett Wein, Brooklyn, N.Y.

There is no fire hazard: Radiators don't get hot enough to ignite much of anything, particularly books. But the heat will dry out their bindings. Leave at least a foot between the top of the radiator and the bottom shelf.

Wind in the Chimney

We live at the bottom of a canyon that gets rather windy in the winter, just when we'd like to use our fireplace. Unfortunately, wind gusts blow the chimney smoke back into our house. Do you have any suggestions for how we could prevent this?

The Hungerfords, Chatsworth, Calif.

You'll see one solution on top of many chimneys along the coast of Oregon, where winters are wet, raw, and often windy. It's a simple device made of sheet metal that pivots like a weather vane to automatically shield the flue from downdrafts (see drawing, below far right). When I had a similar problem at my house for a while, mason Lenny Belliveau solved it by topping the chimney with a bluestone slab that sits on four short brick pilasters. The slab prevents wind from blowing smoke straight down the chimney. There are other types of caps that help, too (see below).

FOR MORE ON CHIMNEY CAPS TURN TO CHAPTER 2: BASEMENTS, CONCRETE, AND CHIMNEYS

Furnace Cleaning Timetable

Our house is so well insulated that we use only about 430 gallons of heating oil a year, so I feel annual furnace cleaning is overkill. Can it be cleaned only every other year (with air filters changed as needed, of course)?

Elizabeth Rye, Cambridge, Mass.

I can't get too specific here without getting more information, but your basic idea is correct: If you don't use your furnace that much, less frequent cleaning should make sense. But to be certain, contact the manufacturer of your furnace. Rich Trethewey, the real expert here, has another slant on this. He says that like any other major mechanical system, it's worth a few bucks every year to be certain everything's in working order. This is particularly true of systems that burn fossil fuel.

Annoying Furnace Noise

My furnace has a real drone to it—you can feel vibrations through the floor. Would switching to a gas-fired system help? Also, my present system takes a very long time to heat up. Is this customary? Our electric bills are running high, too, and still

we don't have a room in the house that's cozy and warm.

Nigel Martin, Marlton, N.J.

Richard Trethewey says that fuel really has nothing to do with the sound a furnace makes. Instead, your system might suffer from a combination of poor design, shoddy installation, and wear. You might have blowers that are out-of-round and wobbling, or maybe they're rubbing against something, or maybe there's a loose or broken mounting bracket somewhere. Shimmying sheet-metal ducts are also a source of noise. Have a reputable service company come in and check for the problems I've mentioned. They can also calculate heat-loss figures for your house and determine if your heating system is correctly sized.

Lifespan of Radiant Floor Heat

My one-story house, built in 1956, sits on a concrete slab embedded with the copper tubing for a three-zone hydronic heating system. It works well, but I'm concerned about the tubing. Other systems installed in this area at about the same time have gone bad and had to be replaced with hot-water baseboard units.

A. Denholm, Akron, Ohio

According to Richard Trethewey, several variables can threaten old-style (copper- or steel-pipe) radiant floors, but don't assume yours will fail just because similar ones have. Temperature control is the main issue. Radiant-heat systems need a steady supply of warm water. Sudden "shots" of hot water stress the tubing; so does boosting the temperature above 140 degrees Fahrenheit, the maximum for safe operation. And where tubing enters the slab, the metal can chafe due to uneven expansion and contraction. Your heating system may have none of these problems, which could account for its longevity.

Richard says you'll know that your system has failed if you suddenly discover a cold or hot spot in the floor, or if you see leaking water or hear hissing. Replacement systems using plastic tubing can be installed on top of your old floor, and they raise the floor level only half an inch.

You'll know that your system has failed if you suddenly discover a cold or hot spot in the floor.

Blow-In Caveat

Blowing in insulation left holes in our aluminum siding. The plastic plugs the contractor provided are unattractive, and we'd like to do away with them when we paint the house. What do you suggest?

Robert J. Fankhauser, Perrysville, Ohio

I'm sorry to say I have no answer for you. If it'll make you feel any better, your letter will warn other readers considering a blow-in job. The drill-and-plug method is one I don't like with siding. It's easy to pop off aluminum and vinyl siding and pop it back

AIR-CONDITIONING *can help in hot weather. But an old cooling favorite—a shaded porch—also lets homeowners enjoy the neighborhood.*

later, leaving no scars behind, and there's no good reason not to do the job that way.

Outside Combustion Air

Here's a problem we've been trying to solve for 17 years. Our two old stone fireplaces use house air for combustion and pull too much heat out of the house. We want to use an outside air supply but have been told by "experts"—stonemasons, chimney sweeps, fireplace dealers, and installers—to put in a fireplace insert. But that also uses house air. You are our last hope. (Talk about pressure!)

Lainie and Sam Goldstein, New City, N.Y.

Pressure? Not if you've been able to wait 17 years. I'd recommend a fireplace insert, too, with glass doors to minimize the outflow of house air. If you don't want any inside air going up the flue, you could install an external vent through the back of the fireplace. However, cutting an opening through fieldstone will be a long, hard job, and you'll still need glass doors to force the fire to draw air through the vent.

Perils of Insulating Sheathing

I'm having a new house built and want to make sure it's insulated properly. Temperatures here range from -30°F up to 100°F, and we expect to run the heating-and-air-conditioning system a good 10 months of the year. Plus, we have high humidity. My builder wants to install double-foil-faced foam insulation panels behind hardboard siding. But I'm concerned that the foil will act like a vapor barrier, causing sweating under the siding and subsequent rot. What do you suggest?

Darlene Forhart, Kansas City, Mo.

I don't like double-foil-faced panels on the outside of a house, period, for exactly the reason you suggest: Moisture can condense inside and rot the frame. I'd rather see the panels put behind the drywall. That's what I did on my own house. Putting foil-faced insulation on the heated side of the wall creates a vapor barrier that should prevent most moisture from penetrating to the frame. All of the joints should be covered with aluminum tape so there is no break in the moisture seal, and the builder will have to use longer finish nails and drywall screws, bigger extension jambs on the windows, and extendable electrical boxes.

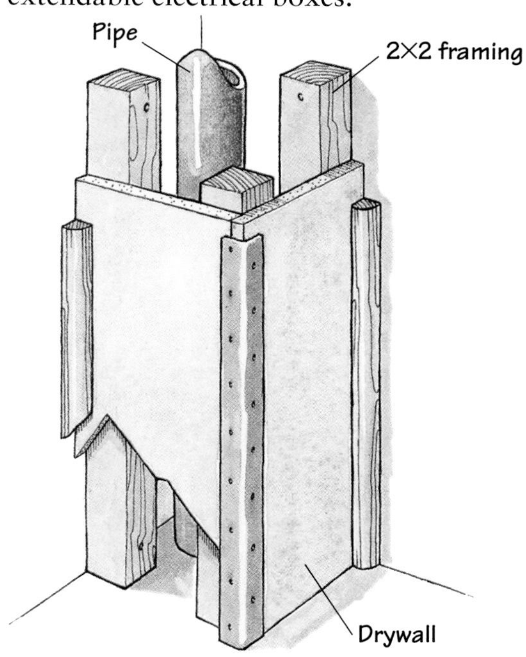

Concealing Pipes

We need advice on covering radiators and the vertical steam pipes running between floors. We like their heat but we don't like their looks.

Maria Stewart, Baltimore, Md.

The radiators can hide behind simple enclosures with full-width openings at the bottom and the top for air circulation. Enclosures can be custom- or ready-made of metal, which conducts heat well, or with an MDF (medium density fiberboard) frame and punched metal grille. Cover pipes in the corners of a room with a lumber-and-drywall box, or chase (see drawing above); pipes next to windows can be hidden behind heat-tolerant curtains.

Asbestos Insulation Hazard

Our house was built in 1938. We think the ducts may be insulated with asbestos, and

there might be some in the ceiling tiles too. Is there a way to find out?

Patrick James Malloy, Evergreen Park, Ill.

There's a potential health hazard here, so you shouldn't risk poking around the ducts or ceiling tiles yourself. Ask your city's environmental agency to refer you to testing labs and licensed removal specialists. Asbestos in good condition can often be encapsulated—covered and sealed in place—which is safe and relatively inexpensive. But if the tiles and duct cladding are shedding dust or falling apart, removal may be necessary but tricky because of the risk of disturbing the material and putting a lot of asbestos particles into the air.

Floors Are Too Cold

I am renovating a cottage built over a dirt crawl space, and in the winter the floors are uncomfortably cold. I'd insulate the underside of the floor, but there's only about 2 feet of clearance at one end and 10 inches at the other. Could we put rigid insulation between the existing plank floor and new flooring?

Melanie Lynn Passauer, Windham, Ohio

To make the effort worthwhile, you'd have to lay on at least a couple inches of rigid insulation over the old floor and then at least one layer of ¾-inch plywood to get a base stiff enough for the finish flooring. As a result, you'd not only lose headroom throughout the cottage, you'd have to cut the bottom off every door, remove and reinstall all the baseboards, and raise the mounting flange under the toilet, to mention only a few difficulties. And your floor joists would still be too close to damp dirt, leaving them vulnerable to rot and insects. In other words, your idea sounds like trouble to me.

To solve your problem, you'll first need to increase the clearance beneath the floor to at least three feet. Have a contractor determine whether it's possible to excavate the crawl space without undermining the foundation. If he can't, you may need to jack up the house. Once that's done, cover the dirt with overlapping sheets of 6-mil plastic, which will help keep down humidity. Now you'll be able to insulate the floor properly from the underside with rigid sheets of foam, fiberglass batts, or, even better, with sprayed foam.

FOR MORE ON FLOORING TURN TO CHAPTER 7: INTERIOR FLOORS, WALLS, AND CEILINGS

Using vapor-barrier paint may ease your mind, but a better idea is to avoid generating a lot of humidity.

Blocking Attic Heat Gain

Our second-floor ceiling (the floor of the attic) is insulated, but the roof is not. Because we store items in the attic and it gets very hot up there in the summertime, we've thought about putting insulation between the rafters. Would this be worthwhile?

John Claflin, Southbury, Conn.

Insulation between the rafters would keep the attic a little cooler, but a better option is to install a thermostatically controlled fan—not a whole-house fan, but a gable-end vent fan—like the one I put in my previous house. First make sure that your gable vents are capable of letting in as much air as the fan will blow out; if they're too small, the fan will suck air out of your house. Even if you end up having to install bigger vents, a fan in the attic will always turn out to be a cheaper solution than insulation.

Retrofit Insulation Choices

I'm in the midst of renovating a two-story house that's about 100 years old. It has a large attic and adequate crawl space. What's the best way to insulate my walls? Is it necessary to remove lath and plaster, or will blown-in insulation do? My plaster is in relatively good condition, and I am receiving mixed messages about the lack of a vapor barrier.

Philip Kroeker, Upland, Ind.

Some people say blown-in cellulose doesn't work because it settles and there's no moisture barrier, but I've found no problems in projects I've checked after five or six years. Using vapor-barrier paint may ease your mind, but a better idea is to avoid generating a lot of humidity. Two musts are: proper installation (no voids) and no exterior leaks. You might also consider insulating the walls with a modified-urethane foam that expands after it's pumped into wall cavities. Originally meant for new construction, this foam is now available for retrofit. We've used it in some of the *T.O.H.* project houses, and it seems to work well. It doesn't require a vapor barrier.

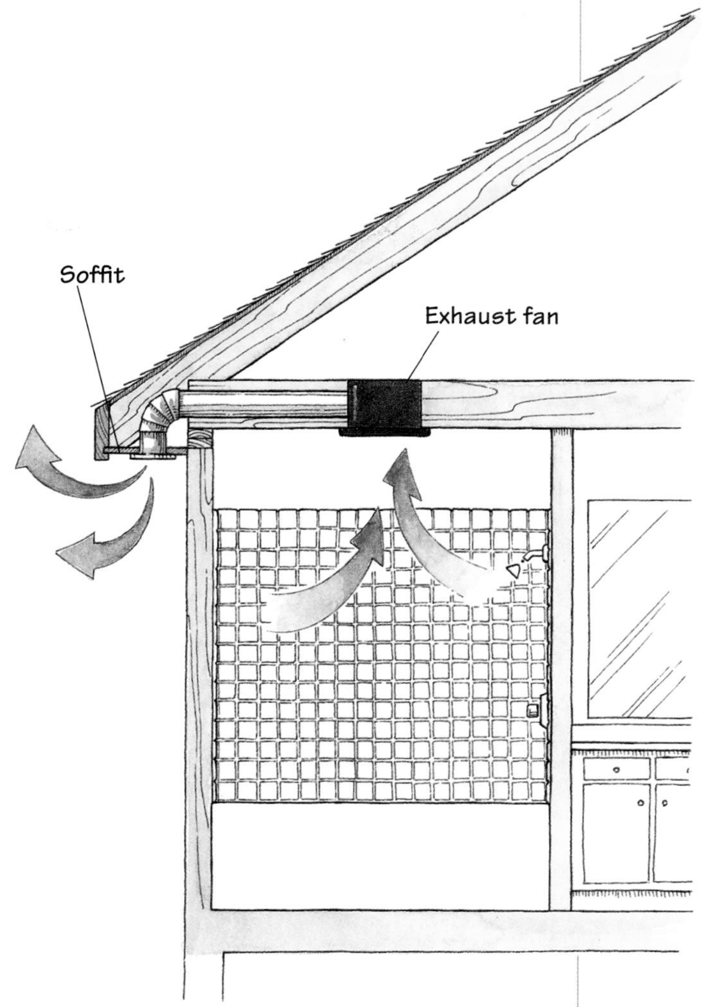

Vapor Barrier Mystery Solved

I've always read that the purpose of a vapor barrier is to prevent condensation inside walls by separating warm, moist air from cold, dry air. My father-in-law, a drywall finisher, swears otherwise, saying the barrier traps moisture and ruins the plasterboard. I've never heard anyone else take that position. But we want to build this year, so I'd like your opinion.

Bob Peterson, Shambaugh, Iowa

The layers of construction should follow this sequence, working from the outside in: siding, sheathing, insulation, vapor barrier, drywall. If they do, condensation won't be a problem. Your father-in-law's objection is valid only if the moisture barrier is close to the outside of the building—the cold side—or if the building is badly insulated.

Venting an Exhaust Fan

I need help with an exhaust-fan dilemma. My mother recently had her upstairs bathroom redone complete with a ceiling exhaust fan. The initial decision was to vent into the attic, but we've since heard that this can lead to condensation and ice buildup in winter. Is this correct? And if we must vent to the outside, can we do it without piercing the roof? Will flexible tubing do, or will it sag and collect moisture?

Adam Drew Lippe, Baltimore, Md.

You can't just blindly vent a fan into an attic: The moisture can rot your roof. To avoid opening the roof, vent through the soffit instead (see drawing above]. Use rigid insulated ducting, and install an exterior damper so cold air doesn't blow in.

Heating System Replacement

Last winter I got the bad news that my forced-air furnace was rusting and would only last one more season. I'm thinking of replacing the whole system with hot water heat. Is that a good idea?

Allen Held, Wheat Ridge, Colo.

Here in the Northeast we've always been big advocates of hot-water heat over hot air, but if your ducts are in good condition, a new furnace is the most cost-effective fix. Putting in a new hot-water system, radiators or baseboard units, with hot pipes going up and cold-water returns coming down, would be an expensive retrofit. ■

C H A P T E R N I N E

Cabinets, Counters + Trim

Deep-Cleaning Cabinets

I'm in the process of renovating the kitchen in my house, a 1948 Royal Barry Wills-designed Cape. (His houses are much sought-after in the Boston area.) We're keeping the raised-panel, solid walnut cabinets, which were custom-built on-site, but we wonder if there's a way to improve their looks a little by cleaning them up. They have a stain finish, but there appears to be no other type of finish on them. Any suggestions?

David Ferrini, Braintree, Mass.

You did the right thing by saving your cabinets. Walnut is a classic wood for furniture, but you won't see it used in kitchens very often, in part because it's so expensive. Oil, rather than varnish, is the customary finish for walnut, so I suspect that's why you don't see the gloss of a protective finish. While oil finishes are more suited to fine furniture than the hard-knocks life of kitchen cabinetry, I think you're better off going staying with what's already on there. Try cleaning the wood with a terry-cloth towel dipped in mineral spirits or turpentine, and then rub on a coat of Danish oil, a thin linseed-oil based finish fortified with synthetic resin. Just don't use household cleansers mixed in water. They are too harsh for the wood.

Oil finishes are more suited to fine furniture than the hard-knocks life of kitchen cabinets.

Biscuit-Joiner Hinges

Where can we get blades for a biscuit joiner that will allow us to cut slots for biscuit hinges? And where can we get the hinges themselves?

Donna and John Heckman, Lanark, Ill.

Biscuit hinges have semi-circular leaves instead of rectangular leaves. That lets them slip into the crescent-shaped slots cut by a biscuit jointer. If you've got a biscuit joiner already, then you have the blades you need. Your manual will explain how to set up

OLD LEADED-GLASS *doors were fit to new built-in cabinets made for the Charlestown project.*

your tool for cutting the slots. You'll find biscuit hinges in the mail-order catalogs of various woodworking supply houses.

Cracks at Ceiling Molding

Two years ago, we added a single-story family room to our 1940 home. Shortly after we completed the work, the three-piece crown molding separated slightly from the ceiling. We caulked this area, but the crack just reappears. What do you suggest?

Art North, Portland, Oreg.

Any molding made of solid wood can expand and contract across its width as the seasons change. And the wider a molding, the greater the movement. I can think of a couple of reasons for this problem. One is that it typically takes a while—even a year or two—for new framing to dry out and stop shrinking. The usual solution in this case is to ignore gaps until the structure reaches equilibrium, then seal the joints with acrylic caulk, which has good adhesion and flexibility.

The fact that you still have a problem after two years tells me that the top edge of your molding may not have been nailed securely into the joists (or the blocking between the joists) in the first place. When nails are only resting in drywall, there's nothing to stop the crack from opening up again. Try locating your joists with a stud finder and renailing the molding to them. But if none of this works, you just may just have to live with this seasonal crack.

Matching Wood Colors

When I remodeled our den, I built and installed bookcases that are nearly identical to one I once saw you build. I made them of birch plywood and gave them a clear finish. I'm planning to trim out the rest of the room in pine, and I'd like to use a clear finish there, too. But I'm afraid the colors of the two woods will look strange

TO DRAW *a straight line on a board, slide a combination square and pencil along the edge.*

together. Is there a way to get the trim and the bookcases to come out the same color, or do I have to go to the expense of installing birch casing?

Michael Brown, Sudbury, Mass.

I've found over the years that there's one foolproof approach to solving complex problems: Simplify them.

Not only will solid birch trim be expensive, it's not a great wood to use when you're planning for a clear finish because its color varies so markedly from blond to dark. That's why most solid birch that you'll find in a house (stair balusters, for example) is painted. However, as you've already discovered, the high-grade veneers on birch plywood take a clear finish just fine.

You could try to stain the pine to match the birch, but getting one species of wood to match another is tough to do even for professionals, let alone someone who doesn't have years of experience at it. You'd have better success if you had put the same stain on both woods, but since you've already put a clear finish on the bookcase, I would just go ahead and use the pine. In the family room of my house, I have cherry, Sitka spruce, and mahogany, and their different colors complement each other nicely. Besides, once you fill the bookcases with books, you'll see a lot less of the birch than you do now. If you were planning to put a pine bookcase next to a birch bookcase, I'd worry a bit about the mix of colors, but when woods are used in distinct ways, as they are in your den and my family room, I think you'll be pleased with the results.

FOR MORE ON FINISHING, TURN TO CHAPTER 6: PAINTING AND FINISHING

Nailing Trim to Angled Walls

We're remodeling our upstairs bathroom—we call it the "turret room" because of its shape—and we have a lot of windows that need trim. But because of the angled walls, I can't figure out how to put it on. The windows aren't perfectly plumb, and I'm afraid that I'll be looking at an ugly, tapered gap between the trim. How would you do it?

Robert Haight, Flemington, N.J.

I've found over the years that there's one foolproof approach to solving complex problems: Simplify them. In this case, start by visualizing all that glass as one big window surrounded by a picture frame of trim: a continuous casing wrapping

around the top, sides, and bottom of the windows (see drawing at left). Of course, you'll actually need separate lengths of casing for the top and bottom of every window, each piece beveled on the ends to make a tight joint with its neighbors. As for the space between each window, I'd cover it entirely with trim: two pieces of wood, beveled so they meet at the crease on the wall. (Using thinner stock here will prevent a clumsy-looking joint where they meet the horizontal casing.) Join each piece of trim with yellow carpenter's glue and biscuits, then finish-nail them into place. That's the simple solution. If it were my house, I'd put in a stool (often referred to as a "sill") and apron instead of a bottom casing because I think they would look better. You'll need to fit the stool first, then the sides, then the head trim. The apron always goes on last.

THE KING *of cabinetmaking power tools is the table saw. To ensure accuracy, align its blade to the saw table on a regular basis.*

Permanent Fix for Loose Knobs

We like the look of our old porcelain knobs for the doors and drawers in our kitchen, but we can't seem to keep the knobs from coming loose. Do you know any tricks I can use for solving this problem?

Debbie Fusco-Gerek, Garden City, N.Y.

If the knobs are held in place by bolts too short to get a good grip, you'll need to buy slightly longer ones. Just make sure the threads match those of the knobs exactly. Or perhaps the hole for the mounting bolt has gotten so big that the bolt's head pulls into the hole. Putting a washer under the bolt head will solve that. Another fix that often solves this problem is to buy a small bottle of thread-locking liquid, a kind of low-strength adhesive. Mechanics use a version of it to prevent bolts from vibrating loose. Just put a drop on the threads in the knob before screwing it onto the bolt. That should do the trick. You'll still be able to remove the knobs later if you want to.

A STICKING *drawer may be the fault of a loose or damaged guide, which is replaceable.*

Imagine your closet as a giant cabinet packed with deep drawers that are as wide as the closet door.

NORM'S FAVORITE *sander for cabinet and countertop work is a 6-inch random-orbit model.*

Storage for VHS Tapes

I have almost 2,000 VHS tapes and need some way to store them. About the only space I have available is in an unused bedroom closet. I thought of building several floor-to-ceiling shelving units and stacking them inside the closet, with some sort of system for having the front ones slide away so I could get at the back ones, but I can't figure out what hardware I'd need to make this work. With all your experience, I thought you could come up with something simple.

Carolyn Arnold, Peoria, Ariz.

Whatever closet you have in mind, I hope it's a big one; 2,000 tapes take up a lot of space. Shelves that slide from side to side could work, but they aren't the most efficient use of your closet space: Half the closet would be filled with shelves, but the other half would have to remain empty because the shelves would have to slide somewhere.

Here's another possibility. Instead of shelves, imagine your closet as a giant cabinet packed with deep drawers that are as wide as the closet door. If you mounted the

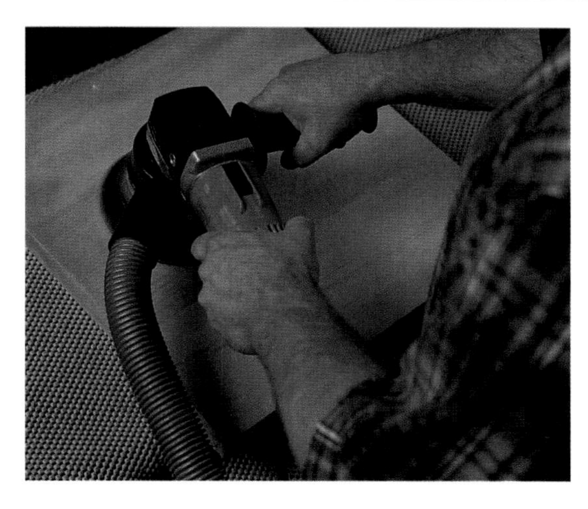

FINE SANDING *dust is the scourge of any workshop. Whenever possible, Norm connects his tools to a shop vacuum (top). Holes in the pad of a random-orbit sander improve dust pickup.*

drawers on full-extension metal slides (readily available at home centers and in mail-order hardware catalogs), they'd pull out completely and still be able to support a full load of tapes. You wouldn't even have to remove the closet door.

Another approach would be to build pantry cabinets with tall, slide-out sections, like those used to hold canned goods in a kitchen. For the hardware, check with a kitchen cabinet supplier or in mail-order hardware catalogs.

If you still don't have room for all your tapes, look for additional storage space under your bed. It's just the right height for storing tapes in wide, rolling drawers, which you can easily buy or build. You should be able to fit about 315 tapes under a twin bed. Or, better yet, maybe now is the time to start collecting DVDs.

Shelves Made of Stone

I'd like to build a set of shelves in my dining room, and I'm thinking about using marble or granite. How should I go about this?

Riva Abrams, New York, N.Y.

Very carefully. Granite and marble look great on a floor, but stone is a bit problematic as shelving: It's heavy and it will crack if not properly supported. (And even then, I wouldn't put much weight on it.) The longer the distance between supports, the thicker the stone has to be. Your best bet is to contact a local stone contractor—there should be a lot of them in your area—to get some suggestions on supports that can handle the weight. Make sure they are fastened to the framing, too, and not just to the plaster or drywall. Actually, I'd rather see you use glass than granite. It's a more uniform material than stone, which is riddled with imperfections that can make its behavior unpredictable when used as you propose.

Painting Plastic Countertops

My house was built in 1960. As befits that era, the kitchen countertops are plastic laminate with a light bluish-turquoise color that I'm not too fond of. They are in almost perfect condition. Can I paint the laminate instead of replacing it?

Laura M. Provost, Clinton, Conn.

I wouldn't. Paint has a hard enough time sticking to smooth surfaces, and with all the hard use a kitchen countertop gets, you'll soon have a peeling, unsightly mess. But that doesn't mean you have to rip out the countertops. Instead, you can glue a sheet of new laminate right over the old unless what's there is loose or bubbled. Plastic

FOR MORE ON PAINTING TURN TO CHAPTER 6: PAINTING AND FINISHING laminate is relatively inexpensive and the installation is straightforward, as long as you work carefully. But unless you're comfortable working with contact cement and and have a router with the appropriate bits to cut and trim laminate, this is a good job to turn over to a countertop fabricator.

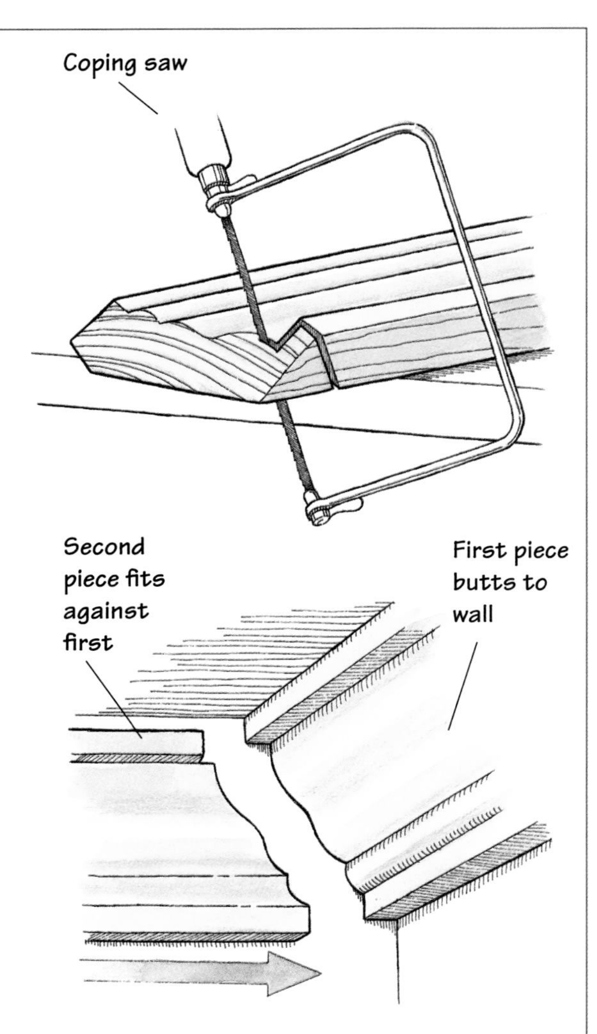

Smoothing Rough Wood

I've just moved into a two-year-old house. The builders used rough-sawn lumber for all the woodwork—window and door casings, baseboards, doors, and trim—and painted it white. Can you think of a way to get a smooth surface on this woodwork, or should I just have it all removed and start over?

Elizabeth Cromley, York, Maine

You could try to sand off the paint with a belt sander and endless hours of elbow grease, but it will be difficult to get the wood clean and smooth. Replacing everything with new wood that matches your taste exactly would be far easier, though more expensive. Any chance you could learn to love white, rough-sawn woodwork?

Joining Crown at Corners

According to everything I've read, crown molding for inside corners must be cut along the back edge for a proper fit after mitering. But if the two pieces of trim meet at a 45-degree angle, why is the back cut necessary?

Randy Noah, Scott, Ark.

Actually, what you're referring to is a coped cut, and it is indeed the best way to handle inside corners on crown molding. Here's why. Mitered joints tend to open up as the wood shrinks, revealing an unsightly gap. That's why you should cope the joint: One piece of molding is simply cut square so it butts into a wall (see drawing above). The adjacent piece is mitered as if it were going to fit in an inside corner, and then the sloped cut is trimmed off with a coping saw, along the contour of the molding's profile. The coped end, being the mirror image of the profile, fits tightly over the first piece, disguising the joint. It sounds tricky, I know. But you get good at it the same way you get to Carnegie Hall: by practicing a lot. Get a miter saw, some molding scraps, and keep working until you get it right. If you take the time now to develop your skills, you'll be able to use them for the rest of your life.

It sounds tricky, I know. But you get good at it the same way you get to Carnegie Hall: by practicing a lot.

Refacing Cabinets

I've been thinking of having my kitchen cabinets refaced instead of replaced. The company I'm considering will replace doors and drawer fronts with solid wood and will cover all exposed edges with wood veneer. My cabinets are solid wood and in good condition. I'm interested because the cost will be a little less than new cabinets, and I'd have no installation charge and no mess. What do you think?

Gloria Dailey, Arlington Heights, Ill.

Refacing is an excellent, economical idea because it uses your original good-quality cabinet carcasses. The thing that struck me in your letter was the cost—"a little less than new." A quick call to Tommy Silva drew this response: "A little? It should be lots less—about half." You should get three or four estimates for the work, and be sure to compare what you're paying for, not just the prices. After narrowing the field to two installers, you want to see some of their jobs—and not new ones, either. See some that are three or four years old, whose owners have lived with the work for a while.

AT THE *Billerica project, Norm and Tom set up shop in an outbuilding to build new cabinets.*

Lost-Cause Cabinet Wood

I have some built-in cabinetry made of applewood, and the doors have begun to warp. Do you have any suggestions?

Guy Butterworth, Miyazaki, Japan

Cabinetry made of applewood is unusual—and with good reason. Apple has a twisty or "figured" grain that's very handsome in projects, such as gun and knife grips, requiring relatively small, thick pieces. But the wood is born to warp, and that makes it a poor choice for the long, slender pieces often used in cabinetry. Sure, it's easy to mill straight boards out of apple logs, but the boards won't stay that way. Because the grain of the wood is so gnarly and wild, it will twist and bend until it's comfortable. A cabinetmaker could straighten your doors but only by measures that are extreme, expensive, and temporary. Sometime after he's done, the grain will simply assert itself once again.

Countertop Fix for Dishwasher

My wife and I recently moved into a new home and found that no one remembered to secure the dishwasher to the granite countertop. Can I do it myself?

Ed Dunk, Marion, Iowa

Maybe. It's easy, but a bit tedious. Take the screws supplied by the dishwasher manufacturer to the hardware store and get matching lead expansion shields—mismatched screws and shields could crack the granite. Chuck a diamond drill bit (available from companies that sell to stone countertop fabricators) into a variable-speed drill at low rpm; cool the bit by pulling it from the hole frequently. Finally, insert the shields and drive the screws.

That's the way it's usually done. But mod-

CABINETS MUST FIT *tightly against a wall and must also be plumb. That's tough to do in an old house without the judicious use of shims.*

ern epoxies are so good that you could probably just glue the mounting clips in place without drilling. That would be the easiest approach, so I'd try it first.

Stained Marble Sink

We have a 100-year-old house with a marble sink in one of the bathrooms. What can we use to clean the stained marble?

LaVonne Klassen, Bluffton, Ohio

I don't know of a better answer to this question than the one given by Jonathan Zanger, of Westchester Marble and Granite, in the third issue of *This Old House* magazine. For routine cleaning, he suggested mild, pH-neutral cleaners like Murphy's Oil Soap or Ivory Liquid. Water-borne stains can be removed with hydrogen peroxide. If these don't work on your sink, try a stain-removing poultice purchased from a stone dealer.

Don't Mix Tile and Oak

I want to build an oak-and-ceramic-tile countertop with sections of tile separated by 1-inch oak strips. I'd like to use cement board as a base. Any suggestions?

Walter M. Lekwart, Washington, Pa.

Yes: Don't. No matter what base you use, the countertop will be nothing but trouble. It's one thing to install oak along the front edge of a tile countertop but it's something else entirely to use the dissimilar materials on the same work surface. Wood expands and contracts at a different rate than grout or tile, and small cracks will eventually form between the wood and the grout as they move over time. These areas will be impossible to keep clean, and the cracks will be a very popular attraction for any liquid that spills on the countertop. In fact, the wood could ultimately expand enough to damage the grout and even loosen the tiles, and that would be the beginning of the end of your countertop. ■

The wood could eventually expand enough to damage the grout and even loosen the tiles.

CHAPTER TEN

Electrical

Plumbing

Keep Old Wiring?

I own a home built in 1935. It's in very good condition, but I'd like to update the wiring, a knob-and-tube system with two-prong outlets and 100-amp service. I've had two electricians check it and both of them say that the wiring looks great so I should leave it alone. The previous owner installed an air conditioner and a new furnace and routed the wiring for both to a separate circuit breaker panel. What do you think?

Brenda Elder, Bridgeport, W. Va.

I've seen a lot of houses where the wiring is old but still sound. But Allen Gallant, an electrician who has done work for some of our *This Old House* projects, says that it's the insulation on the wires, not the wires themselves, that might be a problem. Over time, old insulation turns brittle and crumbly, and if a wire becomes exposed, that can lead to short circuits and fires. He suggests checking back with the two electricians who have already inspected your house and have them make sure the wires' insulation is still in good shape.

Gallant figures that your 100-amp service should suffice. He'd be more inclined to add circuits to serve big appliances than to go through the trouble and expense of upgrading the service to 200 amps, and I'd guess the last electricians who worked on the house felt the same way.

As for the two-prong outlets, Gallant says there's no practical way to ground them: A knob-and-tube system doesn't allow for it. But rather than completely replace the wiring, he suggests that you run new, grounded circuits just to those locations where a stereo, a TV, a computer, or any high-load appliance (such as a refrigerator) might be plugged in. That still leaves the rest of the system ungrounded, but at least the equipment that needs protection most has it.

It's the insulation on the wires, not the wires themselves, that might be a problem.

Running Wire Underground

Our telephone wire extends from a pole off our property, passing over our entire backyard and wood deck. Birds perch on the wire and leave enormous amounts of droppings, particularly on the deck. Since it would be prohibitively expensive to have the phone company bury the wire, are there any simple ways to drive off the birds?

Leonard Dick, Santa Monica, CA

It shouldn't be prohibitively expensive if you bury the wire yourself. I'd call the phone company and say, "Look, if I bury a PVC conduit and put a pull-line in it, will you pull me in a new line?" If they agree, get the specs from them about what kind of conduit you need and how high up it has to run on the pole end. If the phone company wants to charge a lot just for the connection, you might get a better price from an independent installer.

Squirrel Highway

Squirrels are entering my attic by way of a power line from the utility pole. Unfortunately, there's no way to bury the line because it crosses a stream. I've asked the utility to install a baffle on the line, but they say they're unable to do so. Any ideas?

Jack Weiser, Alexandria, Va.

Yes: Stay away from the power line. Amateurs should never mess with large doses of electricity, especially when ladders are involved. Unless you are a gentleman of leisure, the old patience-and-pellet-gun solution is also out. The best thing to do is call an exterminator. He'll handle the problem and spot other possible rodent entrances. That's important: If there are other ways to get in, any squirrel worth his salt will find them.

Insulation Near Old Wire

We bought a beautiful 100-year-old house that has has knob-and-tube wiring and very little insulation. Needless to say, this old house is this cold house during the winter. Is there any type of insulation that can be used around this type of wiring?

Valorie Parent, Lancaster, Mass.

UPDATING WIRES *and pipes is one thing, but getting at them often calls for some demolition.*

Before you add any kind of insulation, have this wiring inspected by an electrician. The covering on wires becomes brittle over time, which can expose bare metal. And you'd be amazed at the convoluted messes I've seen in some old houses, where amateur electricians spliced in new runs whenever there was a need for a light, an outlet, or a switch. Even if your system is in excellent condition, it may be difficult to insulate around it. Batts can't always fit under the zig-zagging runs of knob-and-tube wires, and I'd be reluctant to cover the wiring junctions with blown-in cellulose or cotton because the wires might overheat.

Ceiling Fan Support

We have a 200-year-old house with a kitchen that was remodeled about 10 or 15 years ago and fitted with recessed lights. I have a beautiful ceiling fan with a light that I brought from another house, and I'd like to use it in the kitchen. But my electrician told me I can't hang the fan through the recessed lighting fixture. Is that true?

Michelle Murray, Mendon, Mass.

Absolutely. In fact, electrical codes state specifically that a ceiling fan shouldn't be connected to any standard ceiling electrical box. It's not the electrical load that's the problem, it's that a fan is heavy and moves, so it needs more support than an electrical box provides. There are several kinds of mounting boxes for fans, and some are designed specifically for retrofit applications (see drawing below). One type incorporates adjustable steel straps that support the box between two adjacent rafters, while others use a system of steel plates arranged so that the weight of the fan is supported directly by a single rafter. Both approaches resist the fan's torque—its turning force— and eliminate the possibility of fasteners pulling loose. And both can be installed without the need to remove a lot of drywall or plaster. Assuming you have enough headroom, you should be able to hang the fan in about the same location as the recessed light, but you may have to cut away some drywall to fit the brackets in.

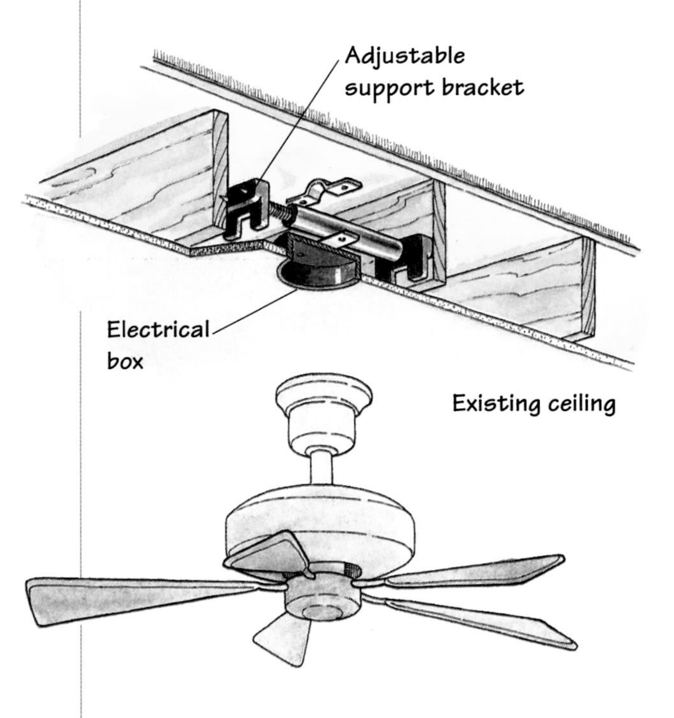

Smoke Detectors Have a Life

I was wondering about the life expectancy of hard-wired smoke detectors. My house is about 15 years old and I think the original detector is still in place. Should I replace it?

Don Hermon, Boise, Idaho

I would. The National Fire Protection Association figures that after about 10 years, the sensors in a smoke detector can no longer be trusted. To keep a younger smoke detector in working order, test it frequently, and vacuum it once or twice every year to remove cobwebs and dust. If you get a battery-powered detector, it will need fresh batteries at least every year, although some organizations suggest replacing them every six months.

Cost-Efficient Wiring Upgrade

I need an unbiased opinion. I have a 1925 house with knob-and-tube wiring. The previous owner put in a new breaker box, but now we're being told we need to change all the wiring too. We have one estimate—and it's $10,000!

Mary Worrell, Asheville, N.C.

Although your wiring is old-fashioned, that doesn't mean it's bound to fail. If the wiring works now, it will probably keep on working. Electrician Allen Gallant says the key is to match the wiring to the breakers or fuses: a 15-amp breaker maximum for 14-gauge wire, 20 amps max for 12-gauge. Provided that the electrician who installed the new box matched the wires and breakers, Gallant says that the only change to consider is installing a separate high-capacity line to handle such things as your dryer, cooktop and other high-demand appliances. That will reduce the load on other circuits, leaving spare capacity in the event you want to add

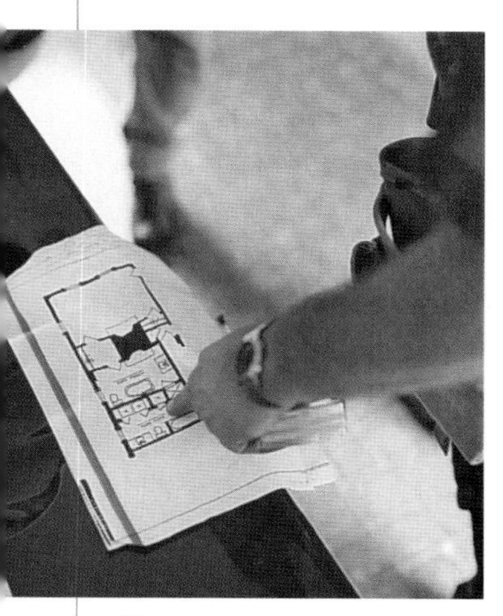

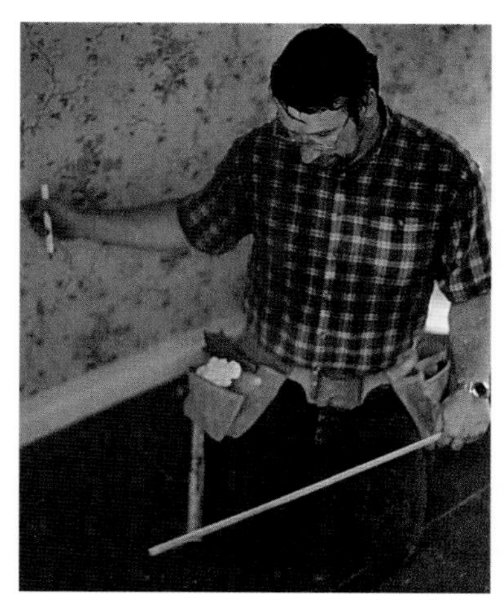

BATHROOM REMODELS *are notoriously complex. Careful planning is the key to success.*

something like a room air conditioner. But Gallant thinks that there's no need to rewire your whole house.

Bulb Burnout Mystery

The lights in our basement burn out too quickly. It seems as if throwing the switch just a few times does it. We're stumped.

R. Zachary Heller, Apollo, Penn.

Since they're basement lights, they're subject to shock and vibration, which come from upstairs traffic and can break the filaments of the bulbs. First, you should try switching to heavy-duty lightbulbs. If the problem persists, you should check to see if you have a localized voltage irregularity or antiquated wiring.

Rebuilding a Shower Stall

The fiberglass base in my shower has cracked, and I'm planning to replace it. I have several questions about the procedure, however. For one thing, I'm not sure how to remove the shower door—it's sealed to the tile with some sort of hardened caulk. I'll also have to remove some of the ceramic tiles around the bottom of the shower where they overlap the fiberglass. Do you have any hints for removing the tiles without breaking them? And what's the best way to support the new shower base? The old one flexed in spots when it was being used.

Ralph Simermeyer, Derwood, Md.

Rest assured that there's more than caulk holding that shower door in place; I suspect you have a metal frame with a gasket or caps hiding the screw heads. After taking the door off the frame, pry these covers up carefully to find the screws beneath. Before removing them, cut through the hardened caulk or grout with a utility knife so that you don't damage the tiles or the substrate when you pull the doorframe away.

Unless the tiles are glued to water-resistant drywall (sometimes called greenboard), I doubt that you'll be able to get them off in one piece. But saving the tiles should be the least of your concerns—you can always replace them with new tiles of a contrasting color. They'd provide a decorative accent next to your new base, or pan, as it's called.

The hard part is getting the old pan out. First, cold-chisel two courses of tile off the bottom. (If its substrate is cement backer board, chisel carefully to avoid damaging it.) Then cut away just enough of the substrate with a utility knife so that you can remove the old fiberglass pan and put in a new one. Bedding it in a few blobs of stiff mortar will help to stiffen the pan and forestall future cracks. Just be sure to lay the mortar on top of a 4-mil polyethylene sheet; this ensures a proper cure and keeps the subfloor dry.

If the substrate is sound, make a clean, straight cut along its bottom edge at a level above or below where the tiles' horizontal grout line will be. (This reduces the chance that a crack in the

FOR MORE ON WALL SURFACES, TURN TO CHAPTER 7: INTERIOR FLOORS, WALLS, AND CEILINGS

Saving the tiles should be the least of your concerns—you can always replace them with new tiles of a contrasting color.

FAUCETS AND DRAINS *are often much easier to install before a countertop is lifted into place.*

grout will let water through.) Next, staple a layer of 15-pound builder's felt to the framing, letting it extend down over the lip of the pan. (By first cutting a kerf in the back side of the old substrate with a keyhole saw, you can tuck the top edge of the felt up behind it.) Then screw strips of cement backer board the same thickness as the original substrate into place over the pan's lip. Finally, seal the joint between the old and new substrate with acrylic caulk and mesh tape, in that order, and cover with thinset adhesive. The day after the joint sets, you'll be ready to tile.

If you do harm the substrate, or if it's already water-damaged, you'll have quite a time fixing it and waterproofing the joints. I've tangled a time or two with shower stalls and have often found that it's better to rip out the old work entirely and replace it with new. Most novices in this situation will find it easier to work with a modular shower unit, which has a single-piece fiberglass wall with interlocking waterproof joints where it connects to the pan.

Barrier-Free Bathtub

My wife and I are at the age when stepping over the side of a bathtub presents a challenge. We would like to turn our combination shower/tub into a stall shower, but the expense of replacing the tub, tile, and flooring is something we can't afford. Is it possible to cut a section out of the side of the tub, providing an entrance that can be closed with a shower curtain?

Jim McConnell, Hollister, Calif.

There are good ways to make a bathroom more accessible, but I'm afraid this isn't one of them. I just don't think it's a good idea to cut away a section of a tub; you run too big a risk of having serious leakage problems. My advice, and that of most experts who specialize in designing for accessibility, is to invest in a shower stall: one with a low door curb or, better yet, without any curb at all. I realize this isn't the answer you were hoping for, but I think you'll be happier with a real shower stall instead of one that invites new problems.

If the expense of this work is too great, you could retrofit the existing tub with clamp-on hand rails to make stepping in a bit easier. Check your phone book for stores that specialize in home healthcare products—they typically stock many products that can make a bathroom safer.

Missing Tub Shutoffs

For some reason, there are no shutoff valves for the bathtub in my 6-year-old home. Has there been some oversight on the plumber's part?

Leonard Clark, Chapmansboro, Tenn.

A shutoff valve for a sink can easily be located in the supporting cabinet, but there's no obvious place to park a shutoff valve for the tub and shower, which often have water lines buried inaccessibly in a wall. Have you checked for an access door on the backside of the wall containing the plumbing? If there's no access door, you should find shutoffs in the basement, either on the supply pipes leading to the tub or at the house

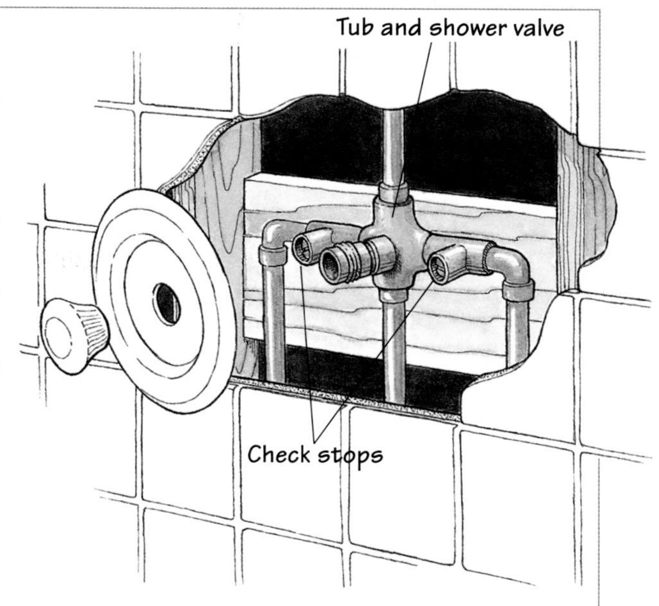

water main itself. *This Old House* plumbing expert Richard Trethewey tells me that some single-lever tub and shower valves incorporate integral check stops, which are essentially the same as shutoffs (see drawing above). If you remove the faucet handle and cover plate, you'll find a slotted stop on each side of the valve; just turn it with a screwdriver to halt the flow of water. Richard believes that these stops should be a standard feature on shower valves.

Installing a Freeze-Proof Faucet

Hard freezes aren't frequent around here, but I want a freeze-proof faucet nevertheless. Trouble is, my brick-faced concrete foundation is 13 inches thick, and I'd have to enlarge the hole for the new faucet's supply pipe to at least 1⅛ inches. To do that without chipping the brick faces I'll need a core bit driven by a rotary-hammer fitted with drill extensions. I also need advice on how to achieve the best results.

L.W. Larson, Birmingham, Ala.

It sounds like you've figured it about right; now you just have to amass the expensive equipment. Why don't you simply use the faucet's shut-off valve inside the house? In warm climates, that's really all you need. Just leave the faucet open afterwards so it drains, and there will be nothing to freeze up. Believe it or

FOR MORE ON FOUNDATIONS, TURN TO CHAPTER 2: BASEMENTS, CONCRETE, AND CHIMNEYS

I've often found that it's better to rip out the old work entirely and replace it with new.

not, I still do that in my house, even though I have freeze-proof faucets.

The story is a little different when it comes to wood wall construction (see drawing below). Richard Trethewey says that the faucet itself is fairly inexpensive and takes

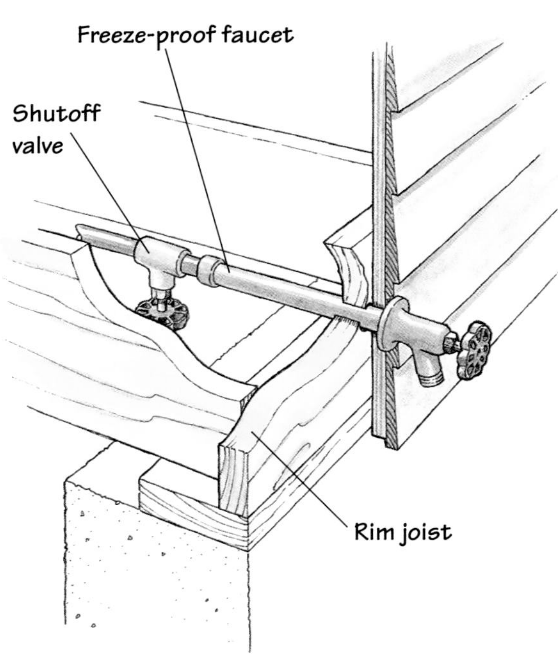

only an hour or so to install in a framed wall. That sounds like a good deal if there's a chance you might neglect to drain your faucets someday. And as Richard says, you won't remember the day your faucets freeze, but you'll sure know it when the ice finally melts in your ruptured pipes.

Point-of-use heaters are great for situations where there is a limited demand for hot water.

Retrofitting Fixtures

I plan on returning the bathroom of my 1903 wooden-frame row house to something like original condition in order to undo an incongruous 1978 renovation. What's your opinion of retrofitting old bathroom fixtures? Also, since many of those available are badly rusted around the drain, how can I remove the rust? Should I replace the faucets?

Janet Merrill, Cambridge, Mass.

Old tubs and sinks work beautifully if they are in good shape, although Richard Trethewey raises one caveat: Using turn-of-the-century fixtures can be tricky because they may not match up with

THIS ELECTRICAL BOX *will house wiring for a vanity light to be mounted on a mirror.*

today's faucets, pipes, and drains. He says your plumber should be able to customize either the fitting or the fixture, but it could get expensive. "Have your checkbook ready," he cautions. To get rid of the rust stains, I'd use oxalic acid diluted 1:10 in water. (Take care, though, because the solution is mildly caustic. Follow all safety instructions on the packaging.) If the surface is rough or pitted from repeated

CHOOSE *the faucet first; only then will you know where to drill through the countertop.*

scrubbings over the years, you can mix up a paste with one of the powder products containing oxalic acid, and let it sit on the stains for a while before rinsing. I think it's a good idea to replace old, worn-out faucets with new ones. They'll be easier to fix if they ever start dripping. Just about every major manufacturer now makes "period" replicas that will complement your classic porcelain fixtures.

Point-of-Use Water Heaters

I'd like to replace my gas-fired 40-gallon water heater with a tankless point-of-use heater, which is supposed to supply unlimited hot water. Can you shed light on other pros and cons, such as energy efficiency, ease of installation, and durability? How large a unit would a family of four require?

Mark A. Schepsis, De Witt, N.Y.

If your water heater is old and the tank is corroded, you may want to replace it with a modern, energy-efficient unit. But otherwise, a 40-gallon water heater should be sufficient to meet the needs of a family of four. Point-of-use heaters are great for situations where there is a limited demand for hot water. *This Old House* executive producer Russ Morash and his wife, Marian, have one at their summer house on Nantucket, Massachusetts. You get continuous water for one person taking a shower, but if you have more than one shower going at once and try to run the dishwasher at the same time, the supply of hot water can slow to a trickle. At times of peak demand, you'll likely need more than one point-of-use heater if you switch from a more conventional system.

TO SOLVE *the problem of hard water at his house, Norm installed a water-softening system.*

Installing a Basement Toilet

We have an old lake house that needs an additional bathroom. The problem is that the logical site is about six feet below grade. I know a pump would be involved, but the mechanics escape me.

A.D. Kite, Pine Mountain, GA

The problem is making water go uphill. You can put in a separate pump or one of the units that have the pump and the toilet built into one fiberglass unit. There are also electric incinerator toilets for residential installations. Check with a good plumbing-supply house. But first check your sewer connection; you may find that it is below the lowest point in your house. If that's the case, you'll have gravity flow even from your basement. ■

THE CLUTTER *of pipes and shutoffs beneath a kitchen sink must be carefully organized.*

C H A P T E R   E L E V

yet there is no wrenchless collet small enough to fit on one; he'd somehow have to use a wrench.

Building a Secret Passage

I'd like to put hinges on a bookcase so that the whole thing will swing away from the wall, revealing a secret storage area. But I don't know how to conceal the hinges or ensure that the case swings smoothly without sagging, even when loaded with books. Any ideas?

Kevin R. Cornett, Saint Bernard, Ohio

You could try the hinges Tom Silva used to create a hidden dining room door at the Billerica project house. They're called SOSS concealed hinges, and fit into holes bored in the woodwork. But to support the considerable weight of a bookcase, you'll need to secure a pair of casters to the bottom of the cabinet—just hide them behind the toe kick. For maximum strength, I'd build the cabinet, including the back, out of ¾-inch plywood (minimum); I'd use fixed shelves fitted into dadoes (square-bottomed grooves), and fasten every joint with glue and screws. You'll probably have to add more plywood on the hinge side to make sure the hinges are securely housed in their mortises.

FOR MORE ON CABINETS TURN TO CHAPTER 9: CABINETS, COUNTERS, AND TRIM

INSTEAD OF *hauling logs to a commercial mill, they can be cut on-site with a portable sawmill.*

Yellow glues are hard to scrape out of a joint after they cure, but they do clean up easily.

FOR PROJECTS, *Norm prefers yellow woodworker's glue or solvent-based polyurethane adhesive.*

Using Woodworking Glue

On your shows, I've noticed that sometimes you use a sponge to remove excess woodworking glue but other times you let the glue dry before scraping the excess off. How do you decide what to do?

Anita Hartley, Berwyn, Pa.

It depends on the glue and the joint. I use two types: water-based yellow (aliphatic) glues, and solvent-based polyurethanes when I need an adhesive that can stand getting wet. Yellow glues are hard to scrape out of a joint after they cure, but they do clean up easily with a quick swipe of a damp sponge or rag before drying. I try to sponge up as much glue as possible without rubbing it into the grain. Once in the grain, glue is hard to get out and, because it fills the pores of the wood, makes for uneven staining. Sometimes I just let the glue dry and then sand it off later to remove any residue. Polyurethane glues only clean up with a solvent like mineral spirits, and only when they are fresh. Once they start to cure, you might as well let them harden and scrape off the excess afterward.

AN EXTENSION *on any table saw makes long stock or large sheets easier and safer to cut.*

Laser Guide for Saw

I've noticed that you use a power mitersaw with a red laser sighting guide, but I've never seen the tool advertised. How can I get one?

J.A. Boland, Moberly, Mo.

After three years on the market, the saw was discontinued in 1996. Although expensive, the design was pretty basic compared to other miter saws that were introduced at about the same time. The laser had to be switched to the left or right of the blade depending on which side of the lumber was the waste side. Old pros who were accustomed to cutting by eye often forgot, and infuriating mistakes occurred. *This Old House* contractor Tom Silva has a laser-guided chop saw, too, and says he likes "everything except the laser. It's hard to see in bright light, and it can't be adjusted." Technology changes, however, and manufacturers will surely try to improve on the model I have.

How Lumber Fails

The floor joists in my home are 2×10s, but they've been notched so the ends rest on a 2×2 ledger board. Does that seem okay to you? I think the notching would actually weaken the joists. I'm also firmly against boring holes through wood joists to accommodate electrical wiring and such. Doesn't that weaken the lumber as well?

Larry Mullenix, Buford, Ga.

Notching is actually pretty common. Back in the days before metal joist hangers were available, I used to set notched joists on ledgers when I framed houses with my father. We couldn't depend on nails alone to hold joists to a beam; the ledgers provided a solid base of support. But you're right—your notched joists are now, in effect, something less than 2×10s, especially if some careless carpenter overran his cuts. The building codes say that end notches are okay as long as they do not exceed one-fourth of the joist's depth, but these

FOR MORE ON FRAMING TURN TO CHAPTER 1: GENERAL REMODELING AND REPAIRS

days I avoid making them at all because the joist might eventually crack at the corner. Toenailing (driving a nail at an angle) through both sides of the joist and into the ledger will restore some of the lost strength and may prevent cracks from forming. As for holes in a joist, they're okay, sort of. You can drill holes large enough for plumbing pipes, as long as you leave enough wood above and below and don't put them too close to the ends. There are too many requirements to cover here, so check with your local building official.

Fix for Glue-Stained Hands

I've been using polyurethane glue a lot in my shop and I think it's great except that it's awfully hard to get off my hands. Any suggestions?

J. Vern Herring, Corpus Christi, Tex.

Getting polyurethane off skin can be quite a problem. In fact, it's a downright nuisance. If you go after the glue within about 15 minutes and scrub it with a washcloth that's been moistened in dishwashing detergent and water, you might get most of it off. But once polyurethane dries on your skin, you'll be stuck with it for a while. I don't know of anything other than patience that gets rid of those dirty-looking splotches; they just wear off in a couple of days. I avoid this problem altogether by wearing disposable latex gloves whenever I work with polyurethane glues or sealants.

PROJECTS *often require many clamps, and it's just as important to have several types on hand.*

Shrink-Resistant Wood

I'm building a tabletop. Should I use flat- or quarter-sawn boards to reduce cupping? And is there any reason to assemble the boards with a tongue-and-groove joint or a finger joint instead of using biscuits? By the way, remember that Lutyens bench you made on *The New Yankee Workshop* some time ago? I saw a similar one in a catalog—it was made of teak and was selling for $7,000!

Lawrence M. Warn, Toledo, Ohio

The first question is easy to answer: Stock that is quarter-sawn resists cupping, and swells and shrinks less than flat-sawn stock. In answer to your second question, you can get a router bit or shaper cutter that makes something similar to a finger joint, but biscuits are quicker and plenty strong. I don't think tongue-and-groove joints are great for tabletops—getting a good glue bond is hard. Regarding that catalog, it's nice to know that some folks can buy benches at $7,000 a pop. But when I build something, making or saving money is beside the point. I love woodworking for the pleasure of it.

FOR MORE ON BISCUIT JOINERY TURN TO CHAPTER 9: CABINETS, COUNTERS, AND TRIM

Best Use for Pallet Wood

Like you, I'm a big believer in recycling, but since I can't find a local dealer in salvaged lumber, I've been recycling old shipping pallets. The wood works fine for some projects and not so well for others. Do you recommend using pallet wood?

Damon E. Lincourt, W. Henrietta, N.Y.

THE CLEAN *lines of a white oak fireplace surround were inspired by Craftsman-era woodwork.*

Quarter-sawn stock resists cupping, and swells and shrinks less than flat-sawn stock.

I built a simple pallet-wood coffee table on *The New Yankee Workshop* some years ago, and it turned out to be a pretty good project. The wood—usually oak—is often second-rate, not good for anything you'd call heirloom quality, and by the time you get all the nails out, the pieces are rather short. But it's useful for small projects and so-called rustic furniture; and it's certainly good to practice on, especially with kids, who ought to feel okay about making mistakes.

Biscuit Basics

What's the best way to apply glue to biscuit joints?

Arthur S. Mulcahy, Perry, N.Y.

I squeeze a bead of glue along the edges of both boards and into each slot, and then I spread it with a disposable glue brush. I don't put glue on biscuits—they're textured, so they'll pick up a good coat from the slots. Gluing both biscuit and slot can cause the biscuit to overexpand and telescope through the wood surface.

AT BILLERICA, *the framing crew paused for a camera check before lifting a wall into place.*

Duplicating Old Moldings

When I owned an 1886 Victorian (with some rather unique detailing I called "Norwegian Sinister"), I could replace moldings with ease; the same profiles were always available. Now I own a late-1940s house—one that aspires to be a Craftsman-style home, and sometimes succeeds—and I find that replacing molding is not only difficult but nearly impossible. I need new "mopboards" (baseboards) with a stepped profile. Do you know of a source, or are there router bits or shaper heads that can do the job?

Ben Leonard, Rapid City, S. Dak.

The source for just about any molding profile you can imagine is a millwork company. Moldings are their business, and if you need enough to make the setup charges worthwhile, they'll make the necessary knives and charge you a fair price. Fifteen years ago this was a slow and expensive process, but now you can fax them a profile and they'll grind a knife quickly. If you don't need much, you can mill your own molding using a a table saw, a shaper, or a router—all sorts of router bits and shaper cutters are also available from mail-order catalogs. Just be careful when cutting. And don't forget that it's possible to build complex profiles using layers of stock moldings.

Old houses, even ones that seem as badly off as yours, seldom just fall to the ground.

Repairing a Rotten Porch Post

I've seen you and Tom Silva repair a porch post with what I believe is called a dutchman. I've never seen anything written about this type of repair. Can you give some more details?

Arlene D. Bell, Salem, Va.

A dutchman is just a small wooden patch used for cosmetic purposes, like the oval "boats" used to fill flaws in construction-grade plywood. In the case of a porch post, a dutchman wouldn't provide the necessary strength for a structural repair, and what Tom and I would use instead is a lap joint, which is formed by placing one piece of wood partly over the other to provide strength in at least two directions.

FOR MORE ON PORCHES TURN TO CHAPTER 12: PORCHES, PATIOS, AND DECKS

Floors Sag Towards the Center

In the 1950s, my father-in-law built a lakeside house made of hand-split fieldstone

with tongue-and-groove hardwood floors. The floor joists, main beam, second-floor beam, and subflooring have now rotted, and the center of the house sags 3 inches. How can I remedy this while replacing the main beam?

Larry D. Hibbs, Laughlin, Nev.

Old houses, even ones that seem as badly off as yours, seldom just fall to the ground. There's a good chance yours can be saved, but don't do anything until you hire a structural engineer. He'll probably notice right away that there should have been a pier supporting the center of the house, just the sort of thing that's left out of a lot of owner-built structures. A decent engineer will propose realistic solutions that fix what's necessary but no more. For example, you might think all the joists have to be replaced. An engineer may suggest cutting off their rotten ends and sistering them instead (bolting new wood on either side), which will save time and money. He may also be able to recommend a contractor who specializes in the rebuilding of old houses and has the jacks and other tools required.

Seasoning Lumber Right

I have some walnut lumber I'm planning to air-dry for a year before using it to make furniture. I stacked the boards in pairs on 1-inch spacers, and now I see that some of the wood has become moldy. How do I get rid of the mold?

Wes Carney, Lawrenceburg, Ky.

If you're seeing mold, the wood isn't air-drying. That means you're storing the wood in the wrong place or you've stacked it improperly. You shouldn't keep the stack on the shady side of the house or cover it so tightly that you don't get any airflow. On the other hand, you don't want lumber in direct sunlight for long periods of time, because it will cook and turn into spaghetti. To properly air-dry, lumber should be stacked well off the ground as well as stickered (separated with spacers). Plus, there should be plenty of room on all sides for good air circulation. But how much mold is there? If you see only a little, that's nothing to worry about as long as the boards are all going to be surfaced later.

Tips for Driving Screws

I've seen you use an electric drill and driver bit on wood and drywall hundreds of times. But when I do it myself, I often find that the screwheads strip out. How can I prevent this?

James Springer, Kettering, Ohio

Cheap, soft-metal screws or a worn-out bit could be at fault. Phillips bits wear quickly, so it's worthwhile looking for hardened steel bits with ribbed tips for a better grip. There are several other causes of stripping, including failure to keep the drill bit firmly pressed to the screwhead and using the wrong-sized bit.

But the most common cause is a failure to predrill holes for the screws. When I hear a bit chatter on a jobsite, I know immediately that someone has stripped a screw. I'll turn around to see a young carpenter struggling with a screw that isn't

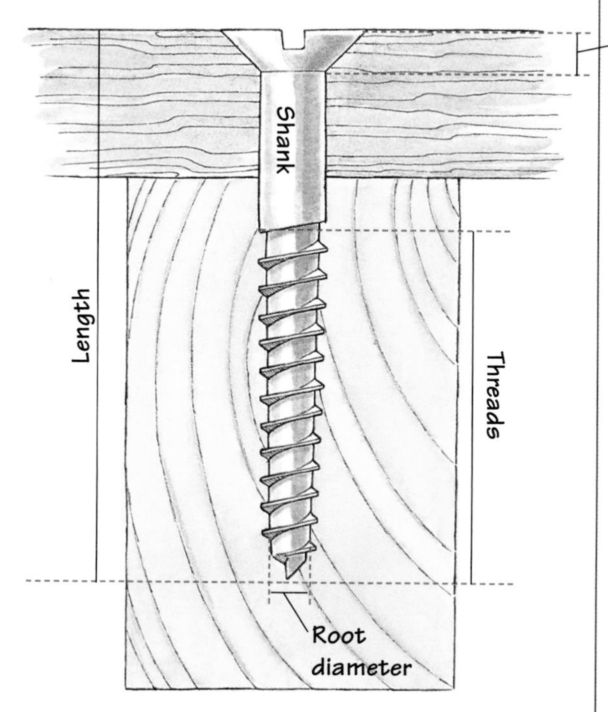

EVEN IN *a shop full of powertools, a rolled scrap of sandpaper is often what solves problems best.*

fully seated yet can't be backed out either. My first question is always: "Did you drill pilot holes?"

Inexperienced carpenters often assume that a power tool will drive screws without predrilling. Ordinary twist drills will do for making pilot holes, and some of these tools now have hexagonal shanks for quick switches from drill to driver. Special pilot bits are better. Many are graduated by screw size—number-8 bits for number-8 screws and so on—and they automatically countersink for flathead screws.

FOR MORE ON FASTENERS TURN TO CHAPTER 1: GENERAL REMODELING AND REPAIRS

To understand how to properly predrill for screws, consider the wood screw. When fastening one piece of wood to another with wood screws, the proper method for drilling pilot holes is a three-step process. In the top piece you'll need a hole no narrower than the screw shank. In the bottom piece you'll need a somewhat smaller hole for the screw threads. It should be about 65 percent of the screw's root diameter in softwood and 85 percent in hardwood. Finally, use a countersink to cut the beveled hole that the screw's head sits in.

When fastening one piece of wood to another with wood screws, the proper method for drilling pilot holes is a three-step process.

Nail Finder Saves Blades

I once saw you use a small handheld device to detect nails in old lumber. Can you tell me where to get one? I plan to run

some salvaged lumber through a planer and want to be sure it's nail-free so I don't damage the blades.

Robert Juday, Portis, Kan.

I have what's called a hand scanner or scanning wand, the same metal-detecting device that security guards use at airports. You can get one by mail order for about $150, a small investment, given the cost of sharpening and replacing planer knives. By the way, you should take your scanner along when you're buying old lumber.

Making the Most of Mistakes

Do you ever screw up the way the rest of us do? And will you ever do a show that explains how and why people make mistakes and then demonstrates the proper way?

Vincent J. Falini III, Dunedin, Fla.

Sure I make mistakes, but I don't think there's much value in a show about correcting them. I always try to demonstrate how to do something right the first time. Over the years, I've learned that the best way to deal with a mistake is to figure out how to correct it yourself. That way you won't make the same mistake twice.

Sharpening Carbide Bits

I assume you use carbide bits for your router. Any advice about how to maintain and sharpen them?

Thom Strunk, Eugene, Ore.

Sharpening carbide bits is not something an amateur should try. There are little diamond stones that you can use to touch them up; basically, you just want to hit the back (flat) side of the blade. But it's tough to do a proper job. I send mine out to a pro and let him worry about them. ■

WITH THE POWER *off, Norm checks the tracking of his bandsaw's blade (top). After additional tuning, the tool will cut square and true.*

CHAPTER TWELVE

Porches, Patios + Decks

Making Curved Porch Trim

I am restoring a 110-year-old Queen Anne house. A porch on the second floor has a piece of curved wood trim that caps a low wall, and I can't seem to find anyone who knows how to replace it. How would you tackle the job?

Debbie Karle, Norwood, Ohio

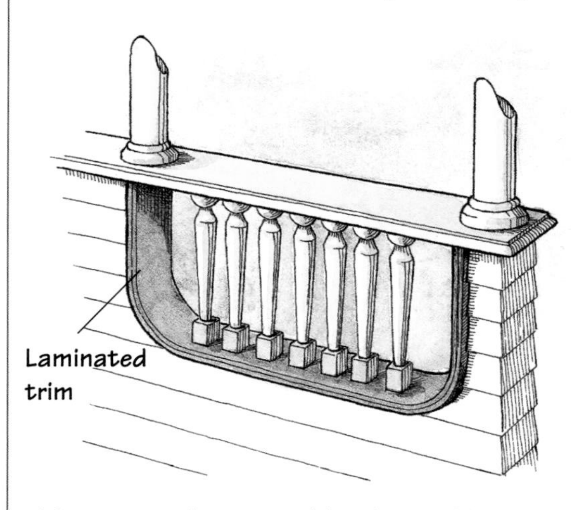

To get wood to curve like that, I'd laminate it in one piece using pliable ¼-inch-thick red cedar strips epoxied together against a curved mold or form (see drawing above). That way, there would be no joints for water to get in. Once you paint it, nobody will know it isn't a solid piece of wood. Any good carpenter or woodworker with a band saw and a planer can make the strips; the most costly and time-consuming part of this project is building the form. If local carpenters are shy about doing this work, try millwork companies, or builders of custom furniture or wooden boats; they tackle these kinds of projects all the time.

"One-offs" like this can get expensive. After going through all the trouble of making a form, you might as well laminate an extra set of parts and tuck them away somewhere. The next person who has to replace this trim will be very grateful.

Sanding is generally the best way to fix a damaged wood surface. Sanding a deck, however, poses a couple of special challenges.

Sinking Porch Steps

I live in a brick house that was built in 1940. It's in pretty good shape, but the concrete steps leading to a door on one side of the house seem to be sinking. Should I have them leveled or should I leave things alone?

Cathye Bullitt, Wichita Falls, Tex.

Steps that tilt not only look bad, they're not safe. And judging by the photos you sent, they are also channeling water directly toward the foundation of your house. You'll need to take care of this soon. The basic problem is that soil around a foundation is never compacted as much as soil farther away; anything not anchored to the foundation simply settles into the relatively softer dirt. Your steps appear to have been cast in place, but they're probably still not so heavy that you can't coax them back where they belong. First, dig out an area 1 or 2 feet wide in front of the steps and next to the foundation so you can slip a crowbar underneath, and lever them upward. Lift them slightly higher than the position you want to end up with, and wedge concrete pavers underneath to hold them up. Continue lifting and wedging until the steps are level from side to side and slope slightly away from the doorway. Now you can begin to pack fine crushed gravel (not pea gravel) underneath. I wouldn't recommend using concrete; it will bond to the underside of the steps and make your work even harder if you ever have to level them again.

FOR MORE ON FOUNDATIONS TURN TO CHAPTER 2: BASEMENTS, CONCRETE, AND CHIMNEYS

Resurfacing Damaged Decks

It looks as if the previous owner tried to pressure-wash the stain out of the wood on the deck. Well, that did get rid of the stain, but it also damaged the top layer of wood. Can I sand out the rough wood? And if I do, will the newly exposed wood take stain and preservative?

Paul Murray, Detroit, Mich.

Sanding is generally the best way to fix a damaged wood surface, and it will actually encourage the wood to take a stain. Sanding a deck, however, poses a couple of special challenges.

The first is the deck's fasteners. If you're lucky, they were driven through from the underside of the deck rather than through the boards' faces. If not, you'll have to set every nail or screw head below the surface to avoid tearing the sandpaper and to keep

TO PREVENT *deterioration, only brick rated SW (severe weathering) is suitable for pathways.*

their protective coatings intact. (Unless they're stainless steel, they'll rust.)

Then you'll need to find out what your deck is made of. Pressure-treated wood is toxic, which means you should wear a respirator, coveralls, and eye protection; and make sure to capture the dust so it doesn't get into the soil or a swimming pool. Sanding a cedar or redwood deck won't require such precautions, although wearing a dust mask is a good idea—the dust from these woods is an irritant for many people. Either a belt sander or a random-orbit sander would be my tool of choice if the damage isn't too deep; a rented drum sander should be able to smooth out deeper, widespread gouges. I'd probably start with 120-grit sandpaper, but you could probably go as low as 80-grit. Anything more aggressive will just make the the situation worse. Sand the deck just enough to remove the damage, then stain it. Hopefully, this experience will discourage you from ever pointing a pressure-washer at wood.

Leak-Prone Outbuilding

When we built a toolshed, we covered it with corrugated roofing because we had used that material successfully on other projects. This time, however, we're getting a lot of leakage. We've tried sealing the roofing with aluminum-fiber stickum, but no luck. We don't know what to do. Please help us.

Mrs. Duane Burgess, Rio Dell, Calif.

Ninety-nine percent of the time, leaks in new doors, skylights, and roofs occur not because of material failures but because the installation wasn't done right in the first place. That's seldom the kind of error you can fix with tubes of goo. On the other hand, the leakage problems you're experiencing could be El Niño at work. A lot of people in my area have discovered leaks they never knew they had, because suddenly it's been raining inches at a time. In either case, you may have to start over in order to get a watertight roof.

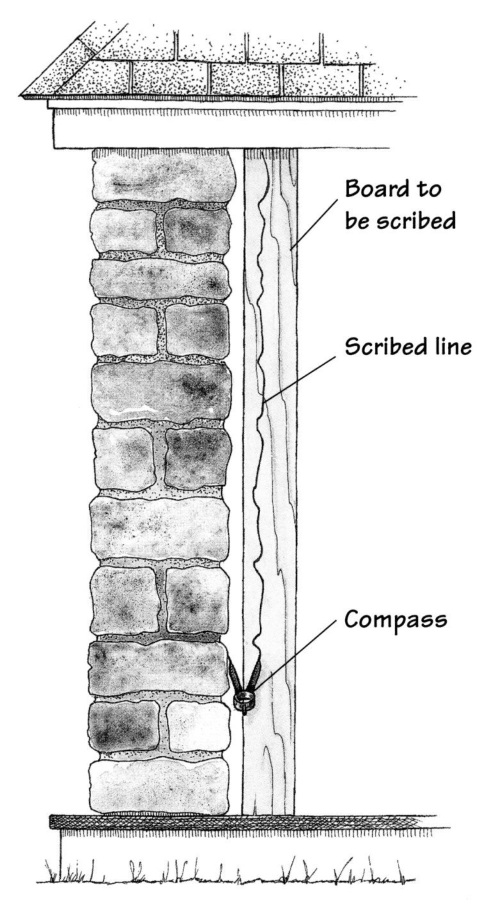

Scribing Wood to Masonry

A mason recently replaced the wood posts supporting our screened porch roof with brick columns to match our home. He used brick that's over 100 years old, and that varied quite a bit in size, so the column faces are quite irregular. Now I'm making screens for each of the openings, and I've been unable to find a way to seal the gaps between the brick and the 2×4 framing of the porch screens. Some of the gaps are two inches wide. Any suggestions?

Jim Belling, Edwardsville, Ill.

Whenever I have to mate a straight piece of wood to an uneven or irregular surface, I use a technique called scribing (see drawing). It can be used to fit the back edge of a shelf against a bowed wall, the bottom of a cabinet to a sloping floor, and wood trim against a rough stone foundation. Anyone who works on old houses needs to know how to do it. All you need is a compass and a saw. A coping saw will work on thin molding, but on thicker stock, a jigsaw fitted with a narrow scroll blade is the best for scribing.

I use a technique called scribing. Anyone who works on old houses needs to know how to do it.

Start by cutting a piece of trim to match the height of the column. The trim should be as wide as the widest gap you have to cover, plus 1½ inch (the thickness of the 2×4 screen frame). In your case, a 1×4 should do it. Place the trim as close to the column as you can while still keeping it plumb, then tack it in place temporarily with a couple of finishing nails. Next, hold the compass horizontally and spread its legs to match the widest gap between the column and trim. Starting at the top of the column, and without changing the compass' spread or its horizontal attitude, set the compass' pencil leg on the trim and hold the other leg against the brick face nearest the trim. Draw the compass downward. As the point of the compass follows the irregular surface of the brick, the pencil will trace a matching contour on the wood. When you've traced the entire length of the column, remove the 1×4 and cut along the pencil line with the jigsaw.

When you put the 1×4 back in place against the brick, the cut edge should match the column's profile fairly well, though you'll probably have to fuss a bit with the fit to make it perfect. And when you're ready for installation, run a bead of siliconized acrylic-latex caulk on the cut edge, slip the trim into place against the brick, and nail it to the framing. I think you'll be proud of the results.

Finishing Hardwood Decking

When Tom Silva built the deck for his brother Dick during the Billerica project, he used a Brazilian hardwood called ipe for the decking. I've heard that ipe wears like iron,

but does it get slippery when wet? If so, could I paint it with a non-skid surface?

Mark Bard, Joplin, Mo.

Tom hasn't noticed any problems on the Billerica deck; he says it doesn't seem any more slippery than one made of pressure-treated wood. And I certainly wouldn't paint it. Why pay for beautiful wood and then cover it up? Besides, the effort would probably be wasted. "I don't think any paint would stick to ipe because the wood is so dense," Tom says. "We put two coats of teak oil on the deck and they just sat on the surface."

Warped Deck Boards

At a local home show we met some deck contractors whose display featured Alaskan cedar decking, which we liked a lot. The wood looked fine as it was going down, but within weeks many knots became visible and many, many cracks developed. After we gave the deck a light pressure-washing—to remove the gray before sealing—the wood seemed to twist in a way we haven't seen before. Would sanding help, or do we need to replace the decking?

Brett and Kathi Miller, Newtown, Pa.

Decks get wet all the time from rain and washing, but they shouldn't be twisting. It sounds to me like the contractor used green lumber—wood with a moisture content above 19 percent—and that the cracks and twisting you see are due to the wood shrinking as it dries. Excessively warped boards won't return to their earlier shape, and sanding won't help either. Your best bet is to replace any pieces that have gone bad with new wood that has a moisture content of no more than 12 percent, as indicated on a moisture meter. Then, I'd recommend that you give the entire deck a thorough cleaning and apply a penetrating, water-repellent preservative that contains a mildicide along with UV inhibitors to keep the wood from turning gray. You can also put on a penetrating semi-transparent stain that colors the wood as it protects against UV. Preservatives last about a year; the stains about two or three, according to the Forest Products Laboratory of the U.S. Department of Agriculture. They recommend that you avoid film-forming products like paint or solid stains, which will eventually crack and peel.

FOR MORE ON LUMBER TURN TO CHAPTER 11: WORKING WITH WOOD

SMALL BUILDINGS, *such as this trash shed, call for walls and floors built just like a house.*

MOUNT DOORS *using high-quality, weather-resistant hardware and compatible screws.*

Choosing a Fence

I have a fence project coming up, and need your advice. I like the looks of wood but am uncertain if it's appropriate because the humidity levels are high around here.

Mike Noelscher, Lexington, Ky.

I vote for building a wood fence like the ones you see everywhere in Bluegrass Country. A second reason, closely related to the first, is that your neighbors might be upset if you build with anything else. You want something that looks as if it belongs there, so it's wise to stick with local styles and standards. If you install posts that have not been pressure-treated, pack gravel around them to allow for proper drainage. (Rotting posts are the chief threat to a wooden fence.) Then protect all exposed wood from sun and rain by brushing on primer and paint or a coat of stain.

Old Brick for a Ramp?

We want to improve handicapped access to our church by adding a walkway made with some of the church's old handmade floor bricks. But they date from the 1700s, and some people doubt they'll hold up.

Jackie Gnann, Springfield, Ga.

The doubters may be right. In the 1700s, brickmakers built scove kilns—basically stacks of freshly molded brick piled around a cavity for burning wood. Bricks nearest the fire came out harder than those toward the outside of the pile, which were confined to indoor or between-wall use. A bricklayer or preservationist with a masonry background might be able to tell if your brick is hard enough to survive the Georgia winter. But even if they pass muster, you may find that their rough, uneven surface makes a poor pathway for wheelchairs.

As indoor work ebbed towards the end of the Milton project, efforts turned towards landscaping and decking work.

If you install posts that have not been pressure-treated, pack gravel around them to allow for proper drainage.

OUTOOR PROJECTS *live longer if assembled with suitable fasteners. Galvanized screws are good, but stainless steel screws are better.*

Tiling Over Exterior Tile

When we removed the artificial turf that the previous owner had glued to the porch floor, we found unglazed 6×6 quarry tiles beneath, set in a concrete slab. Now we have to get rid of the adhesive residue and seal the slab, which covers a wing of the basement where we have an oil tank and a small workshop. When rain hits the floor, water seeps down through cracks in the slab and drips into the basement. We'd like to restore the porch and eliminate the leaks. Do you have any suggestions?

John Siket, West Lawn, Pa.

The previous owner might have glued down the artificial turf in a misguided attempt to stop water from entering the slab, but more likely they were trying to keep people from slipping on the wet tile. Removing the remaining adhesive is the least of your problems. Unfortunately, there's only sure way to stop the leaking, according to tiling contractor Joe Ferrante: Lay new frost-proof tile over the old. He recommends first rolling on a liquid waterproofing such as Hydroment Ultraset, making sure to cover all the edges and up any curb on the porch. Then fill in any unevenness by troweling on a mix of two parts sand to one part cement. The tile can be placed directly on the cement mix using a thinset mortar rated for exterior use. Just be sure that all the waterproofing is covered, otherwise the sun will deteriorate it. Also, the temperature needs to be above 55°F when the tile is laid or the mortar will not harden properly. As you might imagine, this is a job for a expert tile setter.

Adhering Slate to Concrete

Outside the front door of my home there's a concrete slab that I want to cover with slate. How do I get slate to stick to the concrete?

Brian R. Selph, Denton, Md.

What a mason would do is this: He'd clean the concrete with a muriatic acid wash, lay down a "pad" of mortar about an inch thick, then press and wiggle the slates into the pad. Later he'd "grout" the spaces between the slates with mortar, more or less the same way you'd grout bathroom tile. I say more or less because it's a lot trickier than that. Hire a mason; this is not a do-it-yourself job.

Leak-Proofing a Porch

In the course of renovating our 1890 farmhouse, we have found many non-standard construction methods. The most perplexing involves our front porch. About two-thirds of it is over our basement and the rest goes beyond the foundation wall. This encourages heat loss and rot, and lets water into the basement. We plan to replace the rotted porch floor

with pressure-treated tongue-and-groove plywood covered with rubber roofing; the rubber would be topped with pressure-treated tongue-and-groove boards. What do you think?

Mike and Traci Bryant, Orion Twp., Mich.

I've heard of some strange porches, but yours is a new one on me; it's as if your house was put on a foundation that was too big. The problem with your idea is that the"rubber" roofing, called EPDM, won't keep out water once you've nailed or screwed down the floor boards. There may be ways to get around this, but the simpler solution, it seems to me, is to go down into the basement and build a cement-block wall where the foundation should have been all along: underneath the front of the house. You'll have to waterproof the wall's outside face and dump clean, drainable fill into the space between the new foundation and the old one, but when it's all done, you can leave your porch as is and stop worrying about heat loss or water infiltration.

Stiffening a Wobbly Deck

I have a 19-year-old pressure-treated deck attached to the back of my house that's approximately 8 feet off the ground. Recently, I've been feeling slight vibrations in the deck whenever someone walks rather heavily across it. The decking material appears to be in good condition—I treat it periodically with a sealant and pressure-wash it about every second or third year. The outer ends of the joists are nailed into a built-up beam that's supported by three equally spaced 4×4 posts. Is there anything I can do to make the deck stiffer?

S. W. Schuda, Pittsburgh, Pa.

It sounds like you take pretty good care of the decking; it's the framing underneath that needs attention. As part of your yearly maintenance ritual, you'll need to go under the deck and tighten any loose nuts and check for loose nails. But you can't just pound a loose nail back in place; it's already lost a lot of its holding power. Pull it and replace it with a galvanized screw (never a drywall screw) long enough and wide enough to grab fresh wood. Most important, take a close look at the ledger board, which holds the deck to the house (see drawing below). If it's nailed to the house, not bolted directly to the framing, or if water is getting behind it and turning wood soft, you have a serious problem that needs to be corrected immediately. For the sake of your safety, make sure the ledger board is securely connected to sound wood with

As part of your yearly maintenance ritual, you need to go under the deck and tighten any loose nuts.

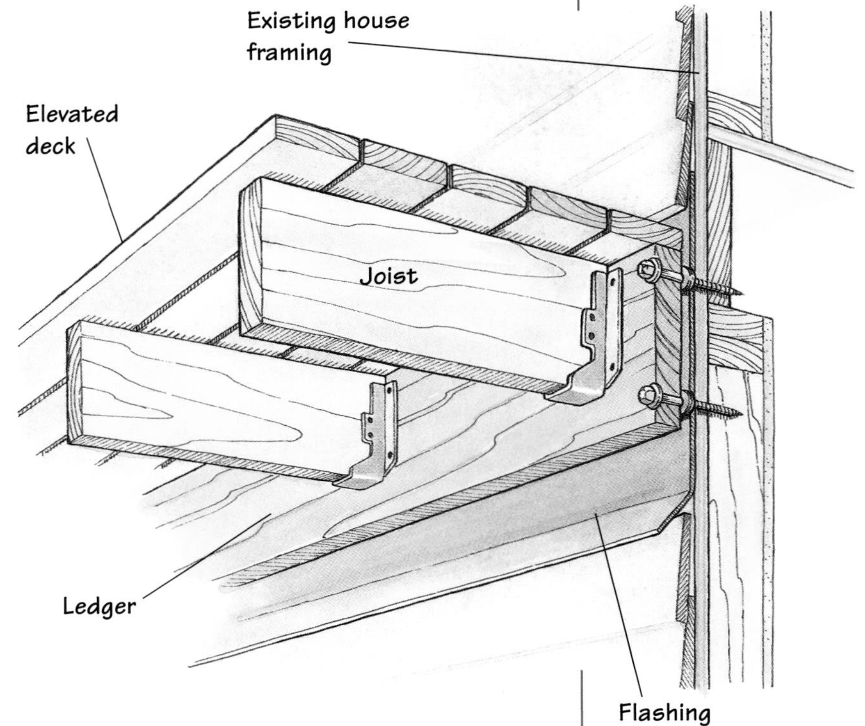

bolts or lag screws—don't rely on nails.

Those posts deserve some attention, too. If the ends are in contact with the ground or embedded in concrete piers, they're probably rotting out and need replacing. They should all be resting on metal anchors to keep the end grain dry. By the way, 4×4 posts seem undersized to me—I'd rather see 6×6s. All this may stiffen the deck to your satisfaction, but if it still shakes you'll have to add some sort of bracing. Knee braces—boards that run at a 45-degree angle from a post up to the beam it supports—are an option. I'd

FOR MORE ON FRAMING TURN TO CHAPTER 1: GENERAL REMODELING AND REPAIRS

FOR PROPER DRAINAGE, *steps should slope slightly forward but be level from side to side.*

make each one from a 2×6 at least 3 feet long. To stiffen the deck horizontally, fasten a long 1×4 pressure-treated board to the underside of the joists. It should run diagonally from corner to corner and be nailed twice into each joist.

Erasing Gray From a Deck

My decade-old cedar deck is dark gray where the sun hits it, but I want a true cedar hue to match the shaded part. If I stained the deck, how long would the color last?

Paul Cangialosi, Brooklyn, N.Y.

Is it in Brooklyn where they say fuggedaboudit? That's what you should do. Gray is the natural color of cedar exposed to the elements—sunlight guarantees that. Why fight nature? Leave your deck alone except to apply a penetrating water-repellent sealer each fall, and maybe again each spring, to preserve the wood. Sealer won't restore the original color, however, and may even darken the wood slightly.

Finishes for Porch Floors

My wife and I are building a new home, and we're having trouble finding flooring for the front porch. The usual material here is painted tongue-and-groove fir, which I've heard often fails almost as soon as it's laid down due to moisture damage. Local retailers tell me they can't get the square-edged fir I've seen you use on various projects. How do I find this flooring and install it for maximum durability?

Robert L. Harmon, Lincoln, Ill.

You're wise to be wary of tongue-and-groove flooring for a porch or deck. The grooves are moisture traps. But I can't imagine why you can't find square-edged fir. If your local home centers don't stock it, try a lumberyard. When you do find the lumber you need, make sure you space the planks so they can breathe; the gap should be approximately the diameter of a 2½-inch long nail. Using painted planks is a problem. For one thing, paint never sticks well to fir. Also, since you're dealing with a horizontal surface, any moisture will sit right on top of the planks and inevitably cause paint to fail. Instead, apply clear wood sealer in the fall and spring for the first couple of years, then annually in the fall. If you use a stain, the results could be blotchy. Fir stains unevenly because it's hard in some spots and soft in others.

Best Woods for Porch Floors

We're thinking of putting a front porch on our house. We want it to have a wood ceiling and floor, both painted. We assume Grandpa used pine. Any suggestions?

Janeen Jensen, Del Mar, Calif.

Using wood outdoors in ways that expose it to standing water can create problems. Tongue-and-groove bead board will give you a nice look for a porch ceiling, but decking is another matter. Pine is a poor choice. Basically a softwood, it requires the most upkeep, and the quality today isn't as high as in Grandpa's day. If you insist on softwood, a good exterior material like western red cedar or redwood will hold up well.

Mouse-Proofing a Slab

Our ranch has a concrete-slab patio that was eventually enclosed to make a year-round room. One wall of the room doesn't rest fully on the cinder-block foundation of the concrete pad; consequently, we get a wind-tunnel effect in cold weather. Also, mice enter readily. We've had several people out for estimates, which range from under $100 to "maybe as high as $5,000"; and completion times that range from half a day to "oh, at least a month anyway." We're not asking for a miracle, just an intelligent diagnosis and sound advice on how we should proceed.

The Grubers, West Salem, Ohio

I suspect that the slab was poured first, and the cinder block was added later as a frost wall. The slab was probably rough on the underside, making it hard to shove the blocks all the way under the edge, so the workmen pushed them in as far as they could and then gave up. This isn't as bad as it sounds. As long as there's no movement in the structure, there's no threat to your house, and the job is small enough to do yourselves. First block every hole—even those you think much too small for mice—with foam-in-place insulation. Don't stop there, though. Mice will go right through foam insulation—they'll probably even like it. The next step: With mortar, cover over everything, finishing with a nice angled cap to shed rainwater.

FOR MORE ON MASONRY TURN TO CHAPTER 2: BASEMENTS, CONCRETE, AND CHIMNEYS

PLANS *for this playhouse can be found in the book New Yankee Workshop Kids' Stuff.*

Invisible Fasteners for Decks

We want to build a 12-by-36-foot deck on the shady north side of our house. Half of the deck will be a screened porch. What's your opinion of the attachment devices for decks that let you fasten planks from underneath without nailing through the top? We also plan to use treated lumber. Can we leave it as is, or do we need to seal it?

Mark D. Campbell, Lexington, Ky.

We used hidden fasteners to install the deck at our project in Milton, Massachusetts, but I have to say they really slowed us down because they had to be screwed in place from underneath. I don't recommend using them. Neither does Tom Silva, who has developed his own approach to installing a deck. "What I'm doing these days is spreading marine-grade adhesive on the joists and then fastening some planks with finishing nails. This is fast, and the planks won't come loose. Just don't put down too much adhesive at any one time. Otherwise it'll dry and get a skin on it, and it won't hold," Tom says. As for applying sealing products to treated lumber, it's smart to use them in spring and fall for the first couple of years and every fall thereafter. ■

Don't stop there, though. Mice will go right through foam insulation—they'll probably even like it.

Credits

This Old House® Books

EDITORIAL DIRECTOR: Paul Spring

Ask Norm Development Team

EDITOR: Mark Feirer
ART DIRECTOR: Sue Ng
COPY EDITOR: Melanie Bush
PICTURE EDITOR: Susan Sung Danelian
PRODUCTION COORDINATOR: Robert Hardin
Special thanks to Anthony Wendling, Anthony Cortazzo, Joseph Milidantri

Illustrations

Heather Lambert

Photographs

COVER: Kolin Smith, Keller & Keller, Michael Myers, Pascal Blancon
FORWARD: Keller & Keller
INTRODUCTION: Pascal Blancon
CHAPTER ONE: David Katzenstein, Dan Borris, Keller & Keller, Shelley Metcalf, Kristine Larsen, Joe Yutkins, Pascal Blancon
CHAPTER TWO: Shelley Metcalf, Pascal Blancon, Kolin Smith, Keller & Keller
CHAPTER THREE: Keller & Keller, Richard Howard, Kolin Smith
CHAPTER FOUR: David Barry, Keller & Keller, Michael McLaughlin
CHAPTER FIVE: Keller & Keller, Michael Grimm, Richard Howard, Joshua McHugh, Michael McLaughlin
CHAPTER SIX: David Barry, Keller & Keller, Michael McLaughlin
CHAPTER SEVEN: Keller & Keller, Michael Myers, Richard Howard, Dan Borris, Kolin Smith
CHAPTER EIGHT: David Barry, Keller & Keller, Richard Howard
CHAPTER NINE: Keller & Keller, Kolin Smith, Furnald/Gray, David Carmack
CHAPTER TEN: Michael Myers, Kolin Smith, Keller & Keller
CHAPTER ELEVEN: Keller & Keller, Joe Yutkins, Shelley Metcalf, Russ McConnell, Michael Grimm
CHAPTER TWELVE: Keller & Keller, Michael Myers, Richard Howard

PRESIDENT: Rob Gursha
VICE PRESIDENT, BRANDED BUSINESSES: David Arfine
EXECUTIVE DIRECTOR, MARKETING SERVICES: Carol Pittard
DIRECTOR, RETAIL & SPECIAL SALES: Tom Mifsud
DIRECTOR OF FINANCE: Tricia Griffin
MARKETING DIRECTORS: Kenneth Maehlum, Maarten Terry
ASSOCIATE DIRECTOR: Roberta Harris
EDITORIAL OPERATIONS MANAGER: John Calvano
ASSOCIATE PRODUCT MANAGER: Victoria Alfonso
ASSISTANT PRODUCT MANAGER: Tristen D'Arcy

Special Thanks To:
Suzanne DeBenedetto, Robert Dente, Gina Di Meglio, Peter Harper, Natalie McCrea, Jessica McGrath, Jonathan Polsky, Emily Rabin, Mary Jane Rigoroso, Steven Sandonato, Tara Sheehan, Meredith Shelley, Bozena Szwagulinski, Marina Weinstein, Niki Whelan

---

Published by

Time Publishing Ventures, Inc.
1185 Avenue of the Americas
New York, N.Y. 10036

First Edition
ISBN: 1-929049-35-8

We welcome your comments and suggestions about *This Old House* Books. Please write to us at:
This Old House Books
Attention: Book Editors
PO Box 11016
Des Moines, IA 50336-1016

If you would like to order any of the *This Old House* books, please call us at 1-800-678-2643.

Please visit *This Old House* on the Web.

PRINTED IN THE UNITED STATES OF AMERICA